Performing Without A Stage

The Art of Literary Translation

by Robert Wechsler

CATBIRD PRESS

CATBIRD PRESS
16 Windsor Road, North Haven, CT 06473
800-360-2391   catbird@pipeline.com

Our books are distributed by
Independent Publishers Group

I would like to thank the people who so kindly gave me feedback on this book:
Peter Glassgold, Nancy Hughes, Floyd Kemske, Peter Kussi, and
Melanie Richter-Bernburg. I would also like to thank the
dozens of people who allowed me to interview them.

Library of Congress Cataloging-in-Publication Data

Wechsler, Robert, 1954-
Performing without a stage : the art of literary translation /
by Robert Wechsler.
Includes bibliographical references and index.
ISBN 0-945774-38-9 (cloth : alk. paper)
1. Translating and interpreting. I. Title
PN241.W43 1998
418'.02—dc21   97-35268 CIP

Contents

Introduction

Lɪᴛᴇʀᴀʀʏ ᴛʀᴀɴꜱʟᴀᴛɪᴏɴ ɪꜱ ᴀɴ ᴏᴅᴅ ᴀʀᴛ. It consists of a person sitting at a desk, writing fiction or poetry that has already been written, that has someone else's name on it. The translator's work appears to define derivativeness. Would anyone write a book about people who sit in a museum copying paintings? Copiers aren't artists, they're students or forgers, wannabes or crooks.

Yet literary translation *is* an art. What makes it so odd an art is that physically a translator does exactly the same thing as a writer. If an actor did the same thing as a playwright, a dancer did the same thing as a composer, or a singer did the same thing as a songwriter, no one would think much of what they do either. The translator's problem is that he is a performer without a stage, an artist whose performance looks just like the original, just like a play or a song or a composition, nothing but ink on a page.

Like a musician, a literary translator takes someone else's composition and performs it in his own special way. Just as a musician embodies someone else's notes by moving his body or throat, a translator embodies someone else's thoughts and images by writing in another language. The biggest difference isn't really that the musician produces air movements while the translator produces yet more words; it is that a musical composition is *intended* to be translated into body and throat movements, while a work of literature is not intended to be translated into another language. Thus, although it is practically invisible, the translator's art is the more problematic one. And it is also the more responsible one, because while every musician knows that his performance is simply one of many, often one of thousands, by that musician and by others, the translator knows that his performance may be the only one, at least the only one of his generation, and that he will not have the opportunity either to improve on it or to try a different approach.

And while the translator is shouldering this responsibility and forcing literary works into forms they were never intended to take, no one can see his difficult performance. Except where he slips up. In fact, he is praised primarily for not being seen. Even when we listen to an album, we can imagine the musician blowing or bowing, but nothing comes to mind when we think of a translator translating, nothing more than what we imagine an author doing. Which isn't much. The Czech writer Karel Čapek wrote of what he did when he wrote: "even if I were to sit on the porch with my work, I don't think a single boy would come and watch my fingers to see how a writer's business is done. I don't say that it is a bad or useless profession, but it is not one of the superlatively fine and striking ones, and the material used is of a strange sort —you don't even see it."* But we don't expect any more of writers. We expect to be excited by what a creator creates, not by the way in which he creates it. Unless he is also a performer, like a jazz musician.

With a performing artist, we do expect the doing to be exciting, because the creation has already been done. The performing artist doesn't create, he interprets. But the translator's interpretation not only takes the form of the original—ink—but it doesn't even depart from the content, the way a literary critic's interpretation does. The only thing that changes is that now we can read the ink. The foreign writer's work looks like gibberish, or would if we ever saw it. Just like a musical score to someone who can't read music. But the musician's performance doesn't look anything like a score; the two couldn't be any more different. The translation is so similar, the result is a palimpsest, two works, one on top of the other, an original and a performance, difficult to tell apart.

*   *   *

Due to the literary translator's odd situation, he is not very well respected. He is expected to submit to his authors and always be faithful to them, never make mistakes, work on a piecemeal basis, and accept bottom billing at best. He is not considered an artist at all, neither a creator nor a performer, but rather a craftsman. And he is generally considered a poor and unimportant one. His work is scarcely mentioned in reviews, and almost never critiqued. His art is rarely taught inside or outside universities, his interpretations are rarely given credence in academia, and his thoughts and life story are not considered worthy of publication. He performs not with hopes of fame, fortune, or applause, but rather out of love, out of a sense of sharing what he loves and loving what he does.

We tend to think that the literary translator's talent lies in being good with languages. Which is like saying musicians are good with notes. Of course they are, but being good with notes won't make you a good musician; it's just one of the requirements. In fact, some of the great jazz musicians never learned to read music; and there are great translations by poets who didn't know the original language. To play music, you have to be able to play an instrument, and you have to be sensitive to nuances and understand what combinations of notes mean and are. Similarly, a translator has to be able to read as well as a critic and write as well as a writer. John Dryden said it best back in the seventeenth century: "the true reason why we have so few versions which are tolerable [is that] there are so few who have all the talents which are requisite for translation, and that there is so little praise and so small encouragement for so considerable a part of learning."* Not much has changed.

Yet Pushkin called the translator a "courier of the human spirit,"* and Goethe called literary translation "one of the most important and dignified enterprises in the general commerce of the world."* Borges wrote, "Perhaps . . . the translator's work is more subtle, more civilized than that of the writer: the translator clearly comes after the writer. Translation is a more advanced stage of civilization."* Well, this isn't really what they said, but this is how their words have been translated into English. On the other hand, translators have been called plagiarizers, looters of other cultures, collaborators to colonialism, traitors, betrayers. They betray their people, their language, the original work, themselves. And all for seven cents a word, if they're lucky.

Whether dignified or traitorous, translators are at least considered modest, especially for artists. What could be more modest than submitting yourself to someone else's vision, characters, style, imagery, even sense of humor? Translators bring something to art that in many other times and cultures has been its core, its central aspect: devotion, service. Yet what could be more boastful than saying that you are capable of writing a work as great as what you so admire, say, a French (or Japanese or Nguni) play the equal of *King Lear?* Odd indeed.

The invisible performance of translation is hard to describe. So translators have come up with all sorts of metaphors and similes for it. The translator is "like a sculptor who tries to recreate the work of a painter," Anne Dacier wrote in the introduction to her 1699 French translation of the *Iliad.** In translating poetry, wrote Petrus Danielus Huetius, a seventeenth-century French bishop and educator, "the most important rule is to preserve the meter and the syntax, so that the poet can be shown to his new audience like a tree whose leaves have been removed by the rigors of winter, while the branches, the roots, and the trunk can still be seen."* Translators have for centuries used the metaphor of pouring wine from one bottle into another. Rosemarie Waldrop, an American translator from French, has taken this image one step further: "Translation is more like wrenching a soul from its body and luring it into a different one."*

More recently and scientifically, the American translator from Spanish Margaret Sayers Peden constructed a complex metaphor out of an ice cube: "I like to think of the original work as an ice cube. During the process of translation the cube is melted. While in its liquid state, every molecule changes place; none remains in its original relationship to the others. Then begins the process of forming the work in a second langauge. Molecules escape, new molecules are poured in to fill the spaces, but the lines of molding and mending are virtually invisible. The work exists in the second language as a new ice cube—different, but to all appearances the same."* And then there is the metaphor metaphor of Gregory Rabassa, an American translator from Spanish and Portuguese: "all languages are metaphor, and translation, instead of a vertical metaphor, is a horizontal metaphor."

Here is how the translators of the King James Version of the Bible described translation:

> Translation it is that openeth the window, to let in the light; that breaketh the shell, that we may eat the kernel; that putteth aside the curtain, that we may look into the most holy place; that removeth the cover of the well, that we may come by the water.

Translation gives us access to the literature of the world. It allows us to enter the minds of people from other times and places. It is a celebration of otherness, a truly multicultural event without all the balloons and noisemakers. And it enriches not only our personal knowledge and artistic sense, but also our culture's literature, language, and thought. All it takes to bring a particular variety of Latin American music to North America is a group of Latin American musicians, or just an album. But to bring a particular Latin American author to America, to those who don't read Spanish or Portuguese, it takes another artist, a translator. Without translations of the early novels of Gabriel García Márquez, contemporary American literature would be a very different thing.

Light, food, water, religion. These are what the King James translators said translation gives us access to: the necessities of life, at least for a puritanical people. Think where we would be if we were not only unable to read the Bible or the ancient classics or Cervantes, Voltaire, Kant, Tolstoy, Freud, and if the writers we could read had themselves read no more than a few of the great

writers and thinkers of history and their time. We would be
unenlightened, thirsty for knowledge, hungry for art.

My intention in this book is to give people access to the people
who give us access, and to the art by which they provide such
access. And to do it with humor and passion. I will talk about
what someone has to have and be to make a good translator, about
how translators relate to the literary works they translate, as well
as to the authors and editors they work with and for. I will talk
about what translators do, about the big and little decisions they
have to make. I will talk about the translator's public image and
what can be done by translators, publishers, reviewers, professors,
writers, and even readers to change it. In other words, I will try
to shake up perceptions about translation and translators.

But my principal goal is to help readers understand what translation is all about, so that they can learn to appreciate this hidden
art. This labor of love and of joy deserves to be loved and enjoyed
itself. In fact, nothing would make me happier than if this book
were to lead readers to try their hands at translation themselves.
Nothing I could say would better show how difficult and enjoyable
translation is.

There are a lot of common misconceptions, not to mention a
good number of real obstacles and a touch of laziness, that have
stood in the way of the enjoyment of literary translation. I will try
to remove some of the obstacles and show why and in what way
the misconceptions are misconceived. And I will also show how
the recent decline in literary translation reflects serious changes in
the way our intellectual culture views literature, especially poetry.
For the most part, I will rely on what translators have written and
have told me in dozens of interviews. But I'll also get my two
cents in.

Since no one can give translators a stage on which to give
their performances, my goal is to give them an audience.

Preparing for the Best

YOU WILL NOTE THAT I REFER TO TRANSLATORS as "them." Let me begin by confessing that I am not a literary translator. Like a professor who writes about literature but has himself written only a few poems or stories, most of which remain in his desk drawer, I have done only a little translation, most of which is sitting where it belongs.

Although I do read three languages in three different language groups (French/Romance, Czech/Slavic, German/Germanic—in order of competence), I am not fluent in any of them and, therefore, translation is a long and difficult process for me. I have, however, very carefully edited numerous book-length translations.

Despite my linguistic limitations, translation is my true love. I can't think of many better ways to spend an evening than to pull out a collection of French or Czech or German poetry, flip through the pages looking for the right author and the right poem for the occasion (usually a short one), and then set myself up at my desk with two or three dictionaries (foreign-English, foreign, English), a thesaurus, the poetry collection, and that greatest of all literary icons, the blank sheet of paper.

My experiences with translation have shown me clearly that it is not a matter of transcription, playing around with languages, or writing somebody else's book. It is a very demanding intellectual and artistic process, and most highly literate people are incapable of doing it at a professional level. I'm proud enough that I can edit translations at a professional level.

Translation is an active way of reading something closely, critiquing it, and writing it, all at the same time. This is the performance. A literary critic also reads closely, critiques, and writes, but his writing takes the form of statements. The translator has to

put his pen where his mind is, not in the terms of a critical statement, but in the termlessness of a literary work.

How does one prepare to do something like this? There aren't any
conservatories for it, or even majors. There are some Master's
programs in literary translation, but most translation programs focus
on technical translation, that is, the translation of documents, scholarly journals, instructions, and other foreign-language writing where
style is of little concern. There are translation seminars and there
are translator-professors who act as mentors, but there is little of
the sort of institutionalism that characterizes most arts today, and
most translators have never studied translation in a class.

Well, I'm going to argue that there is no better way to prepare
to become a literary translator than to go to law school and practice law, something I have done myself but not something done
by any translator I have spoken with or read about, at least in this
century. I hope this will convince you of the likely truth of my
contention.

Why law? One reason is that being a lawyer requires what
being a writer or critic usually doesn't: appreciating the value of
words not just as little wads of meaning or feeling, but as missiles
that can have huge ramifications if you can't tell the difference
between short-range and long-range, between nuclear and chemical
warheads. For lawyers, multimillion-dollar deals can succeed or fail
(for one side or the other) based on the level of ambiguity or
precision of a certain word or phrase, in a certain context, for a
certain purpose. Every word a lawyer uses is a commitment, with
a goal, an interest, and a risk that is—or at least should be—
understood. Therefore, the lawyer is concerned with the finest distinctions between words, not only in meaning but also in tone and
level of clarity.

Translation hardly involves multimillions of dollars or people's
lives, but it too involves commitment down at the nitty-gritty level
and in terms of someone else's goals and interests. Like a lawyer,
the translator does not represent himself, as do the writer and the

critic; the translator is representing his client, the original writer. He has responsibilities, he is committed to fulfilling them, and if he's good he knows how and why he's fallen short, where he's had to compromise to get a deal through.

Central to the study and practice of law is the distinction between process and substance, a distinction akin to that in literature between form and content. The translator supplies not content, but form, and he is usually attracted to translation by the opportunity to work with form. Similarly, lawyers love process; they don't decide what cases to bring or what deals to negotiate, but are attracted by the opportunity to accomplish them, to take them through the necessary processes. Like the lawyer, the translator has to put aside his personal differences with the substance of what he is processing. His job, his fiduciary responsibility—to use legal jargon—is to go through the process of re-languaging it.

Process versus substance, form versus content, are distinctions made by legal and literary theorists, but for lawyers and translators they are matters not to be fought over polemically, but rather to be balanced time and time again. The profundity of these concepts comes from accumulation, the piling up of experience, rather than from theoretical excavation.

The process of translation is a trial, from beginning to end: discovering and building the evidence (knowledge of the author's works, of the cultural and artistic context of his works, and often of his life); interpreting the evidence (figuring out what the original means and what's most essential to it, and then determining the range of alternatives); and making numerous judgments and decisions. It's not particularly ironic that one of the books to be featured in this book, one of the most procedural novels of our century, that is, one in which process is most substance, is Franz Kafka's *Der Prozess*, translated into English as *The Trial*.

A legal education, followed by legal practice, leads one to value words as commitments, to see one's job as the representation of another, and to prefer process over substance, form over content.

One cannot be a first-rate translator without all this, but it's not really a very practical way to prepare. And in the real world it's hard to pass by a hefty legal income, especially with all the school loans to repay. So where do literary translators come from? What kind of backgrounds do they have and why do they translate? Not surprisingly, translators—whether professors or laypeople—get into translation for a variety of reasons and come into it from a range of directions.

One of the most peculiar factoids about translators is that almost no translators are children of translators. Lawyers' children often become lawyers, professors' children often become professors, musicians' children often become musicians. But a translator's children almost never take up their parent's ridiculous lance. Perhaps they learn at an early age that their parent is tilting at windmills (or are these children, like most adults, simply unable to see the dragons?). Perhaps they resent their parent's closing himself up in his study all those evenings and weekends, producing nothing but books with somebody else's name on them. Perhaps it's just that translation is generally a sideline, not a profession, and it's hardly a pasttime in which the whole family can take part, like skiing, gardening, or playing music together. And it's not as if they can watch their parent up on stage and want to share that exciting limelight.

Well, I did find one translator who had the experience of growing up in a family that translated together (and, yes, stayed together). I didn't have to go far to find her either, because she had translated a book for me and she lives and works only twenty minutes away. Her name is Krishna Winston, and her parents were Richard and Clara Winston, a well-regarded, full-time, German-into-English translation team. Winston told me: "My parents worked at home, and they worked together, so they were always talking about their work. They talked about translation problems, they talked about authors, and they talked about books. And when my sister and I got a little older, they would throw out problems for us. 'How do you say such and such?' My father would be preoccupied with some translation problem, and the whole family would get drawn into it.

"What I particularly remember was a later time, when I was already a young teenager, when my parents were translating the Austrian writer Heimito von Doderer's novel *The Demons,* and there was a long section in that book which was written in pseudo-medieval German. So my parents were reading up to try to find some equivalent English diction, and for some reason they lit on William Caxton, and they had the whole family talking in Caxton's English. We all developed roles. We were monks, and I think I was Brother Sebastian and my sister was Brother Ambrose. We used to just go for hours talking in this tongue. And it went on for quite a while, because the chapter was a long one and my father struggled with it. I suppose that with influences like this, one inevitably starts to think, well, this is something I would enjoy doing, too."

Winston also translates German prose, and while she doesn't come close to her parents' output, she does translate about one book a year in addition to being a professor of German at Wesleyan University. And her sister translates from Latin and Greek.

The only other translator I talked with who had a translator-parent is Rosanna Warren. Her mother, Eleanor Clark, translated from French, although far from full-time; she was primarily a novelist. Warren translates from French, Latin, and Greek (ancient and modern), also on the side; in addition, she runs the Translation Seminar at Boston University. The multilingual translator Willis Barnstone has collaborated on translations with both his son and his daughter, and both the father and the grandfather of the poet and sometime translator Rachel Hadas had also done translations themselves, but in no case was this a principal vocation. These are, in any event, exceptions to this curious rule that translators' children, when translators can afford to have them, are not so taken with their parents' vocation or avocation that they follow in their footsteps.

*   *   *

What makes people decide to become translators? Everybody knows why a writer writes. There have been many movies, and countless books about it. A writer has a story to tell, something to express, an urge to put his vision or his life or his anger or his passion down into words. A writer dreams of fame and fortune, the opening of opportunities, the fellowship of other writers, respect, celebrity, immortality.

Musicians fall in love with music, and study hard for many years, learning the great works by heart. Actors want to throw themselves into roles, go up on stage, become part of an exciting world, famous and adored. But a translator has no story to tell, nothing to express, no urge to get himself down into words. He cannot dream of either fame or fortune, or the opening of opportunities, or even in most cases the fellowship of other artists.

Yet some people do end up translating. The reasons they do this range from love to scholarship, from dissatisfaction to political necessity. Since for me one of the things that most distinguishes translation from other arts is the concept of service, I'll start with Richard Howard's reason: "there were some favorite books that I loved, and I translated them so my friends could read them. There were things I liked to read aloud after dinner. There was a text by Giraudoux, and a few other things I thought were enchanting, and then someone said, 'Well, why don't you send them to a publisher.'" At the time, Howard was a dictionary editor and an aspiring poet. Now he is a noted translator of French into English, and a no-longer-aspiring poet.

A different sort of friendship and sharing was behind Richard Wilbur's start as a translator. "My first experience with translation was when André du Bouchet, who's now a rather well-established French poet, and I were fellow graduate students at Harvard. I would sit around with André trying to translate his poems into English, and he sat around trying to translate mine into French. It was fun. He made me sound like Baudelaire. I'm afraid I didn't do quite as well by him. But knowing André, I was able to begin the translation of any one of his poems with a sense that I knew his tones of voice and his preoccupations."* Wilbur, too, became a well-established poet, as well as a translator of such writers as Molière and Voznesensky. This sense of relationship with the trans- lated author continued into Wilbur's future translation work: "I couldn't imagine beginning to translate anybody living or dead without at least having the illusion of some kind of personal understanding—some understanding of the range of his feelings be- yond the particular work."

William Weaver started translating so that he could read the prose and poetry of the friends he was meeting in Italy; he was there driving an ambulance during the Second World War and his Italian wasn't good enough to understand what he was reading without a closer examination. Weaver's first commissioned transla- tion also came out of a friendship. "I did it," he told me, "because it was by my closest Italian friend, and he needed the money to get married. He just assumed that I would translate it, because I watched him write it; I was living with his family." And this trans- lation-out-of-friendship continued. "I was living in Italy at the time and I knew a lot of these writers personally. In some cases I was the only translator they knew. And therefore they would always ask me to translate their books or recommend me to publishers."

One might guess that growing up bilingual—being forced, in effect, to translate in one's head as a natural part of life—would be a good start for a translator, but this is not the way most translators begin, and many feel that it is in fact an obstacle. Actually, multilingual people tend not to translate in their heads, but rather deal with their languages in separate compartments. However, Richard Sieburth, a translator from French and German and professor at New York University, does credit his growing up in a bilingual household (German and English) in a quadrilingual country, Switzerland: "Very early on, you realize that everything has two names and you're living in a double universe. And then being in a country where every product you looked at, your break- fast muesli, everything was in four languages. And absolutely being fascinated by that kind of polyphony, by that plurality of messages."

But once he began to actually do literary translation as an undergraduate, other factors came in to play. "Translation was a way of miming or writing the kind of text you couldn't write yourself." He started out translating a couple of novels by Georges Bataille "for fun," and then as a graduate student and young professor he did translations for literary magazines.

Sieburth himself feels that "bilinguals are often the worst translators. You need that solid anchoring in one language, precisely because you need to respond to the foreignness; with bilinguals that tension gets lost. That tension needs to be maintained." Robert Penn Warren once observed that "those outside of the language, like himself, could appreciate its musicality more than a native speaker—precisely because the outside reader would tend to focus more on (exotic) sound than sense."[*]

American writers lack one principal reason for becoming a translator: suppression. Many foreign writers have turned to translation when their authoritarian government prevented them from publishing their own writing. This is true of Stanislaw Baranczak, now a professor of Polish at Harvard and a translator into Polish of Shakespeare, Donne, Dickinson, and a wide range of other English-language poets. It was also true of Eugenio Montale, the Italian poet who was a dissident to fascism in the thirties. Yugoslav dissident Milovan Djilas is said to have spent his years as a political prisoner translating *Paradise Lost* into Serbo-Croatian, covering 3,000 sheets of toilet paper before finally being given real paper on which to finish his job.

There are all sorts of other reasons a translator starts translating: because he can't find enough translators to do work for his literary magazine, for mental exercise, for the money, because she had a translator for a mentor, because he thinks he can do better than what's out there, for her dissertation, for an apprenticeship, for himself. Even love can turn people into translators; in fact, being blind, in this sense, helps.

Probably the most romantic translation story I've come across is that of Barbara and Benjamin Harshav. Benjamin was born in Vilna, which was then part of Poland but is now part of Lithuania. His first language was Yiddish. After the war he went to Germany, where he edited a Hebrew-language literary journal and did translation for it into and out of several languages, but particularly into Hebrew. Then he moved to Palestine, fought in the War of Independence, and founded a literary journal with the Israeli poet Yehuda Amichai and others. He continued to translate poetry into Hebrew, with the express purpose of bringing individualist poetry into a language whose poetry was primarily group-oriented: religious, socialist, about the Jewish people.

On a visit to Chapel Hill, North Carolina, he met Barbara and together they began translating into English the work of American Yiddish poets. His English was already pretty good, because he had gone to graduate school at Yale (where he currently teaches); but her English was much better. Her weakness was that she did not know Yiddish.

They spent their first two married years in Germany, where she learned both German and Yiddish. She, too, had already done a great deal of translation, although not for publication: in order to keep up the French she had learned in school, she had spent an hour-and-a-half every morning translating French fiction into English—all of Balzac and then all of Zola. In Germany she did the same thing with German writers. Just for herself. Translation can be that enjoyable, that useful, and that addictive.

Octavio Paz, the Nobel Prize-winning Mexican poet, also got into translation via love. He said: "I learned English mainly to read poetry. Then, reading English and French poems, I felt that they should be known in Spanish. You see: it was desire, love—and with love, the desire for participation."* As you will see again and again throughout this book—to the point where you might even begin to believe it—love is in translation, as in so many other (but too few) parts of life, the moving force. But what about "participation"? Was Paz, although fluent in English, not quite saying what he meant to say? I don't think so; Paz is too much in love with words to make a mistake about something as important to him as

his reason for translating. Richard Howard's first reason for translating was to share his passions with his friends; Paz's was to
participate in a worldwide sharing of literatures. They amount to
the same thing, just a different view, a different scale. Howard was
being personal, Paz philosophical.

One thing that does not attract people to literary translation is the
pay. In fact, there's nothing translators complain about more than
the money they don't make from their work. Artists in general do
not make as much money as they would like, but many performing
artists, at least, get regular or full-time work, often with union
wages and protections, and all can look at the great success stories
and tell themselves, I can do that, I'm that good, if only. . . With
so few exceptions they prove the rule, literary translators do not
have full-time work, and commissions are not enough, because
there's no Translators Equity to make one or two good commissions equal a year's salary. And translators have no great success
stories, in the monetary sense, to dream about. Try to take a deep
breath and imagine you're William Weaver, English-language translator of Umberto Eco, Italo Calvino, and other Italian novelists,
one of the giants in his field. Well, he has only scored big once:
with Umberto Eco's *The Name of the Rose*, which paid for his
current apartment. Even Weaver supplements his regular translation income by teaching translation and by writing about opera.
Oh yes, artists also can supplement their income by teaching. But
there are very few translation courses around, and not many
universities try to attract translators to their campuses the way they
do with writers and musicians. No, when translators teach, they
usually teach language and literature courses. And they either fight
for tenure like everybody else or accept the low pay and status
that go with lectureships. I don't know of a single translator who
has been given a short route to tenure due to fame, or even ability,
as many other sorts of artists have. Their names simply don't do
anything for a university's reputation.

So not only does becoming a translator usually start as a labor of love, it remains that. Translators bitch and bitch about not being appreciated, or understood, or respected, or any of the things adolescents complain about every day (yes, not a big enough allowance, as well), but they love their work so much they keep on doing it anyway. And publishers keep on keeping the pay low (and, I should add, losing money themselves on the great majority of translations). But translators *are* organized, and one of their organizations, the American Translators Association (which includes both literary and technical translators), was sued by the Federal Trade Commission for printing a list of recommended fees for translators to request. As if it would really have mattered in a buyer's market.

Money, fame, service. Three things that make the world go round. Money is often a central incentive when choosing a professional career, but this certainly isn't true of translation. Fame is often a central incentive when choosing an artistic career, but this too does not apply to translation. So we're left with service, which is what usually draws educated people to low-paying professions. But it is not the usual kind of service; it's not about caring for the ill, handicapped, young, or deprived. It's about caring for one's literary culture and for writers from other cultures, and bringing them together in the form of a performance. Madame de Staël wrote back in 1820, "The most eminent service one can render to literature is to transport the masterpieces of the human spirit from one language to another."*

But it's not enough to *want* to serve by sharing works of art. It's not like being a publisher, where the act of sharing is not at the same time an act of art and an act of criticism. In gift-giving, it is the thought that counts, but in translation an incompetent result can sometimes be worse than none. It's true that a great work can "shine through" even a mediocre translation, but, especially with poetry, it may not shine brightly enough to seem like a great work.

It's a crazy thing to want to be a writer; very few ever make it, and many thousands of would-be's are frustrated all their lives. It's even crazier to want to be a translator, because almost nobody makes it. The one saving grace is that there's not the same sort of feeling of frustration when you don't make it, because what's being rejected is only your skills, not your self; your take on literature, not your take on life. Yes, it's frustrating to know you probably won't be able to find a publisher for what you want to translate, and that you'll probably have to translate authors you're not so attached to. But you can still enjoy the process, still translate excellent writing, and still share even unpublished results with your friends and students, not as the failed expression of your soul, but as the successful performance of a work you admire. You can, in short, do what you set out to do, what attracted you to translation in the first place. Most of all, people are attracted to translation to share what they love and just for the sheer intellectual joy of doing it.

Because they naturally live at the intersection between language and literature, no one is more likely to be a translator than foreign language and literature professors. But professors who translate differ greatly from one another, just as readers read differently and for different reasons. Or so I am going to argue. Most people read literature primarily for pleasure. They are consumers, consuming the tension of suspense, the release of humor, the escape of adventure, the titillation of sex, the confirmation of beliefs, the tears of another's loss, the joy of another's victory. When a book does not have what they're looking for, or when it asks too much of the reader in order to get at it—as bees keep most people away from honey—the literary consumer turns to something else. In fact, these days the literary consumer almost always turns away from poetry. And from fiction in translation. Needless to say, this sort of reader never becomes a translator. However, this sort of reader sometimes becomes a writer, though usually of genre fiction.

Other readers—usually academics or lifetime students— approach literature the way a doctor approaches a corpse. They see literature as something to dissect, something in which there are things to point out, something that confirms or overturns theories, grist for this or that mill. They are users who see literature primarily as part of an enterprise, a cataloging or theorizing or building of traditions, or lives, or connections. It isn't their feelings they're looking to satisfy as much as it is their minds. And they're usually more interested in aspects of content than of form.

This sort of reader is more likely to translate than any other, but primarily as part of the same enterprise. If you want to use a work as an example, and it happens to have been written in a foreign language and not yet translated into English, there is nothing to do but translate it. If you want to convince people of your political or theoretical or personal values, you will want to share some of what you see as the most important examples supporting them. You translate the work often because you love it, but also because it's important to whatever cause you happen to be fighting for. Thus, a great percentage of literary translation going on in the United States today is done by professors, especially from Spanish, especially of Latin-American writing of a political nature. Or at least it is approached in a political way. The translated authors are less artists than victims or witnesses. Although on the whole very well intentioned, and often reasonably competent, these translators are considered something apart from the mainstream, not because they have different political views, but because they read and translate for different reasons. And this gulf is made worse because many of them do not seem to recognize this distinction—or they deny that it exists.

There are also those professor-translators who work with material from a place and time in which they specialize, from fourteenth-century Japanese drama to Egyptian hieroglyphs. These works might be of great value, even high quality, and today's English-speaking world might be highly fortunate to have access to them. But they are often works that are very difficult to bring into contemporary English-language culture, and the professor-translator often does not have the ability to give them life in the here and now.

Now, please don't get me wrong: not all professors are in the business of literary mummification. Many of our best translators are professors. But their approach to literature is different from the professors I've been discussing. These other professors constitute a third type of reader: the reader who cares more about how it is done than what it is or how relevant it is to their other scholarly endeavors. Not that either of these two things are unimportant: it must have some value and must give them some sort of pleasure. But for these professors, that value and that pleasure lie in such things as the way the original is written, the freshness of the style, the cleverness of the structure, the wisdom of its ideas, the intelligence of the stringing together of words, lines, sentences, paragraphs, stanzas, chapters, poems, the challenge involved in bringing all this into English.

This sort of professor, as well as similar non-professors, reads much more like a writer, analyzes much more like the person in the audience who wants to know how it's done, and not so he can prove it isn't really magic. This sort of reader is like that rare audience member who wants to know *because* it's magic and he wants to be a magician, too. He wants to do to people what the magician does to them, wants to give them that sort of wonder; only he can't pull it out of thin air. For this audience member, wonder is not about the magician surviving the swords thrust through the box, but about how realistically, or with how much panache, the magician does the trick. It's all tricks, illusions, but there are tricks that are done conventionally and tricks that are done spectacularly and tricks that are just done so much differently they don't look like the same trick anymore. This sort of reader loves this last kind of trick the best. And when he is also a writer—or translator—he wants to learn how it's done so that he can do it with his own special twist. This sort of translator-reader is more like a great writer than most writers, because he's not willing to settle for conventional writing. What he wants to translate, what he wants to share with people, are the one-of-a-kinds, what has not confirmed his view of the world, but rather has made him see the world differently. What he hopes will make readers see the world differently. These translators say, in effect, what professor-translator John Felstiner did at the beginning of a talk at Yale: "I'm brimming with things I want to share."

These translators, when they are professors, are often not on tenure track, and they tend to produce more translations than the typical professor-translator. This, however, is slowly changing, as some departments and institutions are starting to recognize translations in their tenure considerations.

Now that I've responded to the question, Where do translators come from? it's time to ask the question, What does it take to become one? I'd like to respond to this question in my usual indirect way, by responding to another question: Why is it more difficult to be a good young translator than it is to be a good young writer?

Of course, a young writer only needs to know one language. But even more important, a young writer only needs to know enough about life to write about what he wants to write about. If he follows his teachers' advice and writes what he knows (or feels or dreams), then it is axiomatic that there will be nothing lacking in terms of his knowledge and experiences. When he describes the way a hockey player attacks a puck—or another player—he is most likely a knowledgeable hockey player or fan, or he'd have his hero play another sport. A young translator, however, has to write about things and experiences he knows nothing about. He might never have attended a hockey game and might not know the language of the sport, not to mention of the fans, even in his own language. A dictionary can't help him with this. This is also true of the young translator's experience of his literary culture and of the foreign writer's literary culture, history, et al. The older a curious person gets (and translators tend to be exceptionally curious people), the more he comes to know about more things. And the more life and literary experiences he accumulates.

A young translator also has limited experience with English. He hasn't read as much, hasn't written as much, hasn't talked to as many people, and is therefore not aware of as many of the possibilities of the English language, of as many different ways of saying something. Life experience may be the writer's principal resource, but language is the writer's medium, and a lack of knowledge of English is more sure to lead to bad writing than a lack of life experience. Yet even with limited knowledge of the possibilities of English, a young writer can find a way to express his vision or experiences; he can write within himself, within his limitations. A translator does not have this luxury. He cannot write within himself; he has to write within somebody else. He has to find a way to express in English what somebody else has expressed, skillfully one hopes, in another language. The more he has at his fingertips a wide range of alternatives, a wide range of styles and solutions to problems, the better a translator he can be. As Petrus Danielus Huetius wrote, "A translator must . . . become like Proteus: he must be able to transform himself into all manner of wondrous things, he must be able to absorb and combine all styles within himself and be more changeable than a chameleon."*

There are young translators who have read voraciously, not only widely but openly, critically, devouring what they read, trying it out in their own writing, trying to figure out how it works. At a young age it is easier, and less painful, to accumulate broad literary experience than broad life experience; the best young translators at least have this literary experience under their belt. But it is few who ever read like this. They make the best literary writers, and the best translators.

Judgment, or instinct, is the crowning achievement of experience, both in the world and in literature. It is the rare young translator who has consistently good judgment, who can fight off his inclinations toward what sounds good to him, who can settle on what is appropriate, who even knows what is appropriate. Judgment requires not only the experience of reading a great deal, but also the experience of writing and, if possible, editing and translating. Nothing trains your judgment—your "ear"—like these last two activities. A young writer might have a good instinct for what he does, but to have good instincts with respect to others' work, you need to be used to listening carefully. And no one listens as carefully as the capable editor or translator.

It also helps to enjoy writing in a range of styles. Being a mimic or parodist can help a great deal with translation. Arthur Goldhammer, a translator of French prose, told me, "I enjoy writing pastiche. I have a French friend to whom I write pastiche of French styles of different centuries. It's one way of keeping myself sharp, and it's also something that amuses me. And I think I have the styles of many times in my ear . . . I live surrounded by books and I read a lot. That's a necessity for any translator: to be familiar with a lot of styles and to try to muster many resources, because you have to give yourself to other people's ways of writing; you can't simply impose yourself on them."

Another thing that can help develop good judgment is memorization, something that has been out of fashion for quite some time now, at least in the United States. Poet-translator Rosanna Warren told me, "I feel so grateful to my parents for uprooting me from the U.S. and throwing me into a French lycée when I was twelve and thirteen, when I had to memorize so much. I think memorization is crucial, absolutely key. It shapes the mind. If you don't shape the mind with something like Shakespeare, then the mind shapes itself out of its baser appetites."

Also central to the young translator's ability is the question of his maturity in terms of his vision of himself as a writer. That is, why he is a writer and what about writing most interests him. There seems to be a rule that the less one has to say, the stronger one's urge is to say it. Most young people want to be writers to express what they feel is their special take on the world. They confuse creativity with originality, and originality with self-expression. Rarely is a young person whose focus is self-expression going to toss all this aside and translate instead. Thus, to be a young translator, one has to be drawn to writing for reasons other than self-expression. In many countries, where there is great demand for translators and most educated people speak another language fluently, translation is a common way for aspiring young writers to pay the rent. Whether they want to or not, they do it because it's there. In the monoglot English-speaking world, there are many fewer opportunities, and few of the opportunities will pay the rent. This is sad, because, as Eliot Weinberger has written, "To translate is to learn how poetry is written. Nothing else is so successful a teacher, for it carries no baggage of self-expression."*

For most people who write, it is only as they age that they realize their take isn't so special, and it thus becomes easier to perform the work of someone who really does have a special vision or style. Translation is, in many ways, a middle-aged art. Translators aren't very good or interested when they're young; when they reach the age most creative writers are starting down the other side of the hill, translators start doing their best work; and then, when they hit their sixties, many realize that it's their last chance to do the original work they've been putting off all these years. Or they don't have the energy to do translation on the side anymore. In any event, they tend to produce fewer translations.

One final thing that makes excellent young translators so rare is the fact that there aren't any child prodigies, any adolescents with a natural aptitude for translation. Alexander Pope, who started his translation of the *Iliad* at the age of twenty-seven, is about as close as anyone has come. Even the best of translators look back at their early work with scorn or embarrassment. This isn't the case with musicians and actors, or even with writers much of the time. It's more like literary critics, who need some seasoning before they start doing their best work. But even critics don't need to develop the sort of instincts that allow them to work at a rate of a zillion decisions per hour.

In summation, it takes a lot to be a first-rate translator. It requires knowledge of a foreign language and a foreign culture, a wide-ranging knowledge of life, a wide-ranging knowledge of English and of English-language literature, excellent judgment and interpretive abilities, a good ear for language and thought, the ability to write not only very well but in a range of styles, and a mature view of writing as something more than self-expression. Add to this attention to details, patience and persistence, self-discipline, a dislike of limelight, money, camaraderie, and a willingness to subordinate yourself to another's creative work, and you have yourself a damn good translator.

The Intimacy of Submission

IN OUR PRESENT INTELLECTUAL CULTURE there is probably nothing as unacceptable as submission. Submission is a willful decision to let oneself be victimized, to not only admit to the superiority of the powerful, but also to admit the powerful into one's life and to serve it.

In terms of writing, to be a translator is to suppress your own voice in favor of another's, to spend your time worrying over the other's problems, manipulating the other's images and characters, expressing the other's vision and ideas. It is to become nothing but a spokesperson for this other writer, when you could otherwise be creating your own fiction and poetry, expressing your own self.

Put this way, translation certainly sounds like something that should be avoided at all costs. But it doesn't have to be put this way. First of all, submission is not all or nothing. We can, for example, be both submissive and dominant. A good example is a pecking order, where we are submissive to those above and dominant over those below. Or we can be submissive in some ways and dominant in others, even with the same person. This is the case with most people, although you'd never know it from all the pointing fingers.

There can also be rewards from submission that offset its costs. You can submit to someone whom you feel does or expresses what you would like to do or express in a way you feel you never could yourself. It is such followers who make leaders what they are. Submission can satisfy needs: the need to take care of people, the need to be good and dutiful, not with the poor or ill (where taking care is an act of dominance), but with one's equals or superiors. There is a reason codependence is so prevalent.

Submission can also involve being a tour guide, taking people to a sight you've already seen and experiencing joy from knowing how much joy they are or, in the case of translation, will be taking in it. The roots of the word to "translate" do, after all, mean "to lead, to transport people somewhere."

The nicest side of submission involves the joys of devotion, admiration, service, humility. As the poet Ben Belitt put it, "there is a vast body of translation in which the enlightened disclosure of admiration is primary—a kind of substantive embodiment of *praise*."* You know the feeling you get when you give a friend a book by a writer you admire, who's special to you? Imagine the feeling you'd get giving the book to your entire culture? Why "enlightened"? Because just *liking* a writer or book isn't enough; the giving has to be done in an enlightened manner, by someone who not only understands the work but has the skills to bring it effectively into English.

And the "substantive embodiment of praise"? This makes translation sound like a prayer. And it is. Think how readers relate to authors in a religious sort of way, that is, submitting to the author without the author's active participation, as if the author were a god. The translator is a very close reader, and there is no praise like spending a year or so translating an admired writer's novel or poetry collection.

Submission can also allow you to be intimate with someone who is, in some ways, superior—more talented, more experienced—someone who would not allow you to dominate him or even be his equal. The student-teacher relationship is the most typical example. This sort of submission allows you to grow both personally and professionally, to gain understanding, to find yourself and become something more. Some writers start out writing like Hemingway or Bishop; saxophonists play like Coltrane; painters try out a few of Picasso's periods. In most arts this is a conscious process, part of the education: copying and performing before painting and composing. Writing, however, emphasizes self-expression over copying, even if a great deal of copying goes on anyway. Translation allows a young writer to dispense with this expressive approach to the world and instead focus on form. Why can't a writer, instead of writing *like* Woolf or Stevens, learn by *writing* Proust or Akhmatova?

A kindred spirit will more likely enable you to understand yourself and your artistic vision and approach more deeply, but the less kindred another writer is, the more a close encounter can lead to growth, to new ways of seeing the world and of expressing what you see. "We translate to be translated," Suzanne Jill Levine, a translator of Latin American prose, wrote in one of the most interesting books on translation, *The Subversive Scribe.**

Finally, submission can be a form of domination itself. It can be a way of getting what one wants while seeming not to, doing something with great hubris while seeming humble and good. In the religious world there is proselytizing, that is, preaching not in one's own name but in the name of God, the Author of Authors. Translators can be proselytizers, too, getting their views, vision, and interpretations across, but in the name of their author, in a way and to an extent they never could with their own work. Gregory Rabassa has referred to translation as "a priestly task."* And many people are more comfortable promoting others than they are promoting themselves, that is, promoting what they revere rather than what they create.

So, submission's not all that bad. In fact, it has its attractions. Which is good, because it's so central to literary translation. In the rest of this chapter, I will look more closely at the various types and levels of submission that are involved in translation.

No one likes to refer to himself as submissive. "Devoted" perhaps, but "affinity," the translator's preferred term, is even better, because "affinity" connotes an equal relationship, a relationship between people with similar interests and similar ways of looking at the world. In some cases—for example, where a poet is translating a poet who is his contemporary—this is an accurate description of the relationship. When Richard Wilbur and André du Bouchet translated each other, this was definitely the case: both were young poets exploring each other's verse and their own poetic abilities. They were literary lovers of the best sort. Their friendship allowed them to express an understanding of the other's writing that strangers could not have had; it also probably blinded them to weaknesses and other possibilities they'd rather not see in the other.

It is often the case that poets translate poets they already know personally. This is less true with fiction writers, because fiction writers are less likely than poets to translate and because nearly all fiction translation is commissioned by publishers, whereas most poetry translation is not. When a translator is a fiction writer, he's usually either young or not successful, that is, not an artistic equal. But fiction translators do often come to know their authors well. After all, they speak the same language.

Richard Sieburth has another way of looking at affinity: as "hospitality . . . receiving someone as a guest . . . with the full formality and etiquette that that entails." Translation for Sieburth is a joyful thing, a greeting and a spending time together; in one essay he calls it "communion." Author and translator are not quite equals, but the unspoken rules allow the meeting to go smoothly and pleasurably, presumably to the benefit of both parties.

More than any translator I spoke with, Sieburth was direct about the joys that accompany the more noble aspects of submission: "I enjoy—maybe that's an old-fashioned part of me—I enjoy feeling useful, that I'm doing something useful. I enjoy serving something that I admire. I enjoy admiration as an emotion. . . . it's at once an attitude of humility and an attitude of overweaning pride that you, on some level, can be the equal of the author." Very succinctly, Sieburth goes through nearly all the aspects of submission I outlined above, including the paradox of translation as both humility and pride.

Sieburth sees submission less in the act of translation than in the way it is perceived. "I think you should look at translators the way you look at performers of music," he told me. "Oddly enough, musicians have a certain status. We recognize a Rubenstein Chopin or a Glenn Gould Bach, but the translator is not seen this way. He is placed in a position of hiddenness or downright emasculation.

The translator is always in an inferior, feminine relationship to a male original." In other words, the translator's submission, or service, is generally considered to be a sign of inferiority. The translator is seen not as a gifted performer of another's written creation, but as an inferior servant, lacking something essential.

The feeling of affinity with an author can, however, lead a translator to feel that he is as singular as the author. As Hans Erich Nossack has said, "My identification with this particular book was so complete, that I imagined myself the only person capable of translating it properly."* Or the translator can identify so closely with the author that he sees himself as being that author, as writing the same book in English. The Earl of Roscommon once wrote a few lines of verse expressing this feeling:*

> United by this Sympathetick Bond,
> You grow Familiar, Intimate, and Fond;
> Your thoughts, your Words, your Stiles, your Souls agree,
> No longer his Interpreter, but He.

This sort of identification, which one can easily imagine in a musician or actor, can also be found among mere translators.

Beyond identification and hospitality is the more unequal relationship of devotion. Translating an author you are devoted to and have always loved as a reader, whose works you've studied and taught and read again and again, can be both a great joy and a great trial. Breon Mitchell, a professor at Indiana University, has recently completed a new translation of Franz Kafka's *The Trial*. Kafka has been a long-time passion of Mitchell's, and of all Kafka's work he is most passionate about *The Trial*. "I had the problem," he said in a talk at the 1994 American Literary Translators Association (ALTA) conference, "of my own reverence for the author. It is not the best thing in the world to translate somebody that you revere so highly. If you feel they're up there somewhere and you're this Kafkaesque, unworthy person, it does not make it easy for you to translate. In a way, it's much easier for you to translate somebody when you can say, Eh, it's a good novel, but I can probably turn out an English version that'll be fairly good, too."

A step beyond devotion is that sort of reverence that takes the words of an author as unchangeable, akin to the words of God. In fact, Fred Jordan, the editor who commissioned Mitchell's translation of *The Trial*, felt this way about Kafka and asked Mitchell to produce a word-for-word translation. This takes us into the issue of fidelity, the subject of a later chapter, but it is worth knowing that devotion can turn into a sort of reverence that hurts the great master by imposing on his work limitations the author never put on himself and would not ask of a translator were he still alive.

Devotion can also lead to feelings of trepidation, worries of letting a writer down. But part of that devotion, and often a more important part, is the sort of love that makes you want to share the author with those who otherwise would never know him. Translators aren't selfish lovers who want to keep their loved ones all to themselves. They give others access to the loved one. Rika Lesser wrote in the introduction to her book of translations from the Swedish, *A Child Is Not a Knife: Selected Poems by Göran Sonnevi*, "These are poems I fell in love with. These are poems that have helped me live, as a human being, in and outside of language. Of course it is my hope they will do the same for you."*

Devoted translators risk losing their own identity to the stronger identities of the writers they translate. Devotion can also lead to closeness bordering on, or across the border into, obsession. As Christopher Middleton once said, "I don't like to [translate] too much because when I'm translating a poem—or any text actually —I pursue this 'other' obsessively and compulsively, and I can't think or do anything else. That's why, when I've been asked to do a longer prose work, I've been very reluctant to undertake the job. . . . it is an incubus."*

For some translators, especially those who specialize in a small number of authors, "affinity" and "devotion" go hand in hand. Eliot Weinberger has principally translated the poetry of Octavio Paz. He told me, "You can really only translate a few people. What I mean is that you have to have a total immersion in the work, you have to know everything about the work, and you have to have some kind of affinity, and I think that's only possible with a few

people. I've done things for an anthology, where I'll translate one
or two poems by a poet I sort of know, but not particularly well,
and the translation is fine, but I feel it lacks a certain kind of
vitality. A lot of people disagree with me on this point. They think
they can translate anything. Usually when you have an anthology
translated by one person, it's a disaster. A few of the poems are
good; the rest aren't."

For Weinberger, love is not enough: "There are writers whom
one loves for all different reasons. Like people, or anything else.
And then there are writers whom I love whom I don't think I
could translate very well. . . . For example, Borges: I was asked to
translate a *Collected Poems* of Borges and I knew I could never
translate that kind of formal poetry at all."

Not all translators seek out writers for whom they feel the
most affinity. For them translation is not only about service and
sharing, but also about personal and cultural growth. Serge Gavronsky, a professor at Barnard College and translator from French into
English, and vice versa, told me, "the poets to whom I have been
attracted are ones that are different from my own writing. I find
that enriching for me; it liberates me from my own preoccupations;
it allows, in a metaphorical sense, a cleansing of myself by the
Other: translation as enema." Here Gavronsky is speaking of his
translations of French poets into English. But he has also been
translating Louis Zukofsky's *A* into French, and here his concern
is primarily with bringing something new into French, "inseminat-
ing" French poetry with foreign genes. Translation as miscegenation.

Affinity is much more common to poetry translation than it
is to the translation of fiction, because, as I've said, most poetry
translation is initiated by the translator and most fiction translation
is done on commission, initiated by the publisher. It is, therefore,
with fiction translation that affinity gives way to something more
akin to acting, where the translator is able to play a range of
authors, including authors who write in a way totally unlike his
own style or approach. In the only review I've ever seen of novels
by different authors translated by the same translator, the reviewer,
novelist Michael Upchurch, wrote that this offers "a perfect oppor-

tunity to gauge how much the translator's art resembles an actor's. In both these translations, John Brownjohn disappears inside his role completely, coming up with prose of such contrasting rhythm and temperament that it's a challenge to remember that Brussig's and Beyer's German-language originals had to pass through the same mind on their way into English. It's a fine accomplishment."*

And even where there is affinity to start with, sometimes intimacy turns the feeling of love into one of annoyance, or even hatred. The Czech translator Zdeněk Urbánek told me how it was translating Dickens: "if you read him, you like him, but if you have to stay too long with one page of Dickens, it is tedious." And William Weaver told me, "I started translating a book and fell totally out of love with it. Not that I was ever really in love with it, but all of its meretriciousness came through, because in translation you can't really cheat. With translators, it's like, no man is a hero to his valet."

In any event, affinity is not always as pure as it seems. Translating a writer you closely identify with is playing with a reflection of yourself, trying yourself on, recreating yourself. Or one could say, as Italian translator Renato Poggioli has, that translators are as narcissistic as poets; instead of contemplating their likenesses in "the spring of nature," they stare at themselves in "the pool of art."* French-into-English translator Rosemarie Waldrop took this image a step further by referring to French writer Michel Leiris's parable of a monk who sees the face of God, and it is his own. The translator, too, has a "sacreligious joy of substituting one's own face for God's."*

Baudelaire, whose translations of Edgar Allan Poe's stories and a few poems, had a major influence on French literature, wrote, "I have been accused of imitating Edgar Poe! Do you know why I so patiently translated Poe? Because he resembles me. I was astonished and carried away the first time I opened one of his books and saw not only things I'd dreamed of, but *sentences* I'd thought of, sentences he'd written twenty years earlier."* But this may have had something to do with the fact that Baudelaire only learned English in order to translate Poe, and therefore could not really understand what he was reading the first time he encountered him. It's much easier to see yourself in a hazy photo.

Saying that one has a close affinity with the author can also be a way for a translator to hide, even from himself, his desire to make over a work of literature in his own voice, a way not to take responsibility for his views, that is, a way to appear submissive while actually dominating. George Steiner has written, "As with a sea-shell, the translator can listen strenuously but mistake the rumour of his own pulse for the beat of the alien sea."*

Most translators do seek out writers with similar interests in such things as form, values, philosophy, and politics. And some take this a step beyond sharing: proselytizing, pushing their own views or style in the name of an author or school of authors. An important example of the proselytizing translator is Ezra Pound. In the ancient, image-oriented poetry of China, he found something that fit his vision of poetry—or at least he saw it in that light—and he considered it part of his mission as an imagist poet to bring this poetry into English, to provide an ancient, foreign repertoire of imagist poetry to supplement what he and his circle were creating themselves. Although he was devoted to the poetry of China, it was actually his own poetic philosophy that he was proselytizing.

Another example is Stanislaw Baranczak, who has been translating into Polish the English metaphysical poets of the seventeenth century, such as John Donne, George Herbert, and Andrew Marvell. "The metaphysical poets are having an effect," he told me. "They're very modern. They're used in literary debates."

This is one of the things that is most wonderful about translation: that old literature can be made modern, can be made to matter not as old literature, but as a way of changing the nature of current literature by introducing into it something totally new. Shakespeare was central to German Romanticism, and he remains a constantly modernized author all over the world. New is modern no matter how old the original is, especially if the translation is done in contemporary language, as is usually the case.

*   *   *

Affinity is controversial these days. It is a major critical stance to see poetry and fiction as consisting of "texts" that stand apart from their authors. Considering the increasingly biographical approach to authors in the popular media, including most book reviews, it seems that "the death of the author" is dead itself. But in large parts of academia, authors are still dinosaurs who, during the Romantizoic era, grew too big to survive. Or perhaps elephants stomping clumsily through life, valuable only for their tusks. In any event, the academics who believe in the death of the author see all literature as, in effect, "translation," that is, making literature out of what is already there; after all, nothing *is* new under the sun. Using approaches determined by contemporary culture, authors manipulate what's out there into something that only seems original, but cannot possibly be. Such academics see actual literary translation as only one of many forms of manipulating a text. Affinity has no place in this scheme, because how can one feel affinity with another manipulator of texts just because you happen to be manipulating the same texts? Fellowship, perhaps, but affinity?

Since I happen to dislike the Romantizoic, biographical approach to literature in which I was educated, and which to some extent placed the literary biography above the literary work, this view of authors is tempting to me. The fact that it is, essentially, true makes it even harder to resist. But it ignores one important fact: original authors do exist. There are just very few of them, and even most of these are unoriginal in many ways, or too difficult to appeal to anyone but readers of "texts." It is also true that even authors who are not essentially original have original aspects: styles, voices, quirks. So, although most authors are little more than manipulators of cultural forms and icons, the authors who really matter rise above this, and it is to them that the translators who really matter turn.

*   *   *

The most intriguing relationship between translator and author that I've come across in my research and interviewing is one of great affinity and devotion, but not reverence. The author is both similar to and very different from the translator. It is this alloyed tension, I think, that makes the affinity so strong.

John Felstiner, a professor at Stanford University, has written two books about translating particular authors: Pablo Neruda and Paul Celan. To put this in perspective, nobody else, to my knowledge, has ever written a book in English about translating a particular author.

I will be focusing on Felstiner's relationship with Paul Celan (whose real name, for the record, was Paul Antschel). Celan (1920-1970) was a great poet of the Holocaust. Although Celan grew up in Czernowitz, in Romanian-speaking Bukovina (a small, once very Jewish area on the edge of the Austrian Empire, Romania, and the Ukraine), lived most of his adult life in Paris, and was emotionally overwhelmed by the Holocaust, he wrote his poetry in German. Although not well known in English-speaking countries during his lifetime, he is now attracting translators like beebalm.

In a talk at Yale University, Felstiner shared a fantasy of his: "It's a fantasy that takes place in the early summer of 1939. I do know that there was one time when Neruda and Celan were in the same place. In the late spring, early summer of 1939, Neruda was in Paris, having gone through his part in the Spanish Civil War. He was receiving refugees in Paris and trying to get them to Chile, and so on. He had lost García Lorca, but he was still a partisan of the Republican government. And Paul Celan, a much younger person, was in Paris to study medicine, but mainly to study surrealism, which is what was happening for him then.

"The fantasy begins at some café on the Left Bank, where I imagine Neruda and Celan sitting down together — they'd probably been introduced by Paul Eluard, who was a friend of Neruda's and a passion of Celan's — and the subject comes around to translation. The question comes up of who can translate this powerful

Latin-American voice and who can translate this as-yet-obscure—because he was still writing love poems to his mother—this poet-to-be from Czernowitz. And oddly enough, a strange thought comes into all their heads at once, and they realize that somewhere in New York—I could have told them exactly where—or in Maine at the time, there is a three-year-old. And it's clear [from a picture of himself as a child Felstiner is holding up] that he's just gotten the news. That's why he's looking up with such a startled frown on his face, because it's bad enough that a three-year-old should be told he has to translate from two difficult Spanish and German poets, but he doesn't know any German or Spanish; he's rather worried. But I think he's up to the task, 'cause as you can see, he's scooping up his crayons and he's getting ready to go to work. So my fantasy continues: Neruda and Celan solemnly rise up, silently shake hands, and walk along into their separate destinies, confident that at one point . . . then I wake up."

Since musicians often feel they were born to play Bach or Beethoven, and actors feel they were born to play Hamlet or Mother Courage, it's nice to see a translator who not only feels he was born to translate the poets he's translated, but who can express it in such a whimsical, self-parodying way. But then Felstiner's first book was about the parodies and caricatures of the English humorist Max Beerbohm. Considering that the only other book I've written is a collection of literary parodies, I feel a sense of affinity with Felstiner myself.

One of the principal reasons Felstiner was drawn to Celan is not quite so whimsical. Felstiner's background, he said at Yale, "has something in kindredship to Celan's own background. If I were born where my father was born, in Lemburg [Germany], I know that my fate would have been much worse than Celan's. One can document that. But I wasn't. As my mother used to say, 'There but for the grace of God go I.'"

Because Felstiner's father came to America, he did not suffer the same fate as Celan's father, who was deported in 1942 and presumably killed in a concentration camp. Celan's mother suffered the same fate. Felstiner said in a talk given at an ALTA conference in October 1994, "Celan came back after one night and found the door barred. He never saw his mother again, and perhaps without reason, one of the pictures I keep over my desk whenever I'm translating is a picture of his mother."

Felstiner has not said very much about his relationship with Celan beyond his stories and the fact that he spent seventeen years of his life translating Celan's poetry, researching his life in great depth, and writing article after article that culminated in the 1995 book *Paul Celan: Poet, Survivor, Jew*. Felstiner's feelings can best be seen obliquely, for example, in his introduction to the book: "in encountering these poems and becoming conversant with them, I have felt a grim energy verging on elation. Does this belie the burden of Celan's voice, or is elation akin to something the poet knew?" There's so much here: the experience of translating Celan, the hope that in translating Celan's poems he felt something akin to what Celan felt writing them, and the concern that his elation was somehow a betrayal, inappropriate to Celan's struggle to voice his grim feelings.

Felstiner's burden was a heavy one, and he clearly worried that he was not bringing all he could over into English. He said in his ALTA talk, "Celan's language was German, the mother tongue which for Celan also became the murderers' tongue. When the only thing he had left — no parents, no homeland, no culture, no family — was his mother tongue, then the alienation that occurs when I translate him is an extra turn of the screw, it seems to me, a loss." And at Yale he noted about a particular translation decision, "I was trying to redeem the loss a little bit."

Felstiner's relationship with Celan can also be inferred from what he says about Celan's relationships with the authors *he* translated, particularly William Shakespeare and Osip Mandelshtam. "Celan translated Mandelshtam like a long lost blood brother, although he never met him," Felstiner said in his ALTA talk. "Many things occasioned this 'shock of recognition' (Melville's phrase) in Celan. Mandelshtam . . . had worked as a translator and had once attempted suicide. Each grew up close to his mother and because of his father harbored ambivalence toward Judaism. Both underwent political and literary persecution not unrelated to their origins. . . . The alienation Celan shared with Mandelshtam and Kafka made them into alter egos. The Russian poet, he once said, offered 'what is brotherly—in the most reverential sense I can give that word. . . . I consider translating Mandelshtam into German to be as important a task as my own verses.'"

"During his time of psychic distress," Felstiner wrote, "Celan translated the author he most esteemed. . . . He began learning English so as to read Shakespeare, tried some sonnet translations, and at eighteen in England went to see the plays performed. . . . When the Germans invaded in 1941, he recited his Shakespeare translations in the Czernowitz ghetto, I'm told, and during his months at forced labor carried a notebook containing his version of sonnet 57."*

I think it would be going too far to say that Felstiner sees Celan as a brother or alter ego. But it isn't the type of relationship that's important; it is much more the "shock of recognition," sharing a feeling of alienation, of tragedy, of psychic distress. In fact, it's the activity of sharing, identifying, empathizing that is most important. Translation, like any relationship, is a process, a getting closer, a learning more, a doing things together, a worrying about, a growing love.

Love and devotion do not, however, necessitate reverence. Celan, for one, molded the poetry of his favorite writers to fit his reactions to their work. "In Celan's twenty-one sonnet translations," Felstiner wrote, "Shakespeare suffers a sea change into something rich and strange, often very strange. I see no contradiction between the esteeming and the estranging."* Celan's style of translation was to break up, add, subtract, question, and argue with the original. Felstiner quotes Celan's 1948 love poem to show what sort of love Celan had for the poetry he translated: "Only faithless am I true. / I am you, when I am I." Felstiner added his own summation: "In love or translation, identifying with an other demands truth to oneself."

Serge Gavronsky has identified two opposite approaches to translation, represented by two very different American translators of poetry. He told me, "One was Amy Lowell, and Amy Lowell did a number of very interesting translations from the Chinese. She is, for many reasons, the archrepresentation of the submissive translator, that is, one who renders honor to the master text. . . . it's very clear that for her the translator disappears, no longer occupies an actual space, which is given over to the original. The other, and the absolute Other, is what I call cannibalism, which was Ezra Pound's theory, that is, when you take those hieroglyphic love poems that he 'translated' or the poems he did from the Chinese, and you ask a sinologist to give you a quicky of at least the meaning of the poems, you realize that Ezra Pound's aesthetics or poetics of translation is a very aggressive one. I exaggerate by calling it 'cannibal.'"

Celan was a cannibal. Felstiner did not, however, feel obliged to copy Celan's approach to translation. Felstiner's goal was not to place his artistic imprint on Celan's poems, but rather to redeem all the loss Celan suffered and all the loss Celan has to suffer being transferred into another language. And for Felstiner too, esteeming does not require copying. He is not at the other extreme, where the translator disappears, submissively crouching behind the author's standing figure. Felstiner is there in front of the author, kneeling rather than crouching, interpreting, teaching, and redeeming rather than either adapting or worshiping the original.

Translating Celan's poetry, as he wrote of translating Pablo Neruda's, is "an oddly subjective experience—one of possessing and being possessed."* In reciting his translations of the Chilean poet's work, he "discovered a strange side effect of translating at its most earnest: the experience of being possessed, the illusion that the lines you've translated are speaking through you and for you." But Felstiner also felt something else: "a strange sense of having authored the lines I am speaking." And so when he looks back at the Spanish original, he is "astonished to find that somehow it now sounds like an uncannily good translation of my own poem, with perhaps a few odd spots."* And when at his Yale talk someone in the audience referred to the Celan original as "the German version," Felstiner responded half-seriously, "Sometimes I think of it as a strangely timewarped version of my own translation."

Felstiner's relationship with Celan is not only with him but also with all the loss Celan felt and with the way that he expressed that loss. There is also Felstiner's own feeling of loss, what the Holocaust means to him personally. Every translator is nagged by what he cannot preserve, but in translating a poetry of loss, any further loss is agonizing. Felstiner felt an obligation to learn everything he could about Celan so that there would be as little loss as possible. At the same time, he was drawn to and excited by this search and by the attempt to capture not only what any translator strives for, but more and deeper and with complete knowledge of what he is doing, and what he is not able to do.

Affinity, devotion, redemption — these sorts of submission give us some of our best, most passionate translations. And they do this by bringing the translator into an exceptionally intimate relationship with the original work of art. Even if Felstiner had written a critical biography of Celan, he could not have become nearly as intimate with Celan's work—and thus the man—as he did by translating him.

Paul Blackburn, an American poet of the 50s and 60s, said it nice and directly: "I don't become the author when I'm translating his prose or poetry, but I'm certainly getting my talents into his hang-ups. Another person's preoccupations are occupying me. They literally own me for that time. . . . In a way you live [the text] each time, I mean, *you're there*. Otherwise, you're not holding the poem."*

"Holding the poem." The way you'd hold a lover. Putting up with hang-ups, living together. Except with a lover, you share each other's hang-ups, and when you hold you get held back. The translator can have this experience only when there is mutual translation. Usually it's a one-way experience, a one-way intimacy. But it's neither masturbation nor one-way giving; there's at least as much taking as there is giving. It's just that the author is not actively doing the giving the translator takes; he's already done the giving, placed the gift under the tree.

This sort of intimacy does not have to turn into published translations, as Rosanna Warren told me: "My practice as a writer is to absorb and study poems that move me, that excite me, that pull me in. And some of them are in foreign languages, and part of the impulse of approaching and entering these works sometimes involves my doing a translation of them, to get truly inside them. . . . Sometimes these translations don't come to anything that's going to be presentable; it was just a practice of intimacy, but sometimes that turns into something that one can show an outside world."

Sometimes the intimacy involves a third party: an earlier translator, or sometimes even multiple translators. This was the case with Jonathan Galassi when he translated the poetry of Eugenio Montale. He told me, "the person I'm in *agon* with is William Arrowsmith, because Arrowsmith has done all these translations. . . . He didn't try to stick to Montale's form; he produced a very strong English, almost a prose text that is a reading of the poems. Mine are trying to do it within the formal constraints of Montale's verse, closer to an imitation of the form as well as the meaning. I have Montale on one side and Arrowsmith on the other. . . . I've borrowed things from him; it's been a dialogue."

It's the intimacy, and all that comes out of it—learning, understanding, expanding one's horizons—that makes the translator's submission such a positive experience. "Is translation as self-transcendence still another version of the paradox: to know yourself, lose yourself in the other?" Edwin Honig wrote in the introduction to his collection of interviews with translators, *The Poet's Other Voice*.* And the answer, of course, is, Yes. Every translator knows that there is no better way to find yourself than by losing yourself; the question is whether you're finding what was there, hidden, or providing new ammunition to articulate what was already there. Or as Herbert Mason, the translator of *Gilgamesh* and other epic works, told Honig in the same book, "translation is a process of gaining intimacy with a work, or a person, or another mode of expression, or another time . . . a process of dragging me out of myself into the open, into a sense of audience."* But then, what each of us considers to be his self is something internal that yearns to be transcended or opened up. Frederic Will has written that the notions of "self" and "other" "are not that unitary or solid. They are intermeshing notions, . . . self meaning among other things what one becomes through others."*

Gaining through submission to another's voice is especially valuable for young writers, but it's useful throughout a writer's lifetime, allowing him to keep growing. The American poet John Hollander discovered the Yiddish poet Moishe-Lieb Halpern when asked to do some translations for an anthology: "they seemed to help me develop a certain tonal mode in my own poems. That is, what I had to do to translate certain poems of Halpern's, I've now retained as a vocal element. Doing Halpern provided a way of unlocking certain things."* In other words, the act of submission does not only involve locking oneself into another writer's mind and style and vision, but also unlocking things in oneself.

But it isn't just what comes out of it, the personal, artistic gains that matter; it's the experience of intimacy, spending time with the loved words of the author, or the loved author's words. The joy that a reader experiences can be multiplied many times in the intimate act of performing a writer's work. Rilke wrote in a letter that he translated Paul Valéry's poetry "with a joyous rapture." Nothing is more satisfying than a book that gets better and richer each time you go through it; few ever have to do this and, therefore, never know the joy of a translator whose ongoing intimacy opens up beauties he would never otherwise have noticed.

A translator, like any reader, can be literally captivated by a poet's sheer beauty. David Wevill noted this in discussing the problems of translating the contemporary French poet Yves Bonnefoy: "the poetry is hypnotic and this hypnosis can affect the translator to the degree that he is no longer re-creating but merely obeying."* Yet what a joy it can be to obey.

*   *   *

The great irony of a translator's submission is that the translator generally gets more rewards than the author. It's not supposed to work that way: the submitting party is supposed to get the brunt rather than the best of the bargain. It's true that the laurels go to the author, but in English-speaking countries it's the rare foreign author who ever gets enough fame to make it worth anyone's while. In fact, most translations—even those competently done— are never published, and most poetry and story translations that are published appear in magazines or books with very small readerships. Even the great majority of published novels in translation reach tiny audiences. So it is the rare foreign author who attains fame, but the translator always gets the rewards he's seeking.

Lost and Found

THE MOST OFT-REPEATED English-language words about translation are those of Robert Frost: "Poetry is what gets lost in translation." This topsy-turvy definition of translation is from one of the few great poets never to have translated. But famous it is, and no one can enter the topic of translation without walking under a gate bearing its words.

Frost appears to me not to have been talking about translation as much as he was using (or abusing) translation to define poetry. But his words have been taken up by those who don't believe in translation. Here's how the sentence looks turned around so that, for the purpose of talking about translation, it's facing front: "Translating poetry loses what poetry is." Or: "In translating a poem, the essence of that poem is lost;" what is preserved are the inessential elements—the images, the basic ideas, many of the words—but not the sounds or the multiple meanings or resonances of the words, the exact way in which the ideas and images are ordered and embodied. In other words, poetry is something that works only in the language it was originally written in and for. Bringing it over into another language is impossible, not really worth doing.

There is a long history to the idea that literary translation is impossible. Frost simply happened to say it in a clever way, a way that would be difficult to translate, just as it is difficult to translate the other most famous expression about translation, the Italian *Tradduttore, traditore*, which literally means "to translate is to betray." This expression is difficult to translate because it is a pun; for a contest I once translated it as "to seed a lay is to lead astray."

Dante wrote, "Nothing which is harmonized by the bond of the Muses can be changed from its own to another language without having all its sweetness destroyed."* In the medieval and Renaissance periods, translation was seen by many as something asymmetrical and therefore, according to minds reared on the symmetrically oriented classics, impossible.* By the end of the sixteenth century, the buzzword for what was lost in translation had become "spirit": the spirit, the soul, of a literary work could not pass through into the translated version.

Shelley was typical of the English Romantics when he wrote in his "Defense of Poetry," "it were as wise to cast a violet into a crucible that you might discover the formal principles of its colour and odour, as seek to transfuse from one language into another the creations of a poet." Note the subtle change from the spirit of a literary work to the more Romantic spirit of a poet's creations.

In the twentieth century, Thomas Mann applied this idea to literary prose: in translation "superior prose . . . is denatured, its rhythm is shattered, all the finer nuances fall by the wayside. Often, in fact, its innermost intentions, its spiritual posture and intellectual aims, are distorted beyond recognition, to the point of total misunderstanding, no matter how hard the translator tries for faithful reproduction."* Mann also wrote that, during Helen Lowe-Porter's work on an English translation of his *Lotte in Weimar*, she said to him with a sigh, "I am committing a murder."

In the introduction to his collection of essays on Shakespeare in translation, Dennis Kennedy wrote, "Everyone knows that a good and faithful translation of Shakespeare's text into another language is an impossibility. . . . At best only approximations can be assembled or an alternative poetry substituted."* He provided a list of what he thought was lost in translation, including subtleties, balances, reflections, insinuations, wordplay, suggestion, resonance, harmony, emphases.

Have you ever heard a musician say that it's impossible, or destructive, to play music, or an actor say it's impossible or destructive to play roles? Challenging, yes, difficult, demanding, certainly, but only for particular performers and particular roles or pieces of music does unplayability actually come into play. Why is translation plagued with the concept of impossibility, not just of the toughest works or of works that particular translators would find impossible, but generally, philosophically, annoyingly all-inclusively?

The greatest difference between performing a translation and performing a piece of music is that while music is written to be performed on instruments, literature is not written to be performed in other languages. No writer thinks, How wonderful this will sound in Swahili! Or worries, Will this come across in Slovak? And the poets of earlier centuries and cultures hardly thought, If I don't rhyme, how much easier it'll be for a twentieth-century American poet to translate me!

It's true that pieces of music are often transcribed for instruments they were never intended for, but these are not performances necessary to give life to the work; they are unnecessary, incidental changes. If they don't work, if they don't capture the spirit of the original, so what. It doesn't make the performances impossible, simply unsuccessful in the particular instance by the particular soloist or group. The original is not destroyed; it isn't even damaged.

Translation is both more and less wrenching than such adaptations. It takes a work of art whose medium is a particular language, and places it in a medium that is at once exactly the same and very different. When someone makes a film based on a novel, the novel has to be wrenched completely out of its medium. When someone writes a poem inspired by a painting, the painting is wrenched into another sphere entirely—there are no more brush-strokes, no perspective, no frame, except metaphorically—and everyone knows it and expects nothing but an interesting interpretation. The translator wrenches a poem into English, but is still stuck with language as his medium. There are words and words, sounds and sounds, expressions and expressions, lines and lines, rhythms and rhythms, images and images, wordplay and wordplay. It is conceivable that every effect in the original can be reproduced in the translation. Every single one. Perfectly. There is no Platonic ideal of an adaptation; there *is* a Platonic ideal of a translation.

And wherever there are ideals, there is the impossibility of attaining them. The perfect anything is impossible.

Impossibility is not only something that critics talk about and writers use to justify their anger at or disappointment with what translation does to their works. It is also something that bothers translators themselves. Translation is what Jonathan Galassi, an editor of translations at Farrar, Straus & Giroux and a translator of Italian poetry, has called "a hopeless enterprise." Harry Zohn, a veteran translator from the German, told me, "Even if it were possible to make a living as a translator, I couldn't because of all the defeats you constantly undergo. Only the translator knows how far short his or her efforts fall from the ideal. It's a compromise very often; it's the art of the best possible failure. And to have that as a full-time thing. . . In teaching, you sometimes see results; you sometimes get accolades. As a translator you tend to take it on the chin. It's a no-win situation, and it's very disappointing."

Richard Wilbur has referred to his translation of Baudelaire's poem "L'Invitation au voyage" as "a less ludicrous failure than the attempts of others."* And Richard Sieburth told me, in reference to his current work on Mallarmé, "you're setting yourself up for the fall . . . It's constantly courting failure, a flirtation with a built-in failure. That's my task: to learn how to fail." It is statements like these that led George Steiner to write, "From the perception of unending inadequacy stems a particular sadness. It haunts the history and theory of translation."*

If I went on like this, the breast-beating would sound increasingly hollow. But as it happens, impossibility is not only an occasion for sadness, it is also one of the translator's greatest incentives. Sieburth says that he is attracted to impossible projects. Willis Barnstone has written, "What seems impossible to translate is truly worth doing. A neutral passage may be easily translated, but the result may also be neutral. But to the translator-poet the untranslatable poem yields the best poem. One tests oneself according to the resistance encountered, and so the untranslatable incites one, forces one, into freedom and invention. If the poem is to be rendered the imagination must soar."*

It's exciting to read Willard Trask's words, "I'd love to translate *Madame Bovary*. It's the greatest novel ever written, and probably the most impossible prose to translate. I'd love to have a try at it."* Or the words of Octavio Paz: "Poetry is 'impossible' to translate because you have to reproduce the materiality of the signs, its physical properties. Here is where translation as an *art* begins."*

Many translators look at literary works in terms of the percentage of its attributes they feel can be brought into English. It's very normal for a translator to feel that eighty-percent of a work can be brought over, but sometimes it's as low as fifty-percent. "If it's one hundred percent," Donald Frame has written, "or even close to that, it may not be challenging or at all interesting."* Eighty-percent might seem low, but then how many novels ever exceed eighty-percent of what they could possibly be?

Despite his beliefs, Shelley *did* translate poetry, and even Mann, after stating his belief in the destructiveness of translation, acknowledged its necessity: "Yet who would wish to discourage the peoples of the world from translating, merely because it is *fundamentally* impossible? . . . I do not know a word of Russian, and the German translations in which as a young man I read the great Russian writers of the nineteenth century were very feeble. Nevertheless, I consider this reading among my greatest cultural experiences."*

Here Mann touched on the essence of why translation, no matter how impossible, is done: it is necessary. How else would he have read Dostoevsky and Tolstoy? How differently Mann would have written with no knowledge of the Russians!

But translation is not only necessary to make great writers greater. It is necessary to remove a terrible curse. The place to turn for the question of translation's necessity is the biblical tale of the Tower of Babel. Let me start by giving the King James Version version, from Genesis 11:

> And the whole earth was of one language and of one
> speech. And it came to pass, as they [Noah's family, after
> the flood] journeyed from the east, that they found a
> plain in the land of Shinar; and they dwelt there. And
> they said one to another, Go to, let us make brick, and
> burn them throughly. And they had brick for stone, and
> slime had they for morter. And they said, Go to, let us
> build us a city and a tower, whose top *may reach* unto
> heaven; and let us make us a name, lest we be scattered
> abroad upon the face of the whole earth. And the Lord
> came down to see the city and the tower, which the
> children of men builded. And the Lord said, Behold, the
> people *is* one, and they have all one language; and this
> they begin to do: and now nothing will be restrained
> from them, which they have imagined to do. Go to, let
> us go down, and there confound their language, that they
> may not understand one another's speech. So the Lord
> scattered them abroad from thence upon the face of all
> the earth; and they left off to build the city. Therefore
> is the name of it called Babel; because the Lord did there
> confound the language of all the earth: and from thence
> did the Lord scatter them abroad upon the face of all the
> earth.

In the beginning, the tale goes, there was no need for translation. There was one people, one language. But people wanted to
do whatever they could imagine. People don't need armies of
workers to do this; all they need are armies of readers. So God
gave each person—in future, each people—a different language, so
that they could not communicate the expressions of their imagination, at least in the form of language. All the other arts communicate fine after the destruction of the Tower of Babel; only those
using the medium of language were cursed, sent into a state of
eternal confusion. And so only the linguistic arts require translation
in order to spread abroad upon the face of the earth. To add insult
to injury, of all the performing arts we consider only translation to
be impossible.

God placed a curse on mankind that could be defeated in only
one way: by translating. Thus translation is ultimately a clever form
of blasphemy, the building of many little bridges instead of one

big tower. Mankind has invented numerous ways to overcome the part of the curse that spread us across the face of the earth: ships, roads, airplanes, the Internet. But translation is the only way that has been invented to overcome the curse of a profusion of languages. *Lingua francas* have come and gone, but they have usually been only regional or imperial. Esperanto was a failure. Only now is English threatening to become the first language understood around the world. Yet at the same time, small languages are being revived and preserved like never before. And English is hardly a worldwide project to build another tower to heaven, to end the curse of Babel. It is fallout from the spread of American entertainment, fashion, and businesses, following on the footsteps of a more conscious spread of British culture in the years before. In any event, most of the people who speak English as a second or third language still read in their first language and watch their movies dubbed. In fact, the greatest literary effects of this growth of English-language culture are the *writing* in English of more works from more cultures and increasing translation out of English into all the world's other languages.

When I spoke with Serge Gavronsky, he had just finished writing a paper on the Babel tale. His thesis, he told me, was that "man has outwitted God. Man has transformed punishment, that is, the multiplication of languages as a result of having built the Tower of Babel, into the only thing that is worth our being on this earth, and that is a literary signature, the growth of literary expression throughout the globe. . . . Had those settlers in the Euphrates delta not transformed clay into bricks, which I will use as a metaphor for texts, and had they not . . . arrogated to themselves the pleasure of creation, which is the Tower of Babel, I would not be a translator, neither would there be any literature, because Genesis is particularly clear on this: there was one language, but there were few words. . . . [U]nderneath the *con*fusion there will be *pro*fusion, the multiplicity of languages. . . . [W]hat God believed was a proper form of the second Fall — it's clear, the first Fall was eating the [fruit of knowledge]. But *Genesis* says also that if you do eat of the fruit of knowledge, your eyes will be opened, and you will have, like Myself, the ability to distinguish between good and evil. That means, metaphorically, that when they ate of the fruit of knowlege, they were then no longer blind, and if they're no longer blind, metaphorically speaking, they can read. That was the first Fall, which allowed them to read, and the second is the Tower of Babel, which allowed them to write. . . . [A]nd the translator is the go-between, the one which allows the mother texts throughout the world to be available. He is the mid-wife, he allows the text to re-emerge under a different national sign, but he does it, he carries, he trans-ports, as the Greek word for metaphor says. That's what a metaphor is: it transports from here to there. That's what translation does, too."

In the New Testament there happens to be a solution to the curse of Babel, which not surprisingly inspired the single most important translation project of modern times. Pentecost is the solution, and the project is the translation of the Bible into every language on Earth. Here's what Acts 2 says, again from the King James Version:

> And when the day of Pentecost was fully come, [the apostles] were all with one accord in one place. . . . And there appeared unto them cloven tongues like as of fire, and it sat upon each of them. And they were all filled with the Holy Ghost, and began to speak with other tongues, as the Spirit gave them utterance. . . . Now when this was noised abroad, the multitude came together, and were confounded, because that every man heard them speak in his own language. And they were all amazed and marvelled, saying one to another, Behold, are not all these which speak Galilaeans? And how hear we every man in our own tongue, wherein we were born? . . . Then Peter said unto them, Repent, and be baptized every one of you in the name of Jesus Christ for the remission of sins, and ye shall receive the gift of the Holy Ghost. . . . And all that believed were together, and had all things common.

Due to the curse of Babel, people around the world could not understand the teachings of Jesus. So the Holy Ghost intervened and gave the apostles the gift of tongues, so that they could translate the teachings of Jesus into all the world's languages. And all that believed would be united again in this belief. The Catholic Church opted for one language, like one Church and one God, to unite everyone. The leaders of the Reformation interpreted Acts as instead calling for the translation of Jesus's words, so that everyone could read them and understand them themselves. Reformation leaders translated the Bible, and then missionaries became language experts, translator-apostles. As a result, the Bible has been the first book to appear in hundreds of languages, and it has radically affected nearly all of them.

Protestant Bible translators are the last people to believe in the impossibility of translation. Translation not only into languages, but also into colloquial language that can be understood by all, is something they have considered absolutely necessary to the spread of Christianity. But this is not true of all religions. Jews have historically been opposed to the translation of their sacred texts. The sacred nature of the Torah is closely tied to the Hebrew language. The words of God were Hebrew words and must remain that. Jewish readers must come to God, rather than God to Jewish readers. But then Judaism is not a proselytizing religion, so it can afford not to reach out through translation. More recently, Conservative and Reform Jews have, however, translated the Jewish scriptures into numerous languages.

To sum things up, translation might seem impossible, but due to the curse of Babel it is necessary. And it is translation's apparent impossibility that attracts many of the best translators and gives them the drive to do their best work. Translation is thus an art of submissive people trying to do the impossible as well as to undo man's second fall. Translation might feel tragically hopeless at times, but it is our only hope and, I feel, should be considered more comic than tragic. As Ben Belitt wrote in *Adam's Dream*, "the translator's vocation is a *comic* one. . . . [one thinks] 'I'm engaged in what I know is an impossible transaction.' . . . Then one immediately sets about translating it, as if all were really possible; *that's* comic!"* Or at least translation is absurd, as George Steiner wrote, "an endeavour to go backwards up the escalator of time and to re-enact voluntarily what was a contingent motion of spirit."*

There are many ways in which translation *is* "impossible." Steiner points out the example of extreme political situations: "when the conceptual reach and valuation of a word can be altered by political decree, language loses credibility. Translation in the ordinary sense becomes impossible. To translate a Stalinist text . . . into a non-Stalinist idiom, using the same time-honoured words, is to produce a polemic gloss, a counter-statement of values."* This is something too often ignored: the fact that words, in particular contexts, have unspoken values attached to them which do not necessarily come across in literal translation. This is true under even less extreme conditions, that is, whenever language is used dishonestly. For example, when Ronald Reagan spoke of "family values," he was referring to a range of ideological positions that had little to do with families. A literal translation of this cynical expression into Russian would have as little meaning as a literal translation of Communist hogwash into English.

Richard Wilbur talked with me about another sort of impossibility that is associated with differing values. "It is difficult to imagine bringing over in translation, for example, the Italian word *pazienza* said in the way in which an Italian says it. If an American says to an American, 'Have patience,' it does not remotely mean what an Italian means by *pazienza*, because of the great American smile, because of the conspiracy to be upbeat, to think upbeat, and to talk upbeat. The Italian expectation of life is much darker, and so the word *pazienza* does not have many ready equivalents in English. Things like 'This too will pass' approach part of the meaning of *pazienza*, but that's not economical or as colloquial."

What is understood easily and deeply by a native reader is often meaningless to the reader of another language, who does not know the original language's history and culture. Jonathan Galassi told me in reference to Eugenio Montale, "so much of his poetry is allusion to the history of Italian poetry. None of that can really come across. You can try to create a language in English that is rich with association, but you're creating a kind of artifact that's not the same thing."

Many people say that today it's impossible to rhyme in translating poetry and still keep it contemporary. Tell that to Richard Wilbur or Willis Barnstone. Barnstone has written, "without the fine craft of using rhyme naturally and invisibly, a rhyming translation is impossible. Few contemporary poets have such craft, and this fact, rather than taste, is responsible for the scarcity of translations in rhyme."*

Taste does come into play, however, in making translation impossible. Some works can simply not be translated into certain languages at certain times. The example George Steiner has given is Aristophanes in Victorian English: Aristophanes' sense of humor was considered too crude by Victorians. Today, few literary Americans would be able to translate a racist work into English, except as a document.

One of the most difficult kinds of poetry to translate is, paradoxically, the simplest poetry. "[T]he more difficult the poem," Michael Hamburger has written, "the more complex and idiosyncratic its structure, the more likely it is that a good deal of its quiddity can be satisfactorily conveyed in translation. It is the plainest, most limpid, poem that may defy translation, because it leaves the least latitude for paraphrase and interpretation, and the plainness that may be a happy reduction in one language and literary convention can sound like an intolerable banality in another."*

Humor is up there with simplicity. Eugene Nida, best known for his books on the theory of Bible translation, has written, "Saying something in a novel manner is bound to have impact. This is precisely what makes Ogden Nash's epigrams so tantalizing and at the same time almost impossible to translate. Note, for example, 'He who is ridden by a conscience / Worries about a lot of nonscience.'"* Wordplay generally has to be totally recreated, which requires a very special sort of translator, one who is a humorist himself.

But probably the most difficult translations are of lyrics.

Ronnie Apter, who translates opera lyrics with her husband, Mark Herman, has written that the translator of poetry "may choose to be tied to a syllable-for-syllable translation, or a stress-for-stress translation, or he may choose to be free of both. The translator of lyrics [meant to be sung] has no such freedom. He must translate syllable-for-syllable, stress-for-stress (although the stress may be ordained by the music, rather than by the original words). He must crest meaning where the melodic line crests. Also, he must [ask] can this syllable be held for two beats without sounding silly? Can the tenor get off this syllable in the space of an eighth note and take a catch breath?"* Nothing is more impossible than meeting all the demands of singing opera, wearing what Apter calls "the strait-jacket of the notes," preserving not only the rhymes but the exact rhythms of a language that has a completely different rhythm than English. And putting words to music, even though opera usually consists of putting music to words. And yet no translators I've spoken with seem to love their work more than Apter and Herman.

According to Edmund Keeley, a translator of modern Greek poetry, W. H. Auden had an excellent response to Frost's dictum: "some would say . . . that what constitutes poetry, at least in the indi-vidual case, is exactly what survives in translation: that which is so essentially poetic in a given poet's voice that it can be heard in any translation, for example, what Auden calls Cavafy's 'unique tone of voice,' unmistakable in English, he believes, whoever the translator may be."* This is definitely the case when a poet's voice rather than his language is the most prominent aspect of his work. Eliot Weinberger echoes Auden, but in a much more general sense: "Poetry," he wrote, "is that which is worth translating. The poem dies when it has no place to go."* It's interesting that both of these translators so concerned about the poet's voice are among the few poetry translators who do not write poetry themselves, who do not have poetic voices, but are excellent writers of prose. Keeley told me that for him this is a conscious choice, not to create his own voice as a poet that would get in the way of his translations. Similarly, Richard Howard is a poet who translates almost exclusively prose, although he did get hooked on Baudelaire. But for most translators, the process is one of melding voices, using aspects of one's own voice to bring a foreign voice into English.

The most direct response to those who quote Frost is George Steiner's: "The defence of translation has the immense advantage of abundant, vulgar fact."* And the most humorous is James Thurber's. Once upon a time, Thurber met a French admirer of his. "I am fortunate," said the admirer, "to speak English well enough to appreciate—and to love—your stories. But, I have also read them translated into French and, believe me, they are even better in French." The modest Thurber nodded and said, "I know. I tend to lose something in the original."*

The courageous translator does not want to merely respond to Frost's dictum; he wants to show him. Probably the most courageous translator, besides those who translated the Bible when it meant being burned at the stake, was a German contemporary of Goethe, Friedrich Hölderlin. Hölderlin translated ancient Greek writers, particularly Pindar and Sophocles, and he got burned in the process. But it was he who did the burning, not an outside authority. Richard Sieburth, who has translated Hölderlin's later poetry, wrote, "it is precisely the intensity of this conflagration that accounts for the dark, charred radiance of his versions. As he writes in one of his late fragments: 'Verwegner! möchst von Angesicht zu Angesicht / Die Seele sehn / Du gehest in Flammen unter.' Reckless! wanting to see the soul / Face to face / You go down in flames."* What Hölderlin was seeking, according to Sieburth, was "the ultimate etymological root (or *logos*) that lay buried beneath all the divisions of language. Yet he also remained keenly conscious of the fundamental hubris of his enterprise: How, given the essential limitation and fragmentation of human speech, could the translator aspire to disclose the unity of the divine Word? The pressures this awareness exerted on Hölderlin's language account for its extraordinary intensity and fragility."* Essentially, instead of building bridges, Hölderlin tried to build another Babel of his own, and he built too close to the sun. His wings were burned, he lost his sanity.

The Romance of Infidelity

FIDELITY IS THE BASIC ETHICAL TERM in translation. Infidelity means a translator's betrayal of the original work and its author.

An artist is expected to be faithful only to himself. An artist can be revolutionary; an artist can reject a tradition or a teacher. This is how schools of art or writing or music come into being. This is what the history of art is all about. Betrayal and promiscuity are respected in an artist.

In the primary arts, there is no original to betray. You can take the *Odyssey* and do anything you want with it—write a play, a ballet, a novel, another poem even—and no one will say you were unfaithful to it, unless you make an absolute mockery of it. And most likely not even then. You have simply interpreted it according to your whims and the times you live in. You are an artist.

What about the secondary arts: performing music, directing plays, adapting novels into screenplays? Here there *is* an original: a musical composition, a play, a novel. A performer can be accused of getting it wrong, a director of going too far, an adapter of missing what made the novel great. But it's rarely a question of fidelity; usually it's a question of eccentricity, incompetence, mis-interpretation, commercialism. A performer's style strips a piece of music of its power; a director's change of gender or time doesn't work or is too clever for everyone's good; an adapter cravenly sands over all the bumpy, provocative aspects of the novel. But even at their worst, they're only misinterpreting, being experimental, selling out. They are first and foremost interpreters, and when they do a poor job, they are simply bad, incompetent interpreters. They have a style, are allowed a style. They take too many risks, or too few, but they are allowed risks. The only thing truly at risk, as with the original artist, is reputation, because the performer, director, adapter is also someone expected to express himself, to be revolutionary, to reject traditions and teachers.

The literary translator is, however, not treated even as a secondary artist in this sense: he is not expressing himself and has no right to be revolutionary. Instead critics ask, Is the translation faithful to the original? Does it do justice to it? Does it betray it? Is it a reasonable facsimile? Are there any mistakes (and if so, they *must* be pointed out)? A director's judgment might be mistaken, but he doesn't make mistakes. A performer makes mistakes, but they do no harm to the original, and his "not doing justice" to the composition is less a matter of ethics than of personal competence and quirks. When a translator makes a mistake, or—even worse—boldly interprets, he has dealt a blow to the original. He is unfaithful, he is an abuser. He screws around, comes home in the middle of the night, and beats his wife. He is expected not to go out and fool around, but to stay home and be submissive. In fact, he is expected not to be a he at all, but a traditional she. The translator is a member of a helping profession, someone who nurses poems and stories into another language. This is what comes with the pleasures of service, the intimacy of submission.

There is a serious double standard going on here: the translator is often unfaithful, the author never is. Why? Because although fidelity is a word that is used with respect to a person's obligations to a spouse, who can be unfaithful himself, in the case of translation it is more a matter of a person's obligations to her father, to someone who cannot be unfaithful back. Unlike in a marriage, the translator is the only one acting, the only one with obligations; the author has already done everything he has to do, and the original is the result of his completed act. The original can now only be acted upon. The original is an old father who must be taken care of, to whom obedience is owed, who has spent his life giving, giving, giving. Now it's the translator's turn to do her duty. Duty is the defining characteristic of a relationship based on one-way fidelity. As John Dryden wrote a few hundred years ago, if a translator's work is successful, "we are not thanked; for the proud reader will only say, the poor drudge has done his duty."* The first commandment of literary translation is, "Honor thy original and thy author."

You might be wondering, What *could* an author possibly be unfaithful to? As I said, the artist is considered to have no obligations except to himself (although various constituencies will attack him for nonartistic acts and statements). The artist is a hero without a country; because he fights for himself alone, he can be a traitor only if he sells out, and even then a traitor only to those who care about such things and can tell the difference. This is not the place to set forth my ideas about an artist's obligations, about his responsibilities to his culture, to ethical standards, to artistic standards. But I think it is worth wondering if there are such obligations. It is worth questioning the Romantic assumption that the artist is a demigod, a father who gives birth to a work of art that has no mother. Even Coleridge's passive image of the author as Aeolian harp gives the author no obligations, no chance of being unfaithful.

When people write or talk about translation, fidelity is always either on the tip of the tongue or in the back of the mind. Some people talk about how important fidelity is, while others try to defend themselves, in advance, against the accusation of betrayal. But in the little world of literary translation, people spend most of their time trying to define it. Fidelity to what or to whom? To what aspects of the original? To what extent?

The question of fidelity in translation is at least as complicated as it is in love, so let me start by giving some background, some history. Throughout most of classical and modern history, the translator did whatever he wanted with the works he translated. This was true of the Romans, who took what they felt like taking from Greek culture and made it theirs. As Friedrich Nietzsche wrote, "In those days, to translate meant to conquer."* Zoja Pavlovskis has written, "[Writers] vied with one another in rewording, paraphrasing, amplifying, reinterpreting, condensing, parodying, and commenting on what their forerunners had produced."* Roman translators did tend to be faithful in terms of form; they brought Greek poetic forms into Latin just as an American translator today preserves every single paragraph of a novel. But the Romans wouldn't have thought twice about leaving out a stanza, or changing it radically to fit their own vision and taste, any more than most translators today would question turning a rhymed, metered stanza into free verse. What they wanted were the verse forms and the vocabulary. Translating quantitative Greek meters into Latin, even then a primarily accentual language, was, according to Peter Glassgold, "a mark of wealth, education, and training to be able to . . . pull it off effectively, to actually get a rhetorical and dramatic effect in the way you wrench your language." Then, literary translation was a matter of pride in creating difficult yet perfect forms; now it is primarily a matter of doing the author justice.

According to translation historian L. G. Kelly, translators during the Middle Ages were "not concerned with anything but intellectual information."* D. P. Lockwood wrote that "medieval translations . . . were not regarded as *belles lettres*. They were a means to an end—a purely professional end."* The eighteenth century also used translation to serve its ends: "What the Middle Ages shared with the Age of Reason," Kelly wrote, "was the conviction that the universally human could only be understood in the familiar terms of their own society."* That is, translators took the content and put it into their own culture's verse forms, cut out what they didn't like, and added in their own moral tenets.

As for the Renaissance, according to Antoine Berman, a French translation theorist, "The lettered public of the sixteenth century . . . rejoiced in reading a work in its different linguistic variants; it ignored the issue of fidelity."* This is an especially difficult thing for us to imagine, but it becomes easier when one realizes that the lettered public of the time was tiny and multilingual. Here were people who actually delighted in reading a work in its Latin, Greek, or vernacular original as well as in its French, Italian, and English versions, often far from what we consider translations. Each work might be in a different form, satisfying different literary tastes, with different voices, tones, even different visions, much the same way different film directors would approach the same novel today. Translators could be much more clearly artists at a time when their role was the same as the author's: to entertain, to express, to expand their art and their language. Translation in Renaissance Europe was not a palliative for the disease of mono-glotism, as it is today; it was a part of literature, a part of the passing of literary traditions and creations from language to language, and a part of the often conscious creation of modern vernacular languages that was central to the cause of the Reformation, religiously and politically. This was a time before copyright laws, before the concept of plagiarism, before one would have to pay to translate or adapt a work. Not long before this, before Gutenberg invented movable type in the fifteenth century, most people who wrote had been transcribers, people who copied out books, who plagiarized in the most basic, slavish, and time-consuming way possible.

Although educated Renaissance Britons were less monoglot than they are today, a principal reason that literary translation, primarily of the classics, began to flourish there was the fact that fewer educated people were learning Latin and Greek. Much of this has to do with the Anglican Church breaking away from Rome: preaching was being done in English, and sermons and other religious books, including biblical and prayer book translations, were appearing in English. At the same time, vernacular poetry was on the rise, although poets still wrote some of their work in Latin well into the seventeenth century. But the English language and poetic forms were not very sophisticated, and there was little in the way of great epics, histories, and philosophical works on a par with Homer, Virgil, Herodotus, Plato, and Cicero. So transla-tion was the logical way to bring these forms and works into English. Translators saw their work as service to their country and their language, not to the author or the foreign culture.

This political faithfulness even went so far as to include the attempt to affect the revolution that was occurring, that is, to prevent it from becoming violent: "[T]hrough the reading of classical literature," wrote C. H. Conley, "the public were to be advised of the general misery and national decline certain to be attendant upon civil strife. . . . [F]ar-seeing members of the nation recognized in translations of the classics instruments for setting up the new order . . . to introduce the rationalistic spirit of ancient literature as the most direct means of transforming national ideals."*

Translating classics was a much more legitimate and effective way than the writing of new works for the primarily young Renaissance English translators to proselytize their ideas and values. In any event, to make a name for themselves as writers, they felt they had to consciously help create a more sophisticated language in which to be known. "So great was the current prejudice against English," wrote Conley, "that the translators at first regarded the employment for literary purposes of 'our corrupt & base, or as all men affirm it: most barbarous Language' as little more than experimental."*

Here is Sir Thomas Hoby, from the dedication to his translation of Castiglione's *Courtier* (1561):

> I wish with all my heart, profound learned men in the Greek and Latin should make the like proof, and every man store the tongue according to his knowledge and delight . . . that we alone of the world may not be still counted barbarous in our tongue . . . And so shall we perchance become as famous in England, as the learned men of other nations have been and presently are.

What a nice view of translation: storing one's tongue, the way you'd store a pantry to prepare for a great feast. And a great feast it has been.

Other than a short period at the end of the Middle Ages, it is only since the advent of Romanticism that fidelity to original and to author has been such a central concern in literary translation. Or, as Kelly puts it, translators began to treat "literary texts as if they were objective."* In fact, until the end of the seventeenth century, fidelity usually meant not being true to the original's content, which it generally does today, but rather being true to the original's poetic form (the novel was still very young in those days).

The concept of fidelity goes all the way back to the classic Roman poet Horace (Quintus Horatius Flaccus for those who don't like to be overly familiar with classical writers) in his handbook on literary style, *Ars Poetica*, which was a favorite among neoclassicists in the sixteenth and seventeenth centuries. Needless to say, a satirist like Horace did not use "fidelity" in a strictly positive sense, but rather ironically: "Do not worry about rendering word for word, faithful translator, but render sense for sense." However, sense fidelity was not very important to Roman translation, and so this origin of the term is important primarily because of the way it was later picked up and at least paid lip service from the sixteenth century on. Only in the nineteenth century was this concept turned into a rule with classical legitimacy.

What happened to make fidelity go from something that had to be mentioned to something that had to be followed? It was the new concept of the artist that Romanticism brought us. It was Goethe, Chateaubriand, et al., and their worship of Shakespeare.

When Voltaire, the great figure of the French Enlightenment, first translated Shakespeare into French, he only published the acceptable parts, and he insisted that Shakespeare's plays be forced into the classical rule system: all action taking place in one day, no ghosts, witches or the like, etc. And it was a long time before the Comédie Française, the leading theater company in Paris, would put on anything but a classical Shakespeare. Even the first German translators did to Shakespeare what they willed. In fact, many of the earliest Shakespeare translators did not speak English at all or very well. But that wasn't the point, for them. The point was bringing the tragedies into their language, not getting everything right.

The following generations did not give themselves such latitude. They didn't see Shakespeare as someone to pillage, but rather as someone to revere, someone whose words were sacrosanct. The translation of the Author's words was an enormous responsibility, a duty not to French or German, but to Shakespeare.

And how could it be any other way? I am a child of Romanticism myself, and I can't imagine why someone would want to redo *Hamlet*, much less classicize, rationalize, or moralize it. Yet there have been many in twentieth-century Europe—at least among the self-consciously avant garde and the political—who continue to use Shakespeare to serve their own interests rather than work to serve Shakespeare. These translators and directors have made Shakespeare anti-fascist, anti-Communist, anti-capitalist, anti-imperialist. They have deconstructed his works and turned them into post-modern pastiches. In English this can be done through casting, clothing, cutting, acting, adapting. But in other languages it can be done through translation, as well.

The translator's attitude toward an author greatly affects the way he translates; it controls his interpretive decisions. This attitude went through a sea-change in the latter part of the eighteenth century, and became institutionalized in the nineteenth century. And this attitude remains institutionalized in America today, except among a small, disrespectful avant garde.

The contemporary American view of fidelity to the content of the original is accepted with as little question today as the Roman translators' fidelity to Greek forms, the English Renaissance translators' use of classic works to push their Protestant agenda, Dryden and Pope's turning everything into heroic couplets, or Voltaire's imposition of classical rules on Shakespeare. Since translators stopped imposing Victorian morality on the works they translated, American translation has pretty much settled down to the fidelity of an old couple: even though there aren't really any more temptations to stray, the concept is strong as ever.

After all this history, translators have settled on the ethical standard of fidelity rather than alternative political or aesthetic standards. Here is what a few translators have said:

> Richard Sieburth: "You have been entrusted with something very important, and very often this may be the only translation this text is ever going to get, and you better

damn get it right. . . . I see this as a responsibility. You're all the more responsible in that it's your work, but not your work. You can be totally irresponsible about yourself. Here, you get into family, kinship relationships, or marriage. There is an unspoken contract that you develop with the text.

Eliot Weinberger: "You have to work from a position of total humility toward the original, and assume that the original author is always right. And you're wrong."

Richard Wilbur: "[The translation] has to work in a faithful way. There wouldn't otherwise seem to me to be any reason not to have written one's own poem, and there wouldn't seem to me any reason to put the name of the victimized author of the original to the translation."*

Fidelity involves contractual and familial responsibility, trust, humility, and decency. Fidelity is ethical, which means that the alternative, infidelity, is unethical.

Nearly everyone accepts the metaphor of fidelity. But fidelity to what? And why fidelity—personal, sexual, ethical—rather than something organic or artistic? And why is there not a recognition of the ambivalence we feel toward someone to whom we swear fidelity? When something is so widely accepted, and with so little reflection, it usually means that there's something wrong with it, that there are questions that aren't being asked, that it's a matter more of power than of truth. In this case, it isn't an imposed power, as in Catholicism or Communism, but the power of our culture, the power of the Romantic ideal of the author and of our interest in content over form.

But before I attack the concept of fidelity head-on, let me look at the question, Fidelity to what? To the content or the form? To the literal meaning of the words or their meaning as the translator interprets them, as Ezra Pound once wrote: "Tain't what a man sez, but wot he *means* that the traducer has got to bring over."*

The distinction between form and content is one of the most

controversial distinctions in writing. Like substance and process in law, or body and mind in philosophy, the distinction between form and content is central to many literary arguments, even when it's in the background. Translation is certainly an area where this distinction is too rarely discussed openly, primarily because it complicates the apparently straightforward fidelity metaphor, which allows fidelity to content to be a given rather than an alternative.

As I said above, throughout most of literary history it was to the original poem's *form* that most translators felt they owed their fidelity. But from the late seventeenth century on, form grew less and less important, and content reared its head higher and higher. Many Victorians aimed to be faithful to both form and content, usually with terrible to mediocre results, usually because of incompetence, often because of the fad for archaic language (as being more faithful to old originals), but sometimes simply because preserving the form did not preserve the effect that form had on the original's readers. That is, a vibrant form often comes across in English as something sterile, without any associations, or even worse, with very different associations.

Then translators began to use the form they chose and to preserve as much content as possible. The most popular choice in America today—of free verse in the translation of formal poetry—throws out poetic form to such an extent that the images and other aspects of content can all be relatively easily preserved. And the results are rarely terrible, but usually mediocre, because the approach is a given and too easy to be inspiring.

There is a continuum of fidelity to various combinations of form and content. In the last two centuries translators have worked all along this continuum of fidelity, e.g., keeping the meter, dropping the rhyme, and trying to keep as many images as possible; changing the meter, being loose with the rhyme, and trying to keep the effect without worrying about all the images; dropping the meter but trying to keep a rhythm and a suggestion of rhyme, while preserving the imagery; and so on. There are an infinite number of possible combinations, and many more formal and content-oriented attributes, which is what makes poetry translation so exciting.

To make this idea of a fidelity continuum concrete, let me share with you three translations, from across the continuum, of a sonnet by the early twentieth-century German poet Rainer Maria Rilke, who is one of the poets most frequently translated into English today. Although Rilke was generally a formal poet, many English-language translators have not preserved his meter and rhyme, or used any meter at all. Some have not even tried to capture his alliteration. Because all three translations below of the sonnet "Archaïscher Torso Apollos" were originally published in 1981 or 1982, there is no question of period differences (although there might be questions of age and attitude toward current trends). The translation by George F. Peters preserves the sonnet's iambic pentameter and its rhyme scheme. The translation by Stephen Mitchell preserves the iambic pentameter, but usually half-rhymes (that is, uses alliteration and assonance) rather than rhymes, and does not preserve the same rhyme scheme. Robert Bly's translation employs a very free version of iambic pentameter and no rhyme scheme (although there is one end-rhyme in the second stanza and a couple of internal rhymes as well). As a sign of respect for the sonnet form, all three translations preserve the fourteen lines and the stanzas. For those who know German, the original can be found in the endnotes.*

> George F. Peters
> Archaic Torso of Apollo
>
> We never knew his body's marvelous crown,
> in which the eyes were growing. All the same
> his torso glows like a candelabra's flame,
> in which his vision, at the most turned down,
>
> endures and shines. Or else his breast's curved force
> could not blind you, and in the gentle flowing
> of his loins a smile would not be going
> to that same center, his conception's source.

Or else this stone would stand deformed and small
under the shoulders' diaphanous fall,
not glistening like fur on beasts of prey;

and would not burst out all along its border
like a star: for all the while his torso's play
is watching you. You must put your life in order.

Robert Bly
Archaic Torso of Apollo

We have no idea what his fantastic head
was like, where the eyeballs were slowly swelling. But
his body now is glowing like a gas lamp,
whose inner eyes, only turned down a little,

hold their flame, shine. If there weren't light, the curve
of the breast wouldn't blind you, and in the swerve
of the thighs a smile wouldn't keep on going
toward the place where the seeds are.

If there weren't light, this stone would look cut off
where it drops clearly from the shoulders,
its skin wouldn't gleam like the fur of a wild animal,

and the body wouldn't send out light from every edge
as a star does . . . for there is no place at all
that isn't looking at you. You must change your life.

Stephen Mitchell
Archaic Torso of Apollo

We cannot know his legendary head
with eyes like ripening fruit. And yet his torso
is still suffused with brilliance from inside,
like a lamp, in which his gaze, now turned to low,

gleams in all its power. Otherwise
the curved breast could not dazzle you so, nor could
a smile run through the placid hips and thighs
to that dark center where procreation flared.

Otherwise this stone would seem defaced
beneath the translucent cascade of the shoulders
and would not glisten like a wild beast's fur:

would not, from all the borders of itself,
burst like a star: for here there is no place
that does not see you. You must change your life.

There are good things to be said for each of these translations, and there are people who lean toward each of them, depending on their taste, where they stand on the fidelity continuum, and what they are looking for from the translation. Bly appeals to readers who like their poetry to have the feel of good prose: simple, conversational, straightforward. This sort of free verse is the leading poetic style of the day, and the style of most translations as well. It happens, however, not to be the style of this poem, the beauty of which appears not only in its images, but also in its sounds and rhythms. And in this case, it does not capture the poem's power.

Peters opted to preserve the form and most of the content, yet still manage to be simple and conversational. His translation displays a serious problem with fidelity to strict forms by today's translators: most are not capable of doing it well. They can write in a form, but few have the experience and resources to do it beautifully.

Peters also, I think, goes a bit too far in being faithful not only to the rhyme scheme, but also to Rilke's feminine rhymes (where the rhyming word's stress is not on the final syllable, as in "flowing" and "going"). A feminine rhyme is weaker and more unusual in English than it is in German, and makes the formal verse that much more prosaic. It also takes away from the poem's power, especially in the last line.

János Csokits explained, with respect to a renowned Hungarian translation of this poem, why even the perfect preservation of form by a highly competent translator can still fall far short of capturing the poem:*

Literary critics have drawn attention to the precision,
style and music of this beautiful translation [by Árpád

Tóth], in which almost nothing of the original form has been lost and even some of the respective rhyming words exactly correspond in meaning. And yet it is not Rilke. . . . one must take into account the artistic temperament and personality of the poets involved. The dynamism and balance of Rilke's sonnet . . . recalls to mind the substance and elegance of Greek marble, whereas the sound and texture of Tóth's language in this translation remind one of an impressionistic painting of a broken statue . . . Tóth must have loved Rilke's sonnet very much, but his verbal chemistry was not compatible.

Stephen Mitchell's is the baby bear of the three translations: he does not opt slavishly for the exact form nor does he swear fidelity to content while choosing the form he likes; instead, he thinks about what form would be most appropriate and possible, and he strives to approximate, rather than copy, the original's beauty and effects. And he does so with competence. Take the twelfth and thirteenth lines of Mitchell's translation. The twelfth's anapestic rhythm (two unstressed syllables followed by one stressed syllable) gives the feeling of the line's principal image, a cascade (Peters does the same); the three stressed syllables in a row at the end of the thirteenth line gives the feeling of this line's principal image, the fur of wild beasts of prey. Note the difference between Peters' iambic "fur on beasts of prey" and Mitchell's "wild beast's fur." The actual meaning of "beasts of prey" is more fearsome (and more true to the meaning of Rilke's phrase) than that of "wild beast," but the sound of Mitchell's words better captures the density and power (as well as the softness of the *felle*, or fur) of Rilke's *Raubtierfelle* (Raub'-tear-fell-a). Bly's "fur of a wild animal" has neither the exact meaning nor sound of the original.

The poet-translator John Frederick Nims put the Mitchell strategy well in describing his own translations of Provençal poetry: "Let me show you how it goes, I imagine myself saying to the reader curious about Provençal—which he has no intention of learning. He only knows that during the twelfth century some great poetry, it is said, was written in Provence; he would be interested in knowing what it was like. Not just what it said—what it was like. . . . The greatest infidelity is to pass off a bad poem in English as representing a good one in another language."*

These, and other translations of Rilke's sonnet, were discussed by German-into-English translators at the American Literary Translators Association conference in the fall of 1995. The translators, some more experienced than others, focused primarily on how each translator captured Rilke's images and interpreted the content of his poem. There was little talk about form and even less about beauty or competence or the quality of the translations as a whole. When fidelity to content is an unquestioned given, this is often the consequence: missing the forest for the trees.

When it comes down to it, the ethical question of fidelity is, I think, usually less important than the practical question of competence. Peters' translation is faithful to form and also as much as possible to content, but it lacks the original's beauty. Bly's translation is faithful to content (according to his interpretation), pays only passing homage to the form, and achieves a beauty currently in favor, but which relates to Rilke's beauty only to the extent that Rilke's beauty was also in favor when and where he was writing, another way to define fidelity. Just as Dryden and Pope did not really choose the heroic couplet for their translations, I don't think Bly chose free verse to capture Rilke's verse. Jean Longland is supposed to have said that turning a sonnet into free verse is like sculpting the Venus de Milo in wet sand.* I think that's a little harsh; a modern material such as plastic is more appropriate.

Mitchell's translation is as faithful to content as Bly's, it suggests the original form, and it captures much more of the original's beauty and power than either of the others. This, however, does not mean that the baby bear is always just right; it only works when the translator appreciates the original, strives to find equivalent effects in English, has the talent to succeed, and is being read by Goldilocks, that is, by someone who insists neither on absolutely faithful form nor on the popular form of the day, but rather on a competent, intuitive balancing of all elements with an eye out for what is most essential. Any inflexible approach hampers a translator: Bly's choice of a free form is just as restrictive as Peters' choice of the same form Rilke used.

To put the use of unfaithful form (free verse, in this case) and faithful content into another perspective, let's contemplate the other end of the continuum: faithful form and unfaithful content. What do you get when you do this? Either the piracy of a tune for a new song (for example, America's stealing of the tune of "God Save the King" for "My Country, 'Tis of Thee") or a burlesque that makes fun of the original's form alone (although here there is usually at least an echo of the original's content). Since foreign-language poetry and prose are unfamiliar to nearly all of us today, we are unlikely to burlesque foreign works outside a language class. An example (necessarily from song) would be the following burlesque of "Frère Jacques."

> Faithless traitors,
> Faithless traitors,
> Boo to you,
> Boo to you,
>
> You write what you want to,
> You write what you want to,
> All day long,
> All day long.

No one would call this translation, yet almost everyone considers the other end of the continuum—all the content and none of the form—translation. This shows a serious taking of sides on the form-content controversy. Adamant moderate that I am, I opt for balance and appropriateness, but if I had to lean one way or the other, I'd lean toward form.

The best way I've found to put my position, although it's still far too simplistic, is to say that when a work is form-focused, the translator should also be form-focused; and when a work is content-focused, the translator should also be content-focused. One problem with this approach is that it is up to the translator's interpretive abilities to determine the extent to which a work is focused on form vs. content. Sometimes it's very clear: a sonnet or villanelle is never accidental; it always shows a conscious formal choice. But even here the translator might be more attracted to the content and be willing to sacrifice some or all of the form (rhyming, the rhyme scheme, meter, the particular meter, the number of lines, the equal length of the lines) to preserve the content. Or as I said above, the translator may consider himself to be (or actually be) incapable of reproducing all or some of the form. Competence is not a prerequisite for wanting to get to know someone or something intimately. We approach a loved one as competently as we can. And often we don't realize how we can best satisfy.

There are modern translators who lean toward the formal end of the fidelity continuum. In the twentieth century, Martin Buber and Franz Rosenzweig translated the Bible into German with the express intent of creating a sensory impression of the original language, to let the reader experience the sound and feel of Hebrew and Greek. Recently an American professor, Everett Fox, did the same thing with the Five Books of Moses, but into English. He wrote in his introduction, "I have sought here primarily to echo the style of the original, believing that the Bible is best approached, at least at the beginning, on its own terms. So I have presented the text in English dress but with a Hebraic voice."*

Modern theorists, as opposed to translators and reviewers, also tend toward the formal end of the continuum. They feel that the reader must be forced to approach the original, not in terms of meaning, but in terms of its forms of thought. The early nineteenth-century German philosopher Friedrich Schliermacher took this position, and the twentieth-century Spanish essayist José Ortega y Gasset agreed with him: "It is only when we force the reader from his linguistic habits and oblige him to move within those of the author that there is actually translation."* Of course, literature should also force the reader from his linguistic habits, but there is no more of this in original writing than there is in translation. The most notable contemporary prose translators taking this approach are Richard Pevear and Larissa Volokhonsky, who have applied it primarily to the work of Fyodor Dostoevsky.

*   *   *

The biggest problem with this discussion is the fact that in all the best literature form and content are inseparable. Who can imagine Shakespeare's greatest sonnets in any other form? Who can imagine Woolf in minimalist prose or even in the lyrical prose that passes as poetic in America today? Milton on lithium, a flowing Hemingway, a Parker that doesn't rhyme? After all is said and done, our opting for content today is as blind, and limiting, as the classical and Renaissance translators' opting for form was then. Yet while our translations are more faithful, in terms of content, theirs are so often much better, or at least more interesting poems.

The age-old goal of inseparable form and content is, in this primarily prosaic age and culture, no longer so important. Many fewer people today read a poem and say, "What beautiful images; if only the poem sounded as beautiful!" When I wrote a book of literary parodies in 1991, I wanted to parody contemporary American poets, but I could think of only one poet whose style was recognizable to a broad range of well-educated readers: Dr. Seuss. We do have some recognizable prose stylists, but not very many. In the English-speaking world today, language is primarily for the communication of information, whether data or confessionals.

Another factor contributing to today's emphasis on content is the popularity of naturalism, or realism. Most writers feel that they should be true to nature. Most readers feel that what they read, unless it's clearly fantasy, should be realistic as possible. They especially like to read novels based on true life and poetry based on the true expression of real feelings. When writers read in public, most feel obliged to tell a story about the poem or prose piece, usually linking it to something that happened in their lives. Often the writing is so confessional that there is no need for this; yet it is still done. Authenticity reigns, and authenticity is mostly about content. Yes, better writers know that it is more important to *seem* authentic than it is to *be* authentic, but in either case what readers see, and what writers talk about, is authenticity. Authenticity is an ethical brother of fidelity.

Serge Gavronsky put the matter of authenticity most baldly: "Readers always want—it's a Romantic preoccupation, never existed before the nineteenth century—authenticity. They somehow believe that if someone signs a text, that text was secreted by that body. Cocteau has a lovely image: he says, 'I shit my books.' In a wonderful way, that's what readers want. They want to smell the feces of authenticity. So when a translator comes on, he appears to be an intercessor . . . because he didn't write it."

It is, of course, possible to be both true to nature and true to art. There is such a thing as authenticity of form, or rather propriety of form, not in an absolute sense, but in relation to content: using the form that best expresses the content. This is what the best writers do. And this is what Richard Wilbur was saying when he told me about the joys he gets from translation: "What excites me is to pursue the illusion of exactitude on all fronts." But today, art usually gives precedence to nature; form becomes secondary, and what we have is writing like Robert Bly's translation: simple, straightforward, formless, free, transparent. Its content is subjective, but its form is objective, unnoticeable. The message sent to aspiring poets is that expression is more important than form, that free verse frees the poet from the restraints of conventions and that the poet need not make a whole host of formal decisions central to the creation of works of art in earlier times. Bly himself made these decisions, at least in his youth, but the result is something that appears as if the decisions had not been made, as if the poem had flowed as naturally out of his pen as conversation flows out of our mouths. This is also true of prose.

The result is that for many poets free verse is no more free than the work of earlier poets, who felt that every poem they wrote had to fit one of a prescribed number of possible forms. In other words, this freedom is not so much an expression of freer choice as it is the following of different conventions. What is different here is that today's conventions contain an underlying message that they do not contain artifice, they do not follow conventions, that we've done away with, gotten beyond, improved on the falseness of artifice and are left with the truer reality of nature and our feelings. Free verse and flat prose also allow writers to be lazy, to not read through the history of poetry and prose, to not try their hand at all sorts of forms and styles, to not build up their skills or their intuition or their ear, to not be able to differentiate between what is good and mediocre. Writing is all expression and experience, the artist has no obligations, and our opinions of the results are equally valid. This is borne out not only by the poetry that is being written and published today, but also by what is not being written and published. And one kind of poetry not being written and published very much today is poetry in translation.

Yes, I've gotten back to translation at last. The fact that our culture (though certainly not all writers, and certainly not the best) has turned its back on artistic form as a form of artifice, as something false, and gotten stuck in its own conventions, has had a serious effect on translation, limiting it both in terms of approach and in terms of how much interest there is in it. For if translation is a matter of working in form (since the content is a given), then a lack of interest in form means a lack of interest in translation. The formlessness of contemporary writing and the contemporary translator's fidelity to content over form are related phenomena that have, I believe, together led to the serious decline of poetry translation in America over the last three decades. I deal later in this book with the recent decline in English-language translation, especially among the younger generations; the focus on content is far from the only element involved.

Another factor contributing to the modern focus on fidelity to content over form is the rise of a scientific perspective. As translator and translation theorist Lawrence Venuti told me, our culture is "tied to science, to concepts of objectivity, but they're ultimately very naive . . . I'm singling out science, but I think economic exchange, the rationalization of the capitalist economy and what that does for the work process, all this has a tremendous impact on language, so that it privileges what I call 'instrumental' concepts of language, which have developed from the Enlightenment on . . . The electronic media have only exacerbated this by evaporating any sense of form and just focusing on the function of language, the communication of meaning. . ." J. M. Cohen has noted a similar relationship between our scientific age and translation: "Twentieth-century translators influenced by science-teaching and the growing importance attached to accuracy . . . have generally concentrated on prose meaning and interpretation, and neglected the imitation of form and manner."*

Ironically, the most controversial English translation of the twentieth century is one that abandoned fidelity for science: James Strachey's translation of Freud's writings. For example, Strachey took Freud's *das ich*, "the I," and *das es*, "the it," and turned them into the scientific terms "the ego" and "the id." He also made up words such as "parapraxis" and "cathexis." Freud did not want to be read only by his fellow physicians, but Strachey's attempt to make Freud more scientific also made him both more inaccessible and more apparently scientific and objective. Especially when you consider how high a percentage of people in the world know Freud, directly or indirectly, from the English translation, Strachey's infidelity in the name of science gave the world a Freud with the same meaning but a different spirit.

The movement away from form and toward language that does little more than communicate content has allowed everyone to feel they could be creative writers. It has democratized literature. Even the writing of children is now being published, while no one is yet buying their paintings or going to hear their musical compositions. (Note, however, that we do attend their performances: their plays and recitals; why, we might ask, are they rarely asked to translate, as they had been for hundreds of years? And if they did, would we read the results? Can we imagine reading other children's translations?) Because it is so much easier to do, our transparent literary language is definitely more democratic, but it is also, as a result, anti-intellectual; to do it or read it requires little practice or thought. The mark of a good poem used to be that it asked to be read at least twice; today, most poems communicate in one reading. Translation is one of the most complete intellectual activities in the arts; to appreciate it, not to mention practice it, requires a great deal. It is an elite activity par excellence, out of step with a world where even well-educated readers happily buy books by people who are only moderately literate.

The modern focus on content is not, however, just about information and democracy; it also has a spiritual aspect. Here is a passage from Goethe's *Poetry and Truth*: "What matters most in all that is handed down to us, particularly in writing, is the ground, the inner being, the meaning, the direction of the work; for there lies what is original, divine, efficient, untouchable, indestructible, and neither time nor outside influences could affect this primal inner being, not any more than a disease of the body can affect a well-built soul. Thus, language, dialect, idiosyncracies, style, and finally writing, should be regarded as the body of any work of the spirit."* For Goethe, a work's content was spirit, its form only the body, a physical manifestation of the spirit. As a result, he felt poetry should be translated as prose, totally stripped of its form, lest the spirit be lost.

The translation of poetry into prose became especially popular in the nineteenth century. Sometimes scholars will translate poetry as prose, usually as a "trot," or series of word-for-word equivalences to teach language students—usually in Latin and Greek—the meaning of foreign words. There are also several English prose translations of Homer and Dante, to name just a couple of frequently translated authors, and these translations are still being made.

Translation into prose horrifies most poetry translators. But there are good arguments for it. For example, D. S. Carne-Ross argued for prose translations of Homer: "If translation is to be more than an academic exercise, it has to be related to living literary interests. Pope could turn the *Iliad* into an Augustan epic because the civilization he belonged to still believed that the epic was [great] . . . the only great living form today is the novel."* In addition, a prose translation is an approach that can more effectively be done by someone who does not have the ability to write poetry. Why translate at all if you can't do it right? Well, that would relegate most practitioners of most professions and arts to the unemployment line.

Most important, however, is the fact that there is a relatively large audience for prose translations of the classics, just as there is an audience for free verse translations of formal verse. One of the major reasons prose translations came to be made is that socially minded intellectuals wanted to introduce the classics to the working class. Then publishers realized that this opened up a huge market. Then professors and teachers joined in when they realized a prose translation is easier to teach and easier to get students to read.

Many people who would never attempt or be able to handle the strangeness or difficulties of a poetic Homer or Dante will be capable of reading prose translations. Goethe wrote that "if you want to influence the masses, a simple translation is always best."* And there are, after all, prose adaptations of Shakespeare in English, the most famous of which is Charles and Mary Lamb's *Tales from Shakespeare* (1807), written to introduce Shakespeare to children and read by generations of adults as well. (The most recent of these books—from a division of the largest American book publisher—is a series called, chillingly, *Shorter Shakespeare*. *Shakespeare for Dummies* is not far behind.) While some people want the entire experience of the original, others are happier with the story being told in the form of a good read.

The novelist Vladimir Nabokov, whose most famous translation is an English prose translation of Pushkin's long Russian poem *Eugene Onegin*, employed the image of one of his most favorite activities—collecting butterflies—to describe the advantages of prose translation of poetry: "shorn of its primary verbal existence, the original text will not be able to soar and to sing; but it can be very nicely dissected and mounted, and scientifically studied in all its organic details."* But then Nabokov is an extreme believer in fidelity to meaning: "It is when the translator sets out to render the 'spirit'—not the textual sense—that he begins to traduce his author. The clumsiest literal translation is a thousand times more

useful than the prettiest paraphrase."* Which leads one to ask why
a translated poem should be useful. That's what trots are for.

The British poet Ted Hughes approached his translation of the
Hungarian poet János Pilinszky's poetry in a similar way. Not
knowing any Hungarian, he worked from line-by-line cribs. He
wrote about his experiences, "my first principle of translating
Pilinszky as literally as possible won out against my meddling self.
. . . [L]iteral renderings, very often, are all one could desire in a
final version. When I go back through the whole poem in [the
crib] version I see once more that the most effective lines in my
final version have come through unaltered, or very little altered."*
Yet, as the cribmaker, János Csokits, wrote, "these poems have lost
the most distinctive feature of their appearance . . . Without the
softening effect of the original metre and rhyme scheme the impact
of some of these poems can be very painful; they sound harsher
and Pilinszky's view of the world appears grimmer than in
Hungarian."* The result is a relatively bare, prosaic, contemporary
English-language poem. Although Hughes did everything possible
to preserve the poet's vision, he divorced this vision from its form
and, therefore, did not truly know the vision. Feeling great affinity
with what he did know, he ended up imposing his own vision on
his translations, without realizing it. This might well have happened even if Hughes did read Hungarian, if he had chosen fidelity
to content over fidelity to form.

There are cases where prose translation completely undermines
the meaning of verse. One such case is Molière's verse plays. As
his English-language translator Richard Wilbur wrote in the introduction to his translations of *The Misanthrope* and *Tartuffe*:
"Molière's logic loses all its baroque exuberance in prose; it sounds
lawyerish; without rhyme and verse to phrase and emphasize the
steps of its progression, the logic becomes obscure like Congreve's,
not crystalline and followable as it was meant to be."*

Although prose translations of poetry are no longer as fashionable as they were in the days when a central goal of social activism
was to give the working classes access to the great things of our
civilization, Goethe in many ways remains the spiritual father of

fidelity. His choice of the content end of the fidelity continuum has remained the choice of most translators and editors, and prose translations have effectively been replaced by free verse translations and even formal translations that, like Peters' Rilke, choose to be flatter and more prosaic than the original.

But is a prose version of Homer really a translation? This question brings us to a practical, although not very popular, solution to the problem of fidelity: differentiating between rather than condemning different approaches. I think the best broad definition of literary translation (here in terms of poetry) is George Steiner's: "the writing of a poem in which a poem in another language (or in an earlier form of one's own language) is the vitalizing, shaping presence."* This definition includes all approaches excludes works that are vitalized by another work, but not shaped by it, for example, James Joyce's *Ulysses* or Eugene O'Neill's *Mourning Becomes Electra*. But I think those works that are both vitalized and shaped by the original should be more clearly differentiated, not in the interest of categorizing as much as in the interest of informing readers.

If the interpreter's goal is to capture the form and content as much as possible, then I feel we can call the result a *translation*. If the interpreter's interest is only in certain aspects of the original—such as its imagery, à la Ezra Pound—then we could call the result a *version*. We could do the same with a poem put into another language's prose or free verse: a *prose version* or *free-verse version*. And if the interpreter is using the original primarily as an inspiration, but effectively going off on his own, then we could call it an *adaptation* or simply say, *based on*. Robert Lowell called his adaptations *imitations*, and this word has been popular for centuries. However, *imitation* gives the impression of something closer than an adaptation: one who imitates tries to do the same thing. I think most readers would consider *imitation* just another name for a translation, especially since they rarely encounter the term today.

All of these are legitimate ways of dealing with a foreign poem, and I feel that all of them should be encouraged. However, fidelity tends to value only the *translation*, viewing the others as betrayals. As an ethicist, I too tend to see infidelity to form and content as betrayal. But the most ethical stance, I feel, is to make sure the reader is told what he is getting. If the reader wants something as close as possible to the experience of the original, then he can pick up a *translation*. If he wants a prose or free-verse *version* of formal poetry, then he can pick up something that is called that. Otherwise, he might end up reading a poem merely *based on* another poem, thinking he is getting someone's best attempt at capturing that other poem. Or he might not know the original was originally in formal verse, or even verse at all.

Unfortunately, however, there is no reason, economically, for a publisher to give out this sort of information, at least in these prehistoric days before there is an appreciation of translation approaches. Such information will scare some readers away, especially from freer versions, because they'll think they can get something more authentic elsewhere. It would have to be explained that the element of authenticity in a freer version involves not its equivalence to the original, but rather the translator's response to the original, the preservation of its content and, possibly, the modernization of its form (authentic, in a sense, because the foreign poet's form was also modern to his readers). There is no reason why a poet will always be inspired by a work to recreate that work, that his performance should necessarily be a re-creation, no more than a singer will want to sing a song just the way the songwriter had imagined it. As we've seen with Celan's *versions* and *adaptations*, the poet might want to make the poem his, refract it through his own eyes, sing it in his voice; and the result might be better than a translation. As with Pound, the poet might want to focus on certain elements of the poem that he wants to bring into English, to confirm his own approach to poetry or just to see what will happen. People like this sort of thing when it comes to music; the question is, could they like this in translation as well? Would enough people be willing to read multiple translations to allow a market to grow in various responses to poetry that are actually sold like that and do not necessarily come from the pens of famous poets?

There are all sorts of responses to a poem, and *translation* is only one of them. It is the most popular one not because it is the best or most ethical in its own right. It is the most popular because we are a monoglot society and most people are looking to read the original in the only way possible. The ethical nature of translation comes less from the requirements of faithfully reproducing an original, and more from the reader's expectations and desires of something as close to the original as possible. When the reader chooses ease over authenticity of form, the modern concept of fidelity embraces that as well, because it is primarily interested in fidelity to content, a more limited ethical position than overall fidelity.

If there were more readers looking for how Robert Bly responded to a poem—in a form other than a *translation*—then he might be even freer with his free-verse *versions*, and the results might be even better. But I think there is an ethical problem in putting forth all of his performances as *translations*, especially because he is, relatively, a celebrity and, therefore, more people will read his Rilke than anyone else's. Readers will likely get a great deal from them, but they will never know that what they are reading bears only limited resemblance to Rilke's verse. If they knew, however, they still might choose celebrity over authenticity; Bly's fame as a poet makes him an artist in the public's eye even when he's "only" translating. But at least the reader would be giving Bly his informed consent.

Where does this leave faithful but mediocre translations, such as Peters' Rilke? Well, no publisher is going to label anything as *mediocre*. In fact, few publishers are even going to recognize mediocrity or incompetence. Mediocre books come out by the bushels, and many of them sell lots of copies. That's what review publications are for. But I won't get into them until the last chapter of this book.

Let me tell a little story to illustrate the concept of free versions and fidelity, this time in terms of prose. A few years ago, my house published Peter Kussi's translation of a 1929 novel by the Czech writer Karel Poláček, entitled *What Ownership's All About*. Poláček's novels had never been translated into English, despite the fact that he was a very popular and well-regarded novelist and story writer, nearly as popular as his contemporary Karel Čapek, nearly all of whose works were translated into English. Many Czechs insisted Poláček was impossible to translate into English, because his language was too difficult and its effects could not be captured in English. Peter Kussi and I agreed that it would be better to capture as much as possible rather than to let Poláček remain unavailable to English-speakers. The result was a work I felt was excellent, but which received lukewarm reviews.

Besides the fact that no one can capture the love another country has for one of its writers, the biggest problem with bringing Poláček over into English is that what was then radical and experimental for Czech, in terms of language, is old hat in English and had largely been accomplished in English even before Poláček's time. What Poláček did was to bring colloquial Czech into literary Czech, with a vengeance. In Czech, colloquial and literary are in many ways different languages, or dialects at least. One was not supposed to use colloquial language on paper. In English, colloquial and literary aren't really all that different.

Poláček also had a very individual way of writing, of presenting dialogue especially, which is hard to capture because it is so deeply rooted in the spoken Czech of his time and his characters' place geographically and classwise. Any dialect is impossible to capture in this sense—evoking a particular place, time, and station—if for no other reason than the foreign reader cannot possibly know anything about the place, time, or particular class characteristics. This further limits how much of Poláček's special genius can be brought into English. Apparently, what could be brought over, although a great deal, was not enough.

One problem here was that both the translator and I assumed that the best thing was to be faithful to the author's work by trying to bring as much of it into English as possible. However, it might have been more faithful to the work to have totally reformulated the book, to have created a work in English that told the same stories and presented the same sorts of characters, but in such a way that the effect on English would be as radical as the original's effect on Czech. This could not, of course, be done in terms of colloquial vs. literary language, at least without doing it in a far more radical way. The goal would be to find a style consistent with the content and as individual as Poláček's, but which was not an attempt to be the same, to be sentence by sentence or expression by expression faithful. This would be extremely difficult, and it would also be risky both in creative terms and in terms of the reaction of reviewers, especially anyone familiar with Poláček's work. Very few lovers of Poláček could bear to see such a version done under his name, even if it were clearly called a "version" or the like.

What I'm getting at here is that faithfulness, especially with works difficult to bring into English, can often best be fulfilled by the translator's freedom to depart from the original. However, few people would consider the result of such freedom faithful, even the same people who love freewheeling versions of Shakespeare or think nothing of dropping meter and rhyme.

One example of a creatively faithful translator is Suzanne Jill Levine, who translated the works of three subversive South American fiction writers with the freedom they expressly gave her so that her translation would be equally subversive in and to English. For her, translation is "a continuation of the creative process" as well as "a critical act which cannot and does not replace but rather complements the original, illuminating its strategies."* As unfaithful as she was to the words of the original, she felt great affinity with the authors and was exceptionally faithful to them.

*   *   *

The concept of fidelity is limiting in several ways. First, it means that nearly all responses to foreign works either take the form of translations or are falsely presented as translations. The goal is authenticity, getting it right. As if translation was about recasting, or even transcribing, rather than intepreting and making decision after choice. Second, fidelity is seen as applying primarily to content, often to words. When a critic rips apart a translation, it is often for its mistakes in understanding words or phrases. Even translators tend to focus on how much of the content is preserved and how it is presented. Third, fidelity holds back the young or occasional translator. As William Weaver told me, "It's like learning to swim: it's easier to swim when you know you can touch bottom. The thing of getting away from a literal approach to the original text and having the nerve to swim out a little further on your own, is realizing that sometimes it's more important to reproduce the fluency and the impact of the original than it is to reproduce this or that word correctly." Fourth, fidelity places the translator in the position of a traditional woman with duties to the male original, and to nothing else. Underlying this view is fidelity's flipside, betrayal. When a translator does a good job, she gets a pat on the back for doing her duty; when she does a bad job, she is attacked for being unfaithful, betraying her husband or father. This leads to a fear of being unfaithful, of incurring the wrath of those who will call her interpretations a betrayal of the authentic master's art. And nothing is worse for any artistic enterprise than fear.

In short, the concept of fidelity makes translation a question of authenticity, content, and duty—getting it right—rather than a question of judgment, knowledge, and competence—doing it well. And the negative focus is on betrayal and mistakes rather than on poor judgment and incompetence.

It's generally not very useful to focus on extreme examples, but in the case of Czech novelist Milan Kundera's views on fidelity, I think the extreme is closer to the norm than most of us would like to admit.

Not only are his views and actions extreme, but he has also done more to bring translation issues to the serious American reading public than anyone has in years. In the form of essays, prefaces, revisions, and retranslations, Kundera has made it very clear that he wants translations of his works to be faithful. He has also made it clear what he means by fidelity. And by its flipside, betrayal, as well.

I will use the Kundera story to make three principal points: (i) that betrayal is important to the notion of fidelity, and hence to our view of translation; (ii) that our Romantic image of the author is both very powerful and central to the fidelity metaphor's continuing popularity; and (iii) that law and power are major considerations not only in determining what fidelity is, but also in its enforcement. I will also use this opportunity to discuss several common misconceptions concerning the application of fidelity to actual translation problems.

First, let me disclose my connections: I know some of the participants rather well (two of Kundera's English-language translators have translated for my publishing house); I know two others of Kundera's translators, who have translated his work from the French; and I am a very minor participant in this story: I consulted with Peter Kussi on his English translation of Kundera's last Czech-language novel, *Nesmrtelnost* (*Immortality*).

Betrayal plays a central role in Kundera's approach to translation. In fact, betrayal has played a central role in Kundera's entire adult life. Czech Communism betrayed the ideals Kundera, like most young Czech intellectuals, held in the late 40s, and then Kundera's work was banned starting in the early 70s. His story of translational betrayal began with the first English translation of his first novel, *The Joke*, which was published in Great Britain without the sections on Czech music and with some of the novel's chapters rearranged. The translators, David Hamblyn and Oliver Stallybrass, have claimed that the deletions were necessary to get a young, unknown Czech author published in the West, and that they repeatedly, and unsuccessfully, tried to communicate with Kundera. Kundera took these changes as a betrayal and, after his first major success in the United States, *The Book of Laughter and Forgetting*, he asked that *The Joke* be translated into English again. And it was, by Michael Henry Heim, who had on his own translated for a literary journal two of *The Joke*'s omitted sections. Kundera later wrote of Heim's act: "I was deeply touched by this noble gesture of solidarity with mistreated, humiliated literature."

Kundera sees not only deletions as betrayals, but also anything he considers "rewriting," something every translator has to do to some extent to make literature work in a language it wasn't intended for. In his essay "Sixty-three Words," in the section "Rewriting," Kundera quotes himself, from his play *Jacques and His Master*, from the words he placed in the Master's mouth: "Death to all who dare rewrite what has been written. Impale them and roast them over a slow fire! Castrate them and cut off their ears!"* Ironically, those words were originally translated into English by Michael Henry Heim, against whom Kundera was to make good his threat, at least figuratively. Kundera did this by revising Heim's translation of *The Joke* without the translator's permission, and attacking Heim in the new edition's preface. Then Kundera asked his American editor, Aaron Asher, to do a completely new version of another novel translated by Heim, *The Book of Laughter and Forgetting*. And the translation wasn't even from Czech, but rather from a heavily rewritten (by the author, fifteen years later) French translation.

What had Heim done to deserve this unusual treatment? He hadn't omitted anything or moved anything around, as had happened with the first translation of *The Joke*. No one had even accused him of doing an incompetent job. What he had done was to be unfaithful. In his "Author's Note" to the "definitive version" of *The Joke*, Kundera describes his experience of reading Heim's translation years later:

> I had the increasingly strong impression that what I read was not my text: often the words were remote from what I had written; the syntax differed too; there was inaccuracy in all the reflective passages; irony had been transformed into satire; unusual turns of phrase had been

obliterated; the distinctive voices of the characters-narrators had been altered to the extent of altering their personalities . . . I was all the more unhappy because I did not believe that it was a matter of incompetence on the translator's part, or of carelessness or ill will: no; in good conscience he produced the kind of translation that one might call *translation-adaptation* (adaptation to the taste of the time and of the country for which it is intended, to the taste, in the final analysis, of the translator). Is this the current, normal practice? It's possible. But unacceptable. Unacceptable to me.

Kundera has produced a litany of fidelity: his work must be translated word for word (which is how he describes his own revisions); the original syntax must be preserved in English; there can be no "mistakes;" and the characters' voices must be captured exactly as he pictures them in English (even though he is not fluent in English).

Like most people, Kundera sees fidelity in terms of words. He wrote the essay "Sixty-Three Words" as a "personal dictionary" for his translators, including his key words, his problem words, the words he loves. (The dictionary, itself an eighteenth-century invention, is one of the culprits in the fidelity debate, because bilingual dictionaries gave people the impression that languages are made up of equivalent words.) On Kundera's list are words such as beauty, being, comic, fate, flow, lightness, value. Words whose several meanings and connotations in Czech rarely match those of the closest equivalent in English. For example, the Czech word for "light" does not mean both bright and without weight, as it does in English, but it does mean easy or effortless much more strongly than our word does. Yet Kundera expects one English word to correspond to all his repetitions of a Czech word.

No translator can use a word fifty times in a novel and give it the same accumulation of meaning it has in the original. It might work thirty-five times, even forty-five times, but the other five or fifteen times, one or two other words must be used or the result will be either gibberish or something very different from what the author had intended. Kundera's rule is right most of the time—and

I, as an editor, often ask for this sort of consistency from my translators—but always repeating a word when the author does so can actually undermine the repetitive use of the word. Why? Because translation is not about words; no translator translates strictly on the level of words, but rather deals with phrases, sentences, concepts, sounds, tones, voices, dictions, etc. A critic who focuses on words will always find the trouble he's looking for. An author who focuses on words will always feel betrayed. It's like seeing every touch on the shoulder, every kiss on the cheek, as an act of infidelity.

In "A Sentence," an essay in *Testaments Betrayed*, Kundera took a sentence from Kafka's *The Castle* and examined the way it was brought into French by three translators. One of the principal things Kundera took these translators to task for was their failure to replicate all of Kafka's repetitions. In his own French version, Kundera faithfully replicates them all, but the result is lyrical, while Kafka's repetition in German is powerful. When the *effect* of repetition in the two languages is not the same, this sort of fidelity to words is actually less faithful than a freer, more thoughtful approach.

In other words, Kundera's view of repetition is just as much a matter of his taste as Heim's view of irony is a matter of his. Every translator "adapts" to some extent, and therefore every translator can be considered unfaithful or falsely peddling his work as *translation*. However, this is a problem not with translation, but rather with the notion of fidelity. The whole of a translation is much more important than its parts. Fidelity is not about the kiss, but about the feelings behind it.

But perhaps Kundera is right. Perhaps the author should call the shots and tell his translators what to do and what not to do. After all, the book does come out under the author's name. Even if a Kunderian translation would not be quite as good, or at least not as readable as it might have been, only the author (and his foreign-language publishers) pay the price. So why not let the author have his way?

Because this places the translator in the position of a transcriber rather than an artist. Translation is interpretation, a series of decisions based upon the translator's knowledge, skills, and sense of judgment. It is only because of the way our laws work that an author can do what Kundera has done, and even then it can be done only because Kundera is that rare animal: a foreign author whose works actually sell in English (despite, or perhaps because of, the unfaithful translations he's been afflicted with). A composer does not control the way musicians play his work; a jazz musician, for example, can turn it upside down and inside out and the composer can just collect royalties. A playwright cannot control the way actors read his lines, although powerful ones do sometimes control major productions. There are simply too many performances of plays and concertos. Kundera's position, then, involves not so much a question of fidelity as it does one of law, power, and the economics of publishing. Or, to play with the fidelity metaphor, the more powerful the author, the easier it is for him to make the translator sign a prenuptial agreement or to divorce the translator quickly and easily when she commits adultery.

Kundera has written of the author: "this unique being . . . should possess all rights over the thing that emanates exclusively from him." Law. And "the ultimate example of the supreme concept of author: one who demands the *complete* realization of his aesthetic wishes."* Power.

This Romantic view of the author as a supreme being —unique, exclusive, ultimate—is to a great extent responsible both for our copyright laws and for our present-day view of fidelity. It's such an overwhelming view today that even Kundera, who has spent most of his literary career attacking Romanticism (as responsible, among other things, for the horrors of Communism) and harking back to the Enlightenment (a time when translation was everything he despises), has embraced the concept of the author as godlike and his creation as something set in stone and handed down from on high.

Most people's belief in fidelity originates in their Romantic view of art, which puts the artist first and the work of art second. "Have you read Kundera?" we say. Or, "He slaved over that sculpture. He nearly starved." Does that make the sculpture any better? Does it matter at all how the artist lived? Think of all the starving artists who never create anything worthwhile, and the rich ones who do the unimaginable. Swann's love Odette, in Proust's *Remembrance of Things Past*, was just this sort of Romantic: "As for Vermeer of Delft, she asked whether he had been made to suffer by a woman, if it was a woman that had inspired him, and once Swann had told her that no one knew, she had lost all interest in that painter."*

Most people still believe in the unique qualities of the author and in the author's precedence over the translator. However, they see other performers—actors, musicians, directors—as artists. In fact, when there's a conflict between artists, today's Romantics even lean toward the performer (the actor over the screenwriter, the musician over the composer). But there is no performer of literature—or so people seem to believe—so there is no conflict and no tendency to favor the translator. Thus a creative translator, even with integrity and competence, can be considered a betrayer, and people will generally side with the author against him—the literary world has certainly not shown any sympathy for Heim. The metaphor of fidelity, which implies that infidelity is bad and should be dealt with, has allowed Kundera to do what he most despises: rewrite the work of artists, ignoring their artistic rights. But then Kundera too does not consider translators artists.

What harm has been done by Kundera's response to what he considers his translators' infidelity? Will readers of the new translations and revisions not get to see what makes Kundera special? No, they'll get all of that, because whatever Kundera thinks, it isn't words and punctuation that make him special; it isn't even his tone, except in the most general sense. It's his images and structures, and only a completely oafish translator or radical revisionist could ruin these; in fact, Kundera's revisions have probably done more damage than a mediocre translator would have done. No, the true harm is that a highly respected writer has taken a strong public position on translation: that the author has all rights and no obligations, either to the translator or to his readers. The fact that future readers will not be able to buy *any* English translation of the original *Book of Laughter and Forgetting* is of no concern to Kundera. Nor does he care to alert readers that they are not reading a translation of the original novel and that they could find such a translation in or through a local library. When enforced and based on power and betrayal, fidelity is no longer an ethical concept, but rather a means of oppression, suppression, and other unethical behavior.

Kundera's view of translation is not the only one held by authors, nor is it the typical one, if only because most authors either can't be bothered or don't know the foreign language well enough to get involved with translations. To put Kundera's views in perspective, let me show some ways other authors who care view the translation of their writing.

The Argentinian writer Jorge Luis Borges was as powerful and insistent an author as Milan Kundera. But he also did a good bit of translation. Here's Ben Belitt on Borges' ideas about being translated into his grandmother tongue, English: "If Borges had had his way—and he generally did—all polysyllables would have been replaced [in English translation] by monosyllables . . . People concerned about the legitimacy of the literal might well be scandalized by his mania for dehispanization. 'Simplify me. Modify me. Make me stark. My language often embarrasses me. It's too youthful, too Latinate. . . . I want the power of Cynewulf, Beowulf, Bede. Make me macho and gaucho and skinny.'"*

Borges was the opposite of Kundera: he insisted on having things his way, but his way was not to respect all of his quirks, but rather to respect the quirks of the English language, a language he loved as much, or more, than Spanish. The Chilean poet Pablo Neruda, who translated a good deal himself, often from English as well, went a step further in talking to his translator Alastair Reid: "Once, in Paris, while I was explaining some liberty I had taken, [Neruda] stopped me and put his hand on my shoulder. 'Alastair, don't just translate my poems. I want you to improve them.'"*

Pablo Neruda wrote about why he felt this way: "English and French . . . do not correspond to Spanish—neither in vocalization, nor in the placement, color, or weight of the words. This means that the equilibrium of a Spanish poem . . . can find no equivalent in French or English. It's not a question of interpretive equivalents. No, the sense may be correct; indeed the accuracy of the translation itself, of the meaning, may be what destroys the poem."*

Since Ben Belitt is not only a translator of Borges and Pablo Neruda, but also a poet whose work has been translated, he can see the other side of the equation: "It is very enlightening for translators to *be* translated in kind . . . There's nothing more depressing than an over-awed literalist at work on your own poetry. Whenever my verse is translated by others, I leave a long, loose rein, and urge translators to follow some powerful lead of their own . . . to find a brio that guarantees a continuum for *them* as well as for me. . . . No one is more tolerant of a translation, I've found, than the poet translated. He is the first to disbelieve in the whole venture, and marvel at the salvage."*

After not wanting to be bothered, probably the most typical position of an author is that of Umberto Eco, the Italian semiotician and novelist best known for *The Name of the Rose.* Here is how his American translator, William Weaver, described Eco's views of translation: "Umberto is not so much interested in getting the translation absolutely correct; he wants the English to work, so often he will say 'use . . . ' or 'put . . . ,' departing radically from the Italian, but helping me smooth out the English period. A far cry from Milan Kundera's notion about translations, which he thinks should not necessarily be smooth or 'read well.'"*

Finally, let me share with you a story about a writer's coming to understand what translation is all about. The writer is Brazilian poet Adélia Prado, and the storyteller is her American translator Ellen Watson: "About a week or ten days into working together, she got out the *American Poetry Review* supplement that had thirteen poems of hers in it, and she said, 'Okay, I want you to put all your books away, close your notebook. Okay. I want you to translate back to me what these poems are, from English back to Portuguese.'

"'What?!'

"'I don't want you to look at my originals, that's the only way I'll know what you've done: if you look at the English and say it to me in Portuguese. . .'

"I'm a little worried, this is the ultimate test. So I did it, and it was really wonderful, because some of the time she'd be grunting and groaning, some of the time she'd be laughing, some of the time she'd go, 'Oh! That sound, that sound'—because she'd have me read it in English and then say it—'it's just not a sound in Portuguese.' Sometimes she'd say, 'Why did you do that?! What did you do there?! That's not what I had!' And just fretting and rejoicing up all over the ballpark.

"And then at the end, a few days later, I showed her a poem of mine that Ivan Angelo had translated into Portuguese. I said, 'Well, here; this will give you an idea of the kind of stuff that I write.' And she read it, and she read it again, and she said, 'Okay, tell me what your original sense was, literally,' and I did. She had felt something was wrong when she looked at the Portuguese. She read the poem and she liked it, but there was a point that she didn't think made sense. And that's the thing she kept asking about, and she said, 'He didn't do it right here; he translated literally what you said, but that wasn't what you were getting at. By staying literal. . .' and suddenly her jaw dropped and she said, 'I get it. I understand it, I know what translation is. I understand now why you had to change things, why you can't do exactly what I did in your language sometimes because it has a different effect.' And that was a really moving moment . . . because she was saying it, not because someone was saying it to her. 'Now,' she said, 'you have total permission to do what you do.'"

Fidelity is as fidelity does. Translation is not a matter of words and inaccuracies, disrespect for authors, or power plays. What Milan Kundera does not understand is that it involves obligations not just to the author or the original work, but also to things he cares nothing about, such as the translator's language and readership. It is about responsibility and it requires belief in and respect for the act and art of translation. As Ben Belitt once wrote, "The operative word is *faith*, and not *fidelity*."

Those who make the loudest noises about fidelity are those who embrace the Romantic ideal of the irresponsible artist, and see the translator as a non-artist who either serves or betrays him. Kundera threatens with castration any translator who dares betray him. And he has castrated. When push comes to shove, this is what fidelity is all about: a theory, a metaphor, that's there to use against a betrayer, to emasculate another artist. Or one that's there for translators who don't want to take responsibility for their decisions, who don't want to have to balance their obligations: I just tried to be faithful, they say, and everybody smiles.

The Obligations of Polygamy

THE GREATEST WESTERN LITERARY WORK on the theme of fidelity is Homer's *Odyssey*. In the *Odyssey* there are three characters who are faithful to Odysseus in very different ways: Argus, his dog; Penelope, his wife; and Telemachus, his son. For Odysseus himself, as for the creative artist, fidelity is not an issue.

Argus simply waits, survives until his master comes back, and then dies. He represents the maker of trots, who simply gives the meaning of the original. He exists totally for the sake of the original.

Penelope cleverly finds a way to allow herself to be faithful to Odysseus in the usual, matrimonial meaning of the word. She weaves every day and unweaves every night, while promising her suitors that she will marry one of them as soon as her weaving is done. It is she, the one with the most clear and simple obligations who is considered the symbol of fidelity. Her fidelity, although clever, takes a narrow, repetitive, and rather absurd form, similar to that of the slavishly faithful translator, who cleverly solves the problems but stays too close to the original to create an equivalent work.

Telemachus is the only one of the three who has multiple obligations: to his mother, to his father, to his island, to himself. Unlike the others, he does not even know his father, so the obligation to him is weaker than the others'. Yet he is the only one who acts on his fidelity to his father. He doesn't simply lie around, like the dog, or come up with a ploy, like his mother; he takes his own odyssey, he speaks and acts cleverly, like his father, and eventually he becomes his father's ally, to save his island, to save his mother, and to find himself. Telemachus, who is not generally considered an example of fidelity, is the true representative of the literary translator, because he fulfills all of his obligations at once, and he acts, he imitates, he travels out of his world and out of himself in order to grow and to help his whole world grow as well. And he does all this while staying faithful to his father.

Translation is not, in short, about being constant, but about the constant balancing of obligations in the form of action.

The fidelity metaphor, accepted by most reviewers, editors, and even most translators, is at best incomplete, at worst a front for the castration of a performer or an excuse for the performer's irresponsibility, and in most cases not very helpful. The metaphor does not allow translators to determine and confront their various obligations, to be free, active, truly ethical artists. It puts them in the position of a traditional woman with one-way obligations to something that is metaphorically both husband and father. It cramps creativity, it makes translators feel like failures, and it denigrates the translator, and translation, in the public eye. And since no one agrees what it is about the original that one has to be faithful to—content, form, spirit, effect—the fidelity metaphor provides little actual guidance. It's simply there and cannot be ignored. So I won't ignore it; I'll suggest replacing it with another, related metaphor: polygamy.

Bigamy has already been raised as an alternative to fidelity by Barbara Johnson in a 1985 essay entitled "Taking Fidelity Philosophically":*

> [W]hile both translators and spouses were once bound by contracts to love, honor, and obey, and while both inevitably betray, the current questioning of the possibility and desirability of conscious mastery makes that contract seem deluded and exploitative from the start. But what are the alternatives? Is it possible simply to renounce the meaning of promises or the promise of meaning? . . . the translator ought, despite or perhaps because of his or her oath of fidelity, to be considered not as a duteous spouse but as a faithful bigamist, with loyalties split between a native language and foreign tongue. Each must accommodate the requirements of the other without their ever

having the opportunity to meet. The bigamist is thus necessarily doubly unfaithful, but in such a way that he or she must push to its utmost limit the very capacity for faithfulness.

One of many problems with translation theorists today, such as Johnson, is that they tend to see translation as primarily an event concerning language. Translators, on the other hand, see translation as primarily an event concerning literature. Johnson considers the fidelity metaphor insufficient partly because there isn't one thing to be faithful to—the original work—but rather two things to be faithful to—the two languages involved. This, too, limits the metaphor.

Polygamy goes beyond bigamous marriage to two languages; it includes obligations to the original work as well as other obligations, for instance to the translator's literary culture. Language is only the medium, the paint, the notes, the steps. What is more important to a translator's obligations are the literatures and the literary cultures he's working in, with, and for.

When your obligations are singular—to one spouse or one parent—then fidelity is the way to fulfill your obligations. When your obligations are plural—to two spouses, two parents, to children and friends, to people at work, to your town and your nation—then it is impossible to be faithful; fidelity is not an issue. The issue becomes responsibility, being thoughtful. The polygamist's obligations can conflict, but there is nothing wrong with this conflict. In fact, that's what marriage is really about, because no one marries thinking that the spouse will have no obligations to anyone else, even though many married people act as though this were the case. This is why sex—one of the few things one is not obligated to do for others—is so central to the concept of marital fidelity. For translators, there is no equivalent to sex. For this reason alone, the fidelity metaphor is inappropriate.

The translator has to seek ways to reconcile these various obligations, while considering the interests of all, to balance his obligations to each so that no one feels too slighted, so that all his obligatees get attention, although not of the same sort or amount.

It isn't the translator's submissiveness that gives him these obligations; it's the fact that he's the one in the middle, the one in charge, the one who's acting.

Recognizing the translator's position, neither the author nor the translator's literary culture should be too demanding of the translator; they should share the translator, be sensitive to the complex situation he's in, and give him the benefit of the doubt. The translator will most likely not be up to completely fulfilling his obligations to all, but it's not because he's unfaithful; it's because he's human, and because his position is a demanding one.

What do I mean by literary culture? It's something one collects over the years, slowly building from the infantile to the adolescent to (hopefully) an adult range of literature. One's literary culture starts with the mother tongue, but it soon becomes more like a series of lovers: lovers you're obsessed with (or were at the time), lovers you come to hate or be bored with, lovers who happened to be there at the right time and place, lovers you meet again years later, lovers who made you feel terrible about yourself, even lovers you haven't had or couldn't get, at least at the time you met them. Each new book—whether read, translated, or written—is approached with all the other books in mind, with all one's experiences, expectations, and desires. One's literary culture forms the background, the information and experiential base, for the translator's decision-making process.

But it's more than this. In terms of obligations, the other most important part of a translator's literary culture is his audience. These are the people for whom a literary culture is intended, and a small proportion of them will be creating the literary culture of the future, partly through their encounters with works introduced to them by translators. The translator has a special relationship with his audience, because (i) unlike the original creator, who writes for the world, the translator writes only for those who read his language and will write his language's literature, and (ii) the translator's readership is handicapped: they can't read the original and don't know the original's literary culture. So the translator's audience and his obligations to it are much more clear and pressing than those of a writer.

One special obligation a translator has to his audience involves understanding. Presumably, the translator, as a foreign-language reader who has to read extremely closely, comes to understand the original as well as anyone. Whereas the author isn't required to understand his own work, a translator has an obligation not only to understand it (because otherwise he won't be able to translate it adequately), but also to communicate his understanding to the audience through the many decisions he makes. And not just by "getting it right," communicating the original's content so that it can be understood. The translator has an obligation to communicate the original at the level at which it was intended, or at least formulated, to be understood. That is, if something is easily understood by a reader in the original language, then it should be easily understood by a reader in English. This is often difficult, because what is common knowledge in one literary culture might be completely unknown in another. On the other hand, if something is ambiguous or difficult to an original-language reader, then it should be ambiguous or difficult to an English-language reader, too. This is one of the toughest things a translator must do, and he is almost never given credit for it, because only someone who has carefully read and understood both original and translation knows to what extent the translator has succeeded, or even tried.

This is only one of several obligations the translator has to his own literary culture. Others include the obligations to introduce new information and forms, and to not unnecessarily distort his language, two obligations that can be seriously in conflict with each other. Imagine a prose style that's odd in German and that, if brought into English via an equivalent oddness, would create a whole new sort of English that wouldn't have existed but for the translation, and which might be picked up and copied by English-language writers. The translator has to decide how much of this oddness he wants to, and can, bring into English—how much he wants his translation to be faithful in this sense—and how much he wants to keep it from being an invasive influence on the English language and, possibly, from putting off English-language readers in a way the original did not put off German readers (contemporary German writing is, for the most part, much odder, that is, more stylized, than what's written, and read, in English). You might wonder why a translator would want to keep out "invasive influences" that would make our literature richer, but there are entire literary cultures—the French, for instance—that are adamant about keeping out, or at least watering down and gallicizing such influences.

Another obligation a translator has to his audience is to produce as good a book as possible. Many translators say that they will not improve a book, that they will recreate all of its warts and scars. If the writer is great, this is probably the best thing, because the English-language reader should see what blemishes the great writer's beauty has. But most writers are not great, and many—at least in terms of form—are more blemished than beautiful. Europeans often use as an example of this the American novelist Theodore Dreiser. The Czech translator and fiction writer Zdeněk Urbánek told me, in reference to Dreiser, "When the original is so awkward, what are you supposed to do with it? Should you try to keep the awkwardness in some form in the Czech?"

Krishna Winston learned early that a translator can sometimes perform best when faced with a poorly written text. "There was a book I did by a German woman," she told me, "about six weeks after I finished my dissertation. Stylistically, it was very annoying, very flippant. And that was actually one of my best translations. I disliked the book and I disliked the author, but I felt I could do most anything I wanted, and I made it into a very good translation. The book still has weaknesses, but I was quite creative with the translation because I didn't feel bound by the original in any way. I played around with the tone and downplayed some motifs and up-played others. I shifted emphases."

I have only published one book where the translator improved on the original. The author was good at everything but his sentences. This book too was German, and since German syntax is so different from English syntax, the translator has to unravel and reravel most sentences anyway. So the translator did improve the writing, and the result was so good that the author himself felt that his book read better in English. If the translator had been more faithful to the original work than to her audience, the translation would have been less successful. But of course, giving the translator this freedom could mean doing a disservice to both if the author is actually a good writer and the translator a poor one. This is one of the risks that goes along with giving the translator, or any performing artist, the freedom to balance his obligations.

An obligation translators of every era have felt they owed to their culture is the obligation not to bring into it things that are offensive. In one age, that might be anything considered crude or barbarous; in another, anything that questions royalty; in our age, anything that is racist or sexist or even uncool. For example, Jasper Griffin, in his review of *After Ovid*, a collection of contemporary translations and adaptations of Ovid's poetry, noted that "One omission is striking. No episodes have been more famous than those in which girls talk themselves into yielding to desires which they know to be wrong."* These episodes are left out or changed so that there are no moral qualms. And even today, many translators are loath to translate crude foreign works into an equally crude English. Ellen Watson told me a story about an extremely scatological excerpt from a Brazilian novel that the author's American agent gave her to translate as a sample of her work. Watson brought it all into English. The agent told her that eight different people had translated the same passage, and that all of them had "cleaned it up and dried it out." She was hired for the job.

Finally, we must remember that the translator is an artist, and that an artist also has an obligation to himself. The translator can hardly impose his vision on a work, but he can impose his vision of translation and his views on literature. He can try to take into account the critical works on a classic novel, but if the work he's translating is new, and even when it's old and the translator is faced with contradictory interpretations, the translator must go with his own views. And he also must go with his skills. If the translator is good at writing humor and the original's humor cannot be replicated when and how it appears, then he should feel free to add in appropriate humor in appropriate places. And every translator balances his obligations to others in a different manner, with different emphases, priorities, and ethics. The translator has to follow his instincts here as elsewhere, although he should constantly question his inclinations and ethical positions.

In a polygamous relationship, obligations to the spouses are not necessarily the same. They're different relationships with different people. This is also true in translation. In the world as it is now, at least in the English-speaking world, the preference is for preserving the original's content and imposing the literary culture's forms. There is a balance, but it is not so much the result of a balancing of obligations as it is a matter of conventional preferences for different aspects of—liking different things about—the spouses. A translator should question conventions just as he questions his personal inclinations. This is one of the things that distinguishes art from craft.

Of course, the original work does have one advantage over the other obligees: it is a sort of newlywed, or new lover. The latest thrill is going to get more attention, and more intimacy, than a long-term spouse. A translator might use, and read in, his language every day and approach the original in the shadow of his history of lovers and for the purpose of sharing it with his audience, but while translating he spends more time, physically, mentally, and emotionally, with the original. Translating a poem or two might just be a quickie affair where the translator gets his kicks, feels little obligation to the original, and moves on. As the eighteenth-century German translator A. W. Schlegel wrote, "I cannot look upon my neighbor's poetry without coveting it with all my heart, and so I am caught in a continual poetic adultery."* But translating a book, especially a book of poetry or quality prose, is much more complicated than this; it's a long-term intimacy. And the translator might keep translating the author's writing, perhaps for the rest of his life, as Schlegel did with Shakespeare. So even though each affair will most likely be short-term, it very well might not, and the translator realizes this. Just as he realizes that his literary culture will always be there for him, giving him context, giving him taste, giving him understanding, giving him its ear and its reactions, giving him stability and joy, not to mention payment for his labors. The translator gives more to the original on many levels, to the extent that he listens to it so closely and gives it his time and attention, but on other, deeper levels, a good translator's heart is with his literary culture. In some cultures, such as France, it is these deeper levels that are controlling, and obligations to the original work take a back seat. One could say that French translators are momma's boys, or that they're always nostalgic for the loves of their youth.

In short, translators do not owe fidelity to one thing, be it spouse or father. Rather, they have different sorts of obligations to different sorts of things: the original work which is trying to find new life in a new language, the language and literary culture in which the original work was written, the literary culture the translator grew up with and works in and cannot get away from, and the handicapped audience for his work, which is especially needy and which the translator's publisher cares about more than anything else. Translation is not about betrayal, but rather about the balancing of, the impossible attempt to fulfill, a variety of often contradictory obligations. A responsible translator will always fall short, but he'll never be unfaithful.

Decisions, Decisions

WHEN IT COMES TO WRITING, I think the old line about perspiration and inspiration is more than something cute that can be smiled at and dismissed. As someone who usually writes in something close to a trance state, I know that writing feels mystical, mysterious, inspired. But then so does playing tennis, and in very much the same way. When I'm writing, I'm often not making conscious decisions about which word to use, how to construct a sentence, how to best put forward an idea or image. I'm often not thinking about the idea or image at all; it just pops up out of nowhere, very much like a passing shot hit on the run. Yes, at some level I have decided that this was the best strategy, but if I'm going to consistently succeed in making the shot, I'm going to have to go with my instincts.

Where exactly is this nowhere that things pop out of? Is it inspiration or perspiration that causes them to pop out? Is it the subconscious, the unconscious, or some other dimension, other lives, whatever you might believe in? Is there something mystical about the process, becoming a vessel for another's voice, getting in touch with the universe?

Me, I think that things mostly pop out of experience, and when we write, no experience is more important than our previous writing and reading experiences, although life experiences matter a bit as well. Instinct, feel, intuition, having a good ear are nice ways of summing up a complex, hidden decision-making process based on the accumulation of experience and the understanding of that experience. Just as without the experience of hitting hundreds or thousands of topspin shots we are incapable of putting just the right amount of topspin on a tennis ball so that it drops in just short of the baseline, without writing and reading hundreds and thousands of sentences we cannot express our thoughts or feelings in a way that works (one thing writing has over tennis is that reading is—or can be—a more participatory process than watching a tennis match; so we can more easily accumulate literary experience). This decision-making process is so mysterious not because it's a mystical event, but because we do it best and most efficiently when we relax and let our past experience rather than our current thoughts and designs run the show. Ditto in tennis.

As Krishna Winston put it, "I think that translation is a matter of intuition, and I would be hard put to it to come up with a polished critical appreciation of a book that I've translated, because I haven't articulated it. I haven't separated my understanding from my intuitive choices of words and phrasing and tone. It doesn't quite reach the level of consciousness."

Writing is neither a mystical event nor a series of conscious decisions. It's a constant process of making decisions, solving problems, partly conscious and partly not. Translating involves every sort of decision a writer makes except for most of the ones critics and readers like to think and talk about, those minor things like characters, plot, imagery, theme. But then translators make a lot of decisions writers rarely have to make, about things extraneous to the original work, such as intent, consistency, essentiality, accuracy, and the relationships and lack of relationships between languages. As Jean Le Rond d'Alembert wrote in 1758, "If we were to measure merit merely according to problems solved, we would often encounter fewer problems in creating literature than in translating it."*

"Translation is above all a pattern of decisions," Richard Sieburth told me, "and every local decision will commit you to decisions elsewhere. The mark of a bad translation is the completely erratic nature of the decisions. . . . Unlike a close reader, as a translator you are stuck with your decisions. You are forced to commit. The thing about translation is that it involves commitment. And another sign of a bad translation is when people are not willing to commit."

Christopher Middleton made a similar point by comparing the

translator to a mime: "What does a mime do? He imitates, yes, but not the actions, gestures, idiosyncrasies of one individual, isolable, human or animal subject. Rather, he takes possession of a total structure by bringing countless small and subtle perceptions into an imaginative configuration. This distinction in effect subordinates all imitation, subordinates it to a spellbinding, independent, and creative action."*

Translation is a *pattern* of decisions, not just a bunch of them. This is one reason why it's impossible to criticize a translation by pointing out isolated mistakes; those "mistakes" might actually be the result of a great deal of balancing, for example, making up in one place for what had to be left out in another part of the work. As Sieburth added, "Someone once asked Richard Howard, 'How would you translate this word?' And he came back saying, 'I do not translate words.' What you translate is a system of relationships." Or, as Ben Belitt has written, "great translation moves by touch, finding the matching shape, the corresponding rugosity even before it looks for the counterpart of meaning."*

Yet even the most minor word choices (although one doesn't "translate" words, one does have to keep "choosing" them) can be difficult for the careful translator in a way they're generally not for a writer. A writer usually just writes down "perhaps" or "maybe," whichever is his favorite word. A translator has to decide which seems *best* in the particular context. William Weaver has written that, "faced with a choice between 'perhaps' and 'maybe,' the translator does not put the words on trial and engage attorneys to defend and accuse. Most probably, he hears the words in some corner of his mind, and likes the sound of one better than the other. Of course, his decision is only apparently instinctive. His instinct will be guided by his knowledge of the author's work, by his reading in the period. It will almost certainly not be guided by any rules, even self-made ones. On Thursday, translating Moravia, he may write 'maybe,' and on Friday, translating Manzoni, he may write 'perhaps.'"*

I started this chapter comparing translation to tennis, at least in terms of decision-making and instinct. But translation's not a game, it's a process, a journey. "Why," Richard Winston asked in an essay, "is the Mock Turtle so funny, while *la Tortue à Tête de Veau* [French for "the Turtle with the Head of a Calf"] is just absurd? Here are mysteries; here the keenest discretion is needed, and the road is not at all wide. It is narrow, crooked, without signposts, and the translator must find his way along it as best he can."*

William Weaver sees the road as less narrow than overgrown, at least when only ten percent of the way through translating a novel, which he describes as "a dense forest into which I have barely ventured. At this point, there seems to be the beginning of a trail, but soon I have to produce my machete and start hacking. With an eye out for wild animals or unfriendly natives."*

John Felstiner likes to refer to the "to and fro" of translation: "If you think how many times when you're translating, even a line or a phrase or even just a word, from one poem to another, when you think how many times your mind goes back and forth and back and forth and back and forth . . . you can get hung up in this transit. You're trying to get from Grand Central to Penn Station and you end up on 42nd Street somewhere, wondering which direction you're going."

No matter how familiar a translator is with the original, literary translation is always an adventure into unknown terrain, whether urban, jungle, or metaphysical, and it's easy to go astray. Translators are constantly warning of the problems of falling asleep at the wheel and letting the original too strictly determine your choices, often with disastrous results. Yves Bonnefoy, a French poet and translator of, among other things, Shakespeare and Yeats, has written, "Words will try to entice us into behaving as they do. Once a good translation has been set in motion, they will rapidly begin to justify the bad poem it turns into, and they will impoverish the experience for the sake of constructing a text. The translator needs to be on his guard."* And what he has to guard against is his very own medium: words.

Not only words, but also grammar can cast a spell on the unwary translator. As Russian-into-English translator Marian

Schwartz said in an ALTA talk, "I think we get so caught up with grammar, we are unconscious of the fact that the achievement is different; we become so enamored with the names of grammatical structures that we want to repeat them. This happens a lot in Russian, which is an extremely compact language. For example, you'll see a sentence in Russian that is a noun in the instrumental, a reflexive verb, and a noun that's a subject, like "Ivan was read the book" or "By Ivan the book was being read," something awful in English. In Russian it would be three words, and the actor would be first, the verb would be second, and the object would be last. . . . there's a great temptation to hold on to the wonderful instrumental. And then there's reflexive verbs—it's astonishing!"

In this chapter, I want to take you down a few of the avenues, paths, and unmarked trails that make up the journey of literary translation, a journey in which prepositions, semicolons, and false friends play the roles of spiders, snakes, and tigers.

I'll start with the pebbles that trip up even the most careful translator: articles, prepositions, and punctuation. "The success of a translation," Eliot Weinberger has written, "is nearly always dependent on the smallest words: prepositions, articles. Anyone can translate nouns."* Very few critics ponder over an author's choice of article, except perhaps in a title. But in translation it can make all the difference in the world. For example, take the first words of Virgil's *Aeneid*, some of the most famous words in all of literature. Historically, they were translated into English as "I sing of arms and the man" or "Arms and the man I sing," but recent translators switched from "the" to "a": "I sing of arms and of a man" (Allen Mandelbaum) and "I sing of warfare and a man at war" (Robert Fitzgerald). Gregory Rabassa wrote of this, "In the one case, Aeneas would seem to be *the* man, the one anointed by the gods for his sacred mission to refound Troy as Rome, while in the other he is *a* man who happened to be picked by fate to fulfill that high endeavor."* This very conscious decision is not so much a critical interpretation as the taking of a contemporary position on the religious and heroic aspects of the epic poem. It sets the tone for the entire translation.

The choice of article often has to be based on interpretation rather than mere transcription, because in many languages—as in Virgil's Latin—either articles are generally not used or are used in different ways than ours. Czech is one of these languages. When a noun is translated, the translator has to decide which article should accompany it, without having anything in the original for guidance, except the context. *Muž kousá psa*, or literally "Man bites dog," is not necessarily a headline in Czech, but a normal sentence, if not occurrence. Should it be translated as "The man bites the dog"? As "A man bites a dog"? Or, if it is actually a headline, "Man bites dog"? (As it happens, Czech journalism uses the past tense for its headlines, but that's another story.)

When translating French, where articles are used as much as in English, one problem is that "the" is often best translated as "a" or nothing at all. "Les traductions françaises sont très excellentes" can either be referring to translations in general, in which case we don't use any article in English ("French translations are very excellent") or we make it singular and use "a" ("A French translation is very excellent" or "A French translation is a very excellent thing"), or it can be referring to particular translations, in which case we use "the" ("The French translations [of Yves Bonnefoy] are very excellent"). You might also note that the literal "very excellent" sounds terrible in English. Exaggeration is more acceptable in French. Most translators would either drop the "very" or change "excellent" to a less superlative adjective, such as "good," that goes better with "very."

And then there are prepositions. There is probably no single sort of stone that trips up more translators more often than prepositions. The problem is that prepositions are central to expressions in every language, and no matter how well you know the meaning of a particular preposition, even one you would get right one hundred percent of the time in the foreign language, it is surprisingly difficult to make the switch to the right preposition in the right English-language expression. There simply aren't any logical rules or relationships. And worse, apparent prepositional equivalences are not to be counted on. The jump from foreign to domestic preposition is one of those things the human mind is simply not good at. This jump, disproportionate to what is being jumped over, has little to do with the art of translation, and more to do with the peculiarities of Western languages. But it is something every translator has to deal with in nearly every sentence; and even the best sometimes don't make the jump successfully, even when they can make unbelievable leaps over boulders.

It is easier to see that it is not words that are being translated (or that words are chosen rather than translated) when you realize that these little words—such as Czech articles—often don't even exist in the original, or that, as with prepositions, the original words hinder rather than help the translator. Thus, you have to translate the sentence, or the thought. And each of the words—even, often especially, the articles—is chosen not just in the context of the sentence, but also in the context of the paragraph, the character or narrator's voice, the work, the oeuvre, and the translator's vision and interpretation of the work and oeuvre.

This is also true of punctuation. The biggest problems with translating punctuation into English are that we use it differently than other languages, and that it is very easy to simply replicate the original's punctuation, even when it doesn't lead the reader to the same effect or meaning, or when it simply isn't appropriate in English. "They tend to use more commas in Spanish," Gregory Rabassa told me, "and they seem to be right—there's a pause there—but even so, in English you don't put a comma in." Many languages also use the semicolon far more than English, where it is used only occasionally, except for stylistic reasons or by eccentric writers.

On the other hand, many languages use the period much less often than we do, finding run-on sentences perfectly acceptable. We find run-on sentences arty and difficult, and our teachers smacked our hands so many times when we used them, it's hard for us to accept them anywhere but in stream-of-consciousness prose. So how do you translate a missing period? You break up the sentence. This is very typical when translating German and Czech, for instance. Although many think this is sinful, most translators find it absolutely necessary, and most copy editors will try to break up the sentences of the overly faithful; their loyalty is clearly to English. But there are many occasions where the run-on sentence should be preserved. Here's translator-editor A. Leslie Willson's example of one such case: "I remember [an] occasion when a translator broke paragraph-long sentences into shorter syntactic units. The work was a story that described the social entwinings and roundelays of an engagement party. The original text consisted literally of paragraphs that were in each instance a single convoluted, meandering, but meaningful sentence. While pondering the translator's choice, I suddenly realized that the entire story was structured as a dance, a ballet of sorts, enacted on the page syntactically. Each complex sentence described another dance step in the partnering and movement of the party. That sort of grammatical mirroring of the events and encounters and characters described required that the translation be syntactically faithful to the original. A revision re-created the intricate social steps and nods and posturing in the syntactic form of the original, changing the mob scene atmosphere of the short sentences of the first draft into the graceful and intricate and *telling* choreography of the original."*

It is easier dealing with run-on sentences in a French work than in German, because run-on sentences are atypical of French. Take Marcel Proust, whose run-on sentences are just as difficult and unusual in French as they are in English; they can be preserved without giving much thought to the matter.

According to William Weaver, there are ways to make divided sentences seem continuous: "Let's say in Italian there's a great long sentence that it's just impossible to maintain as a single sentence in English, because there are just too many bits of information in it and you can't put them into one English sentence, not in a beautiful way, but in any coherent or orderly way. So you have to break it into two sentences. Do you break it into one long sentence and one shorter sentence? Two equally long sentences? What information do you put in one half and what information do you put in the other? What do you want the sentence to end with? . . . The thing is that when you break up a sentence—I tell my students—you have to give the impression that you've written one long sentence, even though you've got a period in there. And you can do this, for instance, by beginning the second sentence with 'and.' . . . These are almost mechanical cheating tricks. But there are other ways of doing it, too: the flow of the sentence can give an impression of length or it can give an impression of concision, depending on the words you use."

Although Weinberger said that anyone can translate a noun, he was, I think, more emphasizing the difficulty of dealing with little words than taking a position on the ease of handling the bigger ones; they can be obstacles, too. Gregory Rabassa has written about translating the Spanish word *rama*, which means "the thing that grows out of the main trunk of a tree." "Who is speaking?" he asks. "Would his Anglophonic equivalent be a branch-man, a bough-man, or a limb-man?"*

John Felstiner described his thought process in translating the German adjective and noun combination *klamme Helle* in a poem by Paul Celan:

> . . . "In the Undivided, there testifies
> the *klamme*
> *Helle.*

"Now, *klamm* is like our clammy: cold and sticky. There is another word in German, *Klamm*, which means 'gorge.' Looking back at the derivation of it, I found out that it has to do with a kind of narrowing. And since Celan was fascinated by *engen*—'to shrink' into your own self—I thought this very late poem needed something more than a 'clammy brightness.' I may be wrong here, but I went from 'clammy' to 'gorgelike' to 'binding' for various reasons. I was a little bit seduced by the alliteration of binding and brightness, also the assonance, and I was a little seduced by the rhythm of it, too. . . . I was a little bit persuaded by the fact that Celan was waiting for a book to be published in 1970, when he wrote this, and that book was called *Lichtzwang,* one of the very unusual compounds he dealt in: 'Light-compulsion.' So 'binding brightness' seemed to me to echo the book he had just titled. What I try to tell students of mine is that sometimes what is expedient can become what is essential."

That is, what could easily be left out—rhythm, alliteration, assonance—is often essential to achieving the right effect and even the right meaning. Because a translator usually cannot capture the exact relationship of the sounds of words such as *klamme* and *Helle,* he tries to relate them in a different but equally effective way. This is especially true when, as here, they are the poem's last words.

There are times when a commonplace word in one language is so exotic in another language, so far from the reader's reality, that it's simply meaningless. A frequently cited example of this is "the lamb of God" for Eskimos. The expression has been translated as "the seal of God," which makes the image equally concrete and therefore more easily accepted and able to become commonplace itself, which is just what a biblical translator wants. A literary translator, however, might not care if such an image is immediate, might not want the image to feel too comfortable, will probably want to provide some foreign flavor; it all depends on the translator's goals and how essential he feels the image's immediacy is to understanding and appreciating the work.

No expression is more immediate than the expletive. "If any form of word can be called untranslatable," Gregory Rabassa has written, "meaning having a close adherence to the word-for-word meaning of the original, it is the expletive. The simplest of sounds and expressions differ most from language to language: the belch, the grunt, the animal sound. . . . I recall an episode in Julio Cortázar's *Hopscotch* in which the hero has pounded his thumb with a hammer as he tries to straighten a nail. 'Puta que te parió,' he addresses the nail. If we leave it at that, we get a Hemingwayish 'whore that bore you,' but the intent is different. My solution was to have him accuse the nail of incestuous proclivities toward its

dam, which is current, ripe, and even maintains a bit of the tone
of the Spanish insult."* Or as Rabassa wrote elsewhere, "when we
translate a curse, we must look to the feelings behind it and not
the words that go to make it up."*

What to do with commonplace words can also be a problem
when translating Romance or Germanic languages into English.
Languages close to ours have subtly false friends, clever little
demons—words and constructions—which mean the same thing in
English (unlike true 'false friends', which mean something totally
different) but which create a significantly different effect or simply
don't work very well in the same context. Unprepared or unwary
translators too often fall prey by going with the easy transcription
of these words into awkward or inappropriate English.

With Romance languages the biggest problem is that latinate
words have a different feeling for them than ours do for us. They
use them because that's practically all they have. When we use a
latinate word, however, we're usually choosing it over a roughly
equivalent Anglo-Saxon word, and often we're doing it to be rather
highblown about something. For example, Italians call a flood an
inondazione; if that were translated as "inundation" (which is the
easy choice) readers would understand what was meant, but it
would sound very stilted in most contexts.

With German, the most common problem is the compound
word. The Germans use them all the time without sounding as if
they were making up words, even on the occasions that they are.
English speakers use them much less often, and it usually sounds
like they're being funny, odd, or making it up. Yet many translators
are lazy and transcribe German compounds into unwieldy English
ones, for example, *Fischschuppe* into "fish-scale" or worse, *Fischzug*
into "fish-catch." Or take something more typical, that is, less concrete. Say, *Seelenleben* as something new-agey like "soul-life" instead
of simply "spiritual life." Or *Seelenruhe* as "soul-peace" instead of
"peace of mind." English compounds might be more interesting,
but they're not very accurate ways of conveying everyday words
for which the English equivalents happen to be phrases.

*   *   *

When it comes to the names of people and places, most translators want to "preserve the flavor" of the original, keep it feeling foreign. But is this best done by preserving the foreign name or by translating it? A translator faced with the Czech place-name *Malá strana* could translate it literally as "The Little Side" (or Little Quarter, or Lesser Town) or just go with *Malá strana*. Most translators' first reaction is to translate such a name, because it actually means something, and the meaning of a name often gives information and an impression that the foreign name itself could not. But does "The Little Side" really mean anything in English? And does a Czech think of what the words mean or just of the place, which is well known to all? I think the latter, and since the translation means nothing in English—in fact, it sounds rather silly—it's best to keep the Czech name in. For flavor.

When the words that constitute the place-name actually mean something even in English, the choice becomes more difficult. *Národní třida* is a major thoroughfare in the center of Prague. (*Malá strana* is an old neighborhood across the river, at the base of the hill on which the castle stands.) It translates as "National Boulevard." The fact that it's called "National" doesn't *really* matter, but most people translate it anyway. And it certainly isn't as meaningless or silly-sounding as "The Little Side." Here, I would say, the immediate context, as well as what works best throughout the book, should determine whether it is translated. And sometimes the sound: who would want to translate Champs-Elysées?

But what if the place-name is familiar to English speakers only in English translation? For example, St. Peter's in Rome. According to William Weaver, "Sometimes you translate the Church in Rome as St. Peter's, and sometimes you should leave it as San Pietro. It depends on whether it's in dialogue or whether it's in narration. It seems weird for a Roman boy to say to another Roman boy, 'Let's go to St. Mary-Major.' On the other hand, when some English tourists are going around Rome, they walk from the Basilica of St. Peter's to the Basilica of St. Mary-Major; it sounds perfectly normal. In E. M. Forster it sounds perfectly normal. In a translation it might not. There's no way you can make a rule about this; you just have to hear it and listen to it and decide."

What about characters' names? Here a translator's decision-making is limited by reasonably strict convention: English-language translators rarely translate characters' names. Keeping names in the original language, usually complete with accent marks, is one of the principal ways English-language translators give their work a foreign flavor. *Maria* does not become Mary, and *Jacques* does not become James (and *Jean-Jacques* can hardly become John-James). But the convention among French translators is just the opposite: names *are* translated. Even Milan Kundera, who insists on absolute fidelity to everything he writes, translates his Czech characters' names into French.

One of the areas in the noun family that can really cause big problems is antecedents to pronouns. Ambiguity about what the antecedent is can cause big problems for the translator who cannot preserve the same level of ambiguity. The following example shows how important a translator's understanding and interpretive abilities are. It is part of a poem by the recent Nobel Prize-winning Polish poet Wislawa Szymborska, which has been translated both by Joanna Trzeciak and by the team of Stanislaw Baranczak and Clare Cavanagh; their respective translations are below:

> Poetry—
> but what sort of thing is poetry?
> More than one shaky answer
> has been given to this question.
> But I do not know and do not know and clutch
>   on to it,
> as to a saving banister.

> Poetry—
> but what is poetry anyway?
> More than one rickety answer
> has tumbled since that question first was raised.
> But I just keep on not knowing, and I cling to that
> like a redemptive handrail.

Trzeciak's solution is somewhat ambiguous, but it does appear that "it" in the fifth line refers to "poetry." Baranczak and Cavanagh make it very clear that "that" refers to "not knowing." As Baranczak told the *New York Times*, "My translation clings to the uncertainty; [Trzeciak] clings to poetry itself."* Trzeciak's Symborska clutches on to poetry despite not knowing what it is; she is a Romantic lover of art. Baranczak's Symborska clings to uncertainty; she's a modern philosopher. This is a significant difference. Baranczak's interpretation seems much more in line with the thought-provoking poet's approach to life, which is rarely Romantic. In short, the decision of which word is the antecedent to a pronoun requires a complete understanding of the poet's work. For a translator, it's not the same sort of problem we had in school making our antecedents clear.

Sometimes the level of ambiguity of the original cannot be preserved. Translating Japanese into English is limited not only by the vast difference between the two languages, but also because Japanese is such a vague language, with many things shown only by subtle differences in verbs and adjectives. As the Japanese-into-English translator Edward Seidensticker wrote, "a quick shift from the original *Tale of Genji* to Dr. Waley's translation can be like the moment in the movies when the London fog lifts and the adversaries stand face to face in the gaslight. . . . On the whole Dr. Waley seems brisk and positive because he lives in a brisker world and writes a more positive language. . . . A Japanese novelist once told me that he had not realized how ambiguous he was until he saw himself in translation."*

Often the limitations of a translator's language hamper him when he's trying to make good time even on the most open roads. Although English is more flexible than other Western languages, at least in terms of vocabulary, there are so many things we can't say in English—not nouns so much as ways of looking at the world. Take how limited our use of diminutives is, compared, say, to diminutive-rich Czech and German. We use diminutives so rarely, most people aren't quite sure what they are, and it isn't very easy to describe them. They are endings to words that show the speaker's or viewer's feelings toward the thing or person involved. In Czech and German, one's family members, friends, and pets are generally referred to with diminutives, but objects can be as well, even days of the week. As Czech novelist-translator Josef Škvorecký has written, "Each [different diminutive] expresses a different stage of intimacy, a different mood, a different depth of amorous intoxication or amorous hatred."*

A translator's inclination is to translate diminutives directly, often with the word "little." "Little father," which readers of translations from the Russian have seen far too much of, does not capture any of the feeling of the various Russian diminutives that can be used with "father." I prefer "dear" as a catch-all solution, but often you just have to dispense with the diminutive and add in the dearness (or other feelings) in other ways. Yes, we have diminutives—endings such as -ie and -kins—but they are cutesy and generally personal pet-names rather than linguistic alternatives. They rarely work ("daddikins"!?), but they must always be considered as a possible alternative.

Another thing English lacks is gender, at least in terms of word-endings. Škvorecký finds this omission astounding: "What an erotic impoverishment it must be not to have feminine endings."*

On the other hand, our enormous vocabulary makes it hard for translators out of English to find the right equivalent; they generally have to go with a word that is less exact or concrete than ours. And our many near synonyms lead translators into English to use words that are more exact or concrete than the original, or to use three different words to represent one repeated original.

Before we leave words and expressions, let me share a few words on the subject from Burton Raffel:*

> Details of all sorts . . . have to be pried like pearls out of their time-and culture/language-bound oysters, to be served up in a new shell. But what may seem eternally pearl-like in one context can seem distinctly odd, even grotesque, in another. Professor Donald Keene informs

me that some Japanese terms of endearment, as spoken by a man to a woman, involve images of sea-slime, slugs, and the like, all repellent to us but wholly positive, even aphrodisiac, in Japan.

How would you translate a Japanese sentence that could somewhat literally be reproduced as "Come closer, my slimy slug"? Would you preserve the foreign flavor, knowing that it would make the reader laugh rather than feel the speaker's love or lust?

Like an adventurer, the translator can't just rely on his vision. Some of the most dangerous creatures in the jungle can only be detected by sound. And the ability to distinguish between rustles and calls and even silences can mean the difference between life and death. In translation, this ability is known as "having a good ear." Like most important things—love, art, joy—it's hard to define. Having a good ear is a subset of having good instincts, that is, it's having good instincts for what sounds or seems appropriate in a certain context. It has, then, to do with sound in the literal sense as well as with "sounding right" in terms of contextual propriety. It involves having a wide range of alternatives at one's fingertips, either in one's head, worked out on paper, or with the aid of a thesaurus or rhyming dictionary. It involves knowing the many ways in which words, sounds, and concepts interact: grammar, rhythm, and logic. But in the end it comes down to "I know it when I hear it." Just as a painter with a good eye knows it when he sees it. Except that I think there are more, or at least more different sorts of relationships involved in writing and translating than there are in painting, primarily because language has other, art-extraneous roles that must be taken into account.

To write, one only needs an ear that can handle one's own register and style—for dialogue, the characters you feel comfortable writing about; for rhythm, the kind of sentences you write; for grammar, the kinds of constructions you use. Does this sound right *for me?* is what the writer asks himself. Does this sound as right in the same way as the original *for a reader?* is what the translator asks himself. The translator who takes on a variety of works and authors has to have an ear for all levels of diction and tone, all types of dialect, class, and other differences. And in order to both recognize differences and convey them into English, the translator has to have a good ear in both languages. And sometimes not just for both languages, but for both languages at different times. Dudley Fitts wrote with respect to translating ancient Greek plays into English: "modern English shuns the kind of rhetorical elevation which one finds in these plays and which was once natural enough in English itself . . . This complicates the translator's task, for he is constantly being tempted to indulge in specious beauties— anything rather than the dreary flatness that his language assumes when he compares it with the original."* After quoting these words, Richard Winston went on to add, "It isn't that English has such strict canons of taste; it's that we feel differently in English, respond differently. It is as though the tonal systems of the two languages were divergent, and the piece in question has to be transposed into a scale our ears recognize."

Here's an example of William Weaver, an experienced translator with a good ear, going through a very minor decision-making process:*

> In the opening sentence, how to capture the force and poetry of the initial repetition? Literally translated ('An idea, an idea . . .'), it sounds wrong to me. How about shifting the negative from the verb to the subject? 'No idea, no idea . . .'? Here the repetition sounds even worse. But perhaps, instead of repeating, I should simply enforce the noun. 'No idea at all . . .' 'Not the least idea . . .' 'No, no idea. . . .'
>
> I like this last solution best, because it allows a repetition, even if not the same repetition as [Carlo Emilio] Gadda's. It is not the perfect solution, but in translating—and especially in translating Gadda—there are no perfect solutions. You simply do your best.

Having a good ear means not only having the experience behind you and the ability to put it into practice. It also means listening carefully to the original and, especially, to the translation.

Eliot Weinberger told me, "People become so obsessed with getting
the literal meaning of the original correct that they never listen to
what they've actually written . . . students often don't read the
translations themselves, they don't hear what they've actually
written because they're still looking at the original. There's this
moment when you have to put the original away and then just
start looking at your translation and working on that. And then in
the end going back to the original again."

Serge Gavronsky seconded this: "Everything I do I read out
loud. I read everything to my wife, abusing her that way, harassing
her that way. To me it is a crucial test . . . It's at that moment
that you will trip or not, that a line will really be a line, meaning
you can follow, it'll carry you. When you read it aloud and all of
a sudden there's something that doesn't function, you hear it.
Whereas a mute reading may not provide you with that."

Rhythm and other aspects of sound, such as alliteration, assonance, and rhyme, are central to poetry. Often a translator has to
give up exact meaning to preserve a sound component. A good
example of this, pointed out by the Mexican poet Octavio Paz, is
in Pierre Leiris's French translation of T. S. Eliot's *The Waste Land*.
Leiris translated

> In the room the women come and go
> Talking of Michelangelo

as

> Dans le salon les femmes vont et viennent
> en parlant des maîtres de Sienne.

(literally "In the salon the women go and come/talking of the
Masters of Siena.") Leiris did pretty well only having to drop
Michelangelo to preserve the rhythm and the rhyme. Since the
point wasn't *whom* the women were talking about, but that they
were talking about high art, this wasn't really a loss at all.

An example of a great poet not capturing the sound of
another great poet's original was raised by John Felstiner in his
book about translating Pablo Neruda's poetry. The instance

involved Pablo Neruda's translation of two lines from Walt Whitman's *Song of Myself*:

> Urge and urge and urge,
> Always the procreant urge of the world.

Pablo Neruda translated these lines as

> Impulso, impulso, impulso,
> siempre el procreador impulso del mundo.

The repetition was preserved, but not the effect. Felstiner wrote, "We hear the dense monosyllabic 'urge' copulating throughout line one; the way the word can (only in English) act as verb and noun at once; the line's taut trochaic beat released into a flow of dactyls in line two; Whitman's astonishing (and Shakespearean) 'procreant' instead of 'proceative'—and all these things leave Neruda's version sounding rhythmically bulky. . . . A friend of Neruda's remembers him working assiduously on his Whitman translation in Madrid in 1935, searching for the right words. Maybe that word-for-word adherence was the trouble, since his own verse at the time, his 'material songs' to wood, wine, and celery, were astir with the procreant urge and the rhythm he did not confer on Whitman."* But capturing the tightness of Anglo-Saxon English is definitely a great challenge for a Spanish writer, who is burdened with long, soft, latinate words. Pablo Neruda clearly felt that the repetition of *impulso* and the strong alliteration of the hard *p* was the best he could do.

Both Felstiner and Alastair Reid have written about how important it is to the sound of a translation to listen to the poet's voice—in both cases, Pablo Neruda's. Reid wrote, "I found I could no longer read a poem of Neruda's simply as words on a page without hearing behind them that languid, caressing voice. Most important to me in translating these two writers [the other being Borges] was the sound of their voices in my memory, for it very much helped in finding the English appropriate to those voices.* Felstiner, who in his lectures plays a tape of Paul Celan reading one of his poems, so that the audience too can hear the original as the author meant it to be heard, wrote in his book on Pablo Neruda, "Perhaps the real 'original' behind any translation occurs not in the written poem, but in the poet's voice speaking the verse aloud. . . . a translator may also pick up vocal tones, intensities, rhythms, and pauses that will reveal how the poet heard a word, a phrase, a line, a passage. . . . what translating comes down to is listening—listening now to what the poet's voice said, now to one's own voice as it finds what to say."*

Just as it is often the smallest creatures—bacteria and viruses—that can be the most lethal, it is the simplest writing that is often the most difficult to translate. You can squash a spider or shoot a tiger that crosses your path, but there's not much you can do to keep a virus at bay, nor do you have a lot of alternatives when faced with a simple (in form, not necessarily in meaning) poem that works perfectly in another language. With simple writing, there just isn't much room for maneuver, fewer alternatives to choose from.

Jaroslav Seifert, the Nobel Prize-winning Czech poet, is the simplest and most difficult poet I've ever tried to translate. His poetry is especially difficult when it rhymes; because of its endings, simple Czech verse can rhyme and be beautiful in an easy, acceptable, musical way English poetry—especially today—cannot. If we keep the rhyme, Seifert's poetry seems forced, which it certainly isn't. But when we drop the rhyme, what seems beautifully simple in Czech come across as simply flat in English.

Without the beauty of Seifert's verse, the focus becomes the images, and the images aren't nearly as exciting, especially for non-Czechs who don't understand the allusions to Czech history and literature. For not only was Seifert a simple lyrical poet, he was also a dissident, and some of his poetry is in a code that got by the Communist censors, and also goes right by us. Ewald Osers has done a good job bringing Seifert into English, but he chose to keep away from the rhymed poems as much as possible.

Similarly, Edmund Keeley, with Philip Sherrard, has done a good job faced with similar problems in the poetry of C. P. Cavafy.

This was his approach: "[Y]ou do have the problem of losing some of the poet's linguistic texture, and of seeming to render him too flatly, prosaically, but I think that's a chance you have to take; the less artificial strikes me as the more honest and effective mode. You find the right stance by remembering that Cavafy was a very dramatic poet . . . [the poems] always somehow offer speaking voices, voices that allow the translator to introduce a colloquial richness, I think, that doesn't cheat on either the poet or the tradition of living poetry in English, and that can be found at least to some degree in the original. That's what Sherrard and I finally decided."*

When it comes to complex, baroque prose, on the other hand, people marvel that anyone could translate someone like Gabriel García Márquez. But, as his first English-language translator, Gregory Rabassa, has written, "he is so exact in his choice of words, getting ever so close to what he wants to say, that, indeed, it is difficult to make a botch of a translation of his work as he leads you along to a similar closeness in English of metaphor (word) and object."* Where Seifert suggests, García Márquez says it straight, even though his prose style is so much more lush.

But in general, even though complex sentences cause head-aches, it is easier to give an equivalent impression of a particular sort of complexity than it is to give an equivalent impression of a particular sort of simplicity. Because complexities are more clearly unlike each other, they can be easily recognized and turned into English complexities that seem very individual. It requires much more fine discrimination, not to mention writing ability, to capture the distinctiveness of a particular sort of simplicity.

Humor can be even more difficult to translate than simplicity. Let's start with the least funny, but most essential part of humor, irony. Stanislaw Baranczak, who has, among other things, translated a collection of English-language light verse into Polish, told me, "Irony is a problem, because the whole issue with irony is that you don't say something that you intend; you say something else. . . . You have to determine what [the author] tried to conceal under-neath this . . . irony." Even recognizing irony is difficult for many people; and the reason for this is what makes recreating it so tough: there are subtle, contextual signs that the author is being ironical. It is difficult to recognize and to create these signs so that the reader will realize (at least as much as the reader of the original) that the author is being ironic. Sometimes it just doesn't work culturally. Take understatement, which is a sub-category of irony. It's natural for a Briton to use understatement, to say less than he means. The double negative "Not bad!" is a compliment in England. But in many languages compliments are not something to be ironic about; they tend to be overstated rather than understated.

As with irony, humor is about getting it. It's usually not a matter of bringing subtle signs over into another language, but of creating the same combination of laughter and understanding. Rarely will witticisms, puns, jokes, parody, or satire work the same in one language or culture as they do in another. That is why so little humor is ever translated; even if the humor isn't very word-oriented—that is, not dependent on puns and other sorts of word-play—it rarely can make the cultural leap. A lot of British humor doesn't make it across the Atlantic to America, and vice versa. So why should foreign-language humor be able to make a double leap? Familiarity is essential to getting it—familiarity with what the humor is making fun of and familiarity with the style of humor, as well. This is a special problem in the U.S., where little is known about other cultures, especially contemporary ones. Yet everyone knows a lot about us, which is why at least our comedy films, and some of our more popular humorists, are able to be popular abroad.

So what does a translator do when face to face with humor? Well, the first thing he should do is forget the idea of running and hiding behind literal translation; it just won't cut the mustard. He has to be exceptionally creative, to transform the humor into something that works just as well in English and that conveys pretty much the same idea. For example, if the author is parodying a popular song (and the translator is knowledgeable enough to recognize this), then the translator should parody a popular song that is recognizable to his readers. If he can find one from the foreign culture, all the better; but it doesn't have to, and will rarely be, the same one, unless it's very important to the novel that it is. On the other hand, it can't be *too* American, or it will sound as if the author is making fun of us rather than of his own culture. If this is the case and we don't know of any, say, Japanese popular music, then the translator might want to make fun of music in general (at least we've heard of karaoke), make fun of something equivalent that we have heard of (say, a Japanese novel or film), or drop the whole thing and add in some parody somewhere else. There's nothing worse than making a lame joke or parodying something unknown.

Dialect creates similar problems. To the original-language reader, dialect gives a concrete impression of place and class. But dialect has meaning only in its language. The translator is placed in a difficult dilemma: does he use a recognizable English-language dialect that is roughly equivalent (say, Appalachian for Slovak mountain folk) or does he try to create something that suggests the original but does not exist in English. Gregory Rabassa opts for the latter solution: "People try to take, say, a class dialect from Spanish and put it into a class dialect in English, and it doesn't work, because you made that person into an English speaker, and that's not it. What I would do with, say, a gaucho, is not try to make him into a cowboy. Make him into an English-speaking gaucho. You've got to invent. It has to sound like English, but also sound like a gaucho. There are ways."

The pavement of the translator's journey is syntax, or word order. Syntax is the best way to see how differently peoples and authors think. Every language has its own basic syntax, and each author embraces it and departs from it in his own manner. For an English-language reader to truly understand a foreign work, it is important that he understand the way the author thinks and sees the world. A translator tries to bring across this reflection of different forms of thought, both those of the author and those manifested in the foreign language's syntactical conventions.

Willard Trask told Edwin Honig in an interview, "I'm very strong in the belief that one of the important things is the order in which thoughts enter minds. As nearly as possible—although you certainly can't do it for very long with German, or at all with Latin—one should try to keep somewhere near the word order of the original in the translation. . . . But obviously you can only do this to a certain extent or no one would read it. But I'm very strong on trying it. And I think that the way you can do it is to have your English be *so* English in the passages that don't matter that you can get away, where it does matter, with something foreign. . . . gradually I think that people will feel at home with more foreign constructions than they now admit." I would agree with Trask that, where this difference in vision is important to the work, it should be reflected in the translation, either by an odd syntax or by some other means that does the job. But this requires both excellent interpretive skills and perfect control of English. In other words, it's something that is, I think, as much an issue of competence as theoretical approach. Most translators play it safe by at least trying to use normal English syntax, because it's more acceptable to publishers and less likely to be construed as amateurish "translationese." Most inexperienced translators, that is, tend to preserve the original's syntax much more than English can bear, not because they have any theoretical goals, but because they can't make the leap between languages. Translators have what Richard Pevear calls an "inner editor" to keep them from falling into translationese. Pevear, who tends to keep closer to the original than most translators, told me, "there's this little editorial voice that's constantly preaching cowardice, saying 'You don't dare to do that.' And I have to say, 'No, I do dare. I'm going to do that. I like it.' And I do it."

To unravel a German sentence and put it back together again means effectively recreating every sentence. As Edwin and Willa Muir, best known as the translators of Kafka's German, have written, "The very shape of thought has to be changed in translation, and that seems to me more difficult than rendering words and idioms into their equivalents. . . . From its first word a classical

German sentence is purposively controlled until the verbs come down at the end of it to clinch the statement . . . The English statement has not this control; it cannot wait, or does not choose to wait, for the end of the sentence to convey its meaning. . . . To construct an English sentence is not unlike stringing beads one after the other. But to construct a German sentence—what image can best describe that?" The Muirs settle on "a great gut, a bowel, which deposits at the end of it a sediment of verbs."* Never believe that, just because a translator works closely with a language, he loves it uncritically.

Japanese is even more difficult, according to Edward Seidensticker, who has translated a lot of it into English: "A Japanese sentence prefers to keep one guessing. The last element in the sentence reveals whether it is positive or negative, declaratory or interrogative. 'I do not think that . . .' begins an English sentence; '. . . this I do not think' ends a Japanese sentence, having coyly held off the fact of belief or disbelief to the end."*

There are some cases where difference in thought goes beyond mere difference in syntax, where there is a difference in the perception of what poetry is. This has been a serious problem in the translation of classical Chinese poetry, where simultaneity rather than logic is central. Also, this poetry, although lyrical, does not contain an "I". It is not, as is our lyrical poetry, about an individual's experience in the world, but about the world itself. Most translators have ignored this and added an observer. This was shown clearly in an enlightening little book by Eliot Weinberger called *Nineteen Ways of Looking at Wang Wei: How a Chinese Poem Is Translated*. Chinese poetry clashes with our view of poetry and our philosophical view of nature. I agree with Weinberger that one should accept the poet's philosophy and bring it into English as best one can; in fact, that seems to be the most important thing to preserve in order to truly experience this part of Chinese culture. The alternative is to write English-language poetry based on or inspired by Chinese images, without the other essential aspects of Chinese poems. The results might be good poems, but they should not be called *translations*.

*   *   *

To determine an author's thought processes, where they go beyond the conventions of his language, a translator must also determine the author's intent. But this is a thorny subject: critics hate to get into it, and writers tend to say it doesn't exist, that a book is what it is, not what its author intended. But it's hard to understand a book without at least speculating about intent. Suzanne Jill Levine has written, "An awareness of a book's intended effect on its original reader is obviously necessary in order for us to understand the difficulties of repeating that effect. The author's intentions, overdetermined by her or his own context, may or may not be verifiable, or even relevant, but the translator—like all interpreters—has to decide, within a given context, what function she or he is trying to fulfill."* [By the way, I hope you will forgive me for using masculine pronouns alone instead of using both masculine and feminine (or grammatically awkward plurals); I just can't bear to write sentences that read like this last one.]

You can know all the tricks of the trade, have the ammunition and aim necessary to take on the fiercest of beasts, but if you don't have the balance to cross logs over streams, hug the edge of cliffs, and just plain walk, you won't get very far. In translation, balance is even more important. "The art of literary translation," Burton Raffel has written, "and above all the translation of poetry, might almost be defined as the art of balancing different claims."* The translator must choose not only what in the original to preserve and what to give up, but also what to add. All the elements I've been talking about—rhythm, sound, vision, allusion, humor, effect, syntax, familiarity vs. foreignness, ease vs. difficulty, ambiguity vs. clarity, meaning vs. form—not only have to be dealt with, but they have to be balanced against each other, one preserved, the other lost, two given up to keep one that is more important in the particular context. Balancing encompasses all of this chapter, because few of a translator's decisions are made in isolation, even though it's very hard to describe them in any other way. So much is lost in going from one language to another, and yet it's hard to compensate for this loss without feeling unfaithful. Balancing, rather than fidelity, is the central ethical act of translation, the act that allows for the redemption of losses, for respecting a work's integrity, for the recreation of another, freestanding work of art. Balancing is the way in which a translator meets his obligations. Yet this crucial and complex process is often described as "doing what works," hardly something to make audiences ooh and aah.

The difficulties of balancing are most pronounced in the translation of poetry, and there is one collection of essays that focuses on a nitty-gritty look at balancing, Daniel Weissbort's *Translating Poetry: The Double Labyrinth*. But good prose also creates a host of problems. So instead of talking on and on about all the considerations there are to consider, I'm going to turn the page over to Breon Mitchell, a professor at Indiana University and former president of the American Literary Translators Association (ALTA), and let him talk about translating what he has called "the sentence that has been written about and talked about more than any other sentence in German literature," the first sentence of Franz Kafka's *The Trial*. Mitchell has recently completed only the second English translation of this novel (although the first translation has appeared in a revised form).

First, let me give you the German original and the English translations. First the German: "Jemand mußte Josef K. verleumdet haben, denn ohne daß er etwas Böses getan hätte, wurde er eines Morgens verhaftet." Then the first English translation, by Willa and Edwin Muir: "Someone must have been telling lies about Joseph K., for without having done anything wrong he was arrested one fine morning." And the revision by E. M. Butler: "Someone must have traduced Joseph K., for without having done anything wrong he was arrested one fine morning." I should note that the only revision Butler made to this sentence, the word "traduced," was an alternative to something Mitchell sees as only a minor problem, and which Butler made into a major one by using a word few readers will recognize, thus unnecessarily putting them off in the novel's first verb (the German word is more familiar, equivalent to our word "slander").

The following combines what Mitchell said in a speech to ALTA in November 1994 and what he said in an interview with me in April 1995: "When I approached Kafka again, for *The Trial,* I expected his language to be exactly what it is, because I knew it well from years and years of dealing with the German. But when I was really faced with translating it, I was surprised at how hard it is to translate practically any sentence. It's because in spite of the apparent simplicity of the language and the relatively simple structure of the sentences, he just builds so much into each sentence, in terms of the way in which the words are arranged and the richness of the relationship between the words. I think it's so powerful in the original, and it's just extremely difficult to carry that power across so simply in English. . . .

"[This sentence] has been gone over and over and over, and for me it's a stumbling block, a hurdle that's almost impossible to get over. First of all, because it is so well known. Second, because the English version is almost as well known. And thirdly, because the English and the German seem to be doing two very different things.

"Many of the problems of Kafka come up in this sentence. At the end of the first sentence, it says that Joseph K. must have been slandered because *ohne daß er etwas Böses getan hätte, wurde er eines Morgens verhaftet,* and this *getan hätte* [having done] is a subjunctive form that is tied up with the construction *ohne daß* [without. . .]. It requires the subjunctive. But that is a very subtle thing, and the standard English translation just says, . . . 'for without having done anything wrong.' . . . In the German, it begins with the feeling something like, 'Without his *perhaps* having done anything wrong.' Maybe he didn't really do anything wrong, or maybe what he did wasn't really wrong. But in the English translation . . . well, the trial's over. He's been slandered, he didn't do anything wrong, he was arrested. This opens the novel on a note of total injustice. And it's not the feeling you get in the German at all.

"The other thing that's complicated to me is that use of *Böses*. Because there I think immediately of Nietzsche, and so, I think, do most German readers now and even at the time: *Jenzeits von Gut und Böse, Beyond Good and Evil*. It's a real duality of good on the one hand and something much more than wrong on the other. It has overtones that include morality much more strongly, and also religious dimensions. Almost the notion of sin built into it in some way. Right and wrong's not good and evil. But to turn that into evil? You can't say that 'without having done anything evil, he was arrested one morning.' So you might want to say something like, 'without having done anything truly wrong,' . . . and to build into that first sentence the notion of uncertainty that I see in the use of the subjunctive, the overtones of moral weight that I see in *Böses*, without making a sentence that sounds extremely odd and strange in English. 'Truly wrong' elevates 'wrong' into a stronger sense. And the use of the word 'truly,' I hope, would call up the whole question, What is the truth in this? I thought of using the phrase 'it seems' or 'apparently.' But these create only doubt, without heightening the sense of wrong. So I've become enamored of the word 'truly.'

"And then we have *eines Morgens* [one morning], and the sentence builds toward the final word: *verhaftet*. It's like a nail at the end of the sentence. He is arrested. The sentence builds toward that, and it's sprung on you like a surprise. Then it seems that the sentence in English ought to end with the word 'arrested,' too. The standard English translation ends with 'one fine morning.' In a little detail like that, you've changed the whole feeling of the sentence. My other objection here is that the standard translation says 'one *fine* morning.' That is an interpretation that gives an ironic overtone, makes it sort of humorous. That's not present in the German. There is another sentence in which *eines Morgens* is used, another famous sentence, the opening sentence of 'Die Verwandlung,' 'The Metamorphosis,' where Gregor Samsa finds himself *eines Morgens* turned into this *ungeheuer Ungeziefer* [enormous vermin]. The Muirs, who translated both texts, simply translated the words in 'The Metamorphosis' as 'one morning.' Why it's 'one fine morning' for them in *The Trial* and just 'one morning' in 'The Metamorphosis' is not clear. They should have said, This is an echo of some sort, one of those intertextual connections or threads you want to maintain. You translate it the same way unless there are strong reasons not to. So I don't want to say 'one fine morning.'

"We could start the sentence 'one morning,' but then you have to get in 'someone must have been slandering Joseph K.' My tendency is to work it in earlier in the sentence, but not at the beginning. So I would opt for something like, 'Someone must have slandered Joseph K., for one morning, without having done anything truly wrong, he was arrested.' I'm thinking now still, because I'm still working on it, of taking the word 'truly' and working it into the sentence—or 'really,' but it sounds so American—to give the subjunctive sense to it. If I say 'without really having done anything wrong' it indicates maybe he did something wrong, but it really wasn't wrong or he really didn't do it. But what I don't want to do is just leave it 'without having done anything wrong.'

"This can't be done in English with a sentence that attempts to be close and literal and exact. Of course, you could rewrite it. An English novelist could think of another way to write a sentence that would do it. But then it would be removed from the German to the extent that it would not be necessarily, or read like, a translation. I feel this old tension between fidelity to the text, reverence for every word that Kafka wrote, and then the desire to create an English sentence that does something like what the original does, isn't an awkward and offputting sentence, and doesn't misinterpret the situation from the very beginning. That's the way in which Kafka is hard for me, not just with the first sentence but with most of the sentences."

Balancing all the elements of a sentence, even a relatively simple sentence of only a few words, is not an easy thing. Imagine doing justice to an entire work.

Most examples given in writing about literary translation consist of great literature like this. When the author isn't quite up to snuff, the balancing process is somewhat different. The translator can be in the position of an editor. But does a translator have the freedom to say, as an editor would, "The penultimate paragraph in Chapter 3 doesn't make sense. Strike it."? Can he go through the entire manuscript, fixing things up here and there, making the prose read more clearly or making the verse more rhythmical or less forced?

The translator has to decide how to deal with the fact that a paragraph doesn't make sense. Does he too write a paragraph that doesn't make sense (and possibly get blamed for this fact)? Does he make the paragraph make sense? Does he try and find some place in between? Or does he give up and strike the paragraph as if he were the original's editor (if the author is still alive, he can ask for permission to do this)? Whose interest is most important in this instance? The reader's in understanding what he's reading, and not being unnecessarily put off by it? Or the reader's in having an authentic experience of the original? The author's in having everything brought over that possibly can, even the mistakes? Or the author's in having the best version of his work brought over, even if it means editing?

It should be noted here that not all countries, not to mention all publishing houses, are equally attentive at editing the books they publish. American books tend to be better edited than those from other countries. It is not uncommon for American translators to be faced with practically unedited books filled with errors, poor grammar and the like.

Decisions, decisions. There are so many approaches to a literary work, so many obligations, so much to win and lose, and all the while what you're doing is impossible, unappreciated, unmarketable. One wonders why there are so few experimental approaches and instead so many attempts to just get it right, attempts that are almost always failures, are always failures to some extent. When it really comes down to it, the major differences between translations—at least those reasonably close in time—involve the translators' ethics, competence, and goals more than they do a lot of the things discussed in this chapter. Everyone faces the same hurdles, but some jump over them, some run around them, some crawl under them, and some don't see them and fall flat on their faces. Most do a little of each.

And the obstacles change over time; some become easier to see, others become taller, and new ones appear. Think of the poor Muirs. They were given Kafka as an author to translate. They didn't know what he would become. For them, it wasn't a matter of scholarship or reverence or getting every little thing right; it was a matter of doing a job on time, and getting on to the next one. They had never taught Kafka and never would. They were running a footrace rather than taking on hurdles.

Some translators go to the other extreme, needless to say, in terms of the care given to the work being translated. Take Robert Fitzgerald, who translated Homer and Virgil: "The translator . . . does one draft after another; he's a sedentary craftsman trying through repeated trials and failures to arrive at a readable English page. I did it by writing out the Greek of each book in a ledger-type notebook: each Greek line followed by two blank lines. While I did this, I would use the dictionary and what scholarship I could find to clear up puzzles in the text. When I went to work I had nothing but my own Greek in my own hand before me to try to match with English in the blank lines underneath the Greek. Then the typewritten drafts began, and every evening I would destroy half of what I had done every morning, and often a day's work would be only a few lines. I had from the beginning a sense that I didn't care how long it took and if I had to wait a week for a suitable version of one exclamation I would wait a week and, you know—no hurry. Patience. Patience."* But then Fitgerald, like Mitchell and like most American translators of great literature, was a professor, someone with a regular income and flexible hours.

Richard Sieburth summed up this feeling of taking one's time when he told me, "Translation is an art of artisanal rhythms." The poet-translator Rachel Hadas used another sort of image in the introduction to her collection of translations: "Rash as I had been to encroach at all, I had entered each stanza, no, every line of each stanza of those twenty-one poems as a careful servant would enter a room, polishing facets, highlighting ornaments without displacing any important documents, restoring its primal luster to all the crucial and artful original disorder. The surface of each separate syllable gleamed as I gingerly advanced."*

The process doesn't necessarily stop when the translation's all done or even when it's been published. Translators, even more than writers, are never satisfied. Since translators work in the realm of alternatives, there are always other ways it could have been done. It can be painful to read again or, worse, read in public. Eliot Weinberger completely redid his first translations of Octavio Paz's poetry. And over twenty years and six or seven editions he has continued to revise his translation of Paul Blanco's poetry. His feeling about this is indicative: "You have to start somewhere."

A translator's doubtfulness about his work is the flip side of the balancing he's required to do. Gregory Rabassa wrote, "the choices made in translation are never as secure as those made by the author. Since we are not writing our own material, we are still unsure whether or not the word we have used is the best one, either for meaning or for sound or for ever so many other reasons. I am always distressed when I receive the usually handsome copy of a book I have translated. . . . I start having second thoughts about word choice and how it would have been so much better had I said this instead of that."*

One of the most important factors to be taken into consideration in making a pattern of translation decisions is, What is the result going to be used for? And whom is it going to be used by? If the answer is that it is intended for contemporary poets to learn about contemporary poetry in India, or about fourteenth-century Provençal poetry, then writing with an ear to contemporary poetry is important. If the translation is intended to be used by students studying ancient Egyptian poetry, then giving them a feeling of the form of the original verse is important, and free verse is out; if it's for students studying ancient Egyptian society or language, then prose would probably do.

If the translation is to be presented *en face*, that is, with the original on the page across from the translation, then there is more pressure on the translator to keep his lines the same as the original, and not be quite so free with his translation. Traditionally, *en face* presentations were used primarily with trots, that is, literal translations meant for students of the foreign language, so that they could more easily read the original. Recently, this has been in fashion principally, I think, because of our obsession with authenticity. 'Here it is,' the *en face* format seems to be saying, 'the real thing. See, they're both right there in front of you; we're not pulling any wool over your eyes.' I think this is bad for translation, because it's restrictive. It's hard enough to get some distance from the original in order to be successfully creative, without knowing that the original will always be there, casting a shadow over your work, practically begging critics and readers to question your decisions. Those who favor *en face* presentations argue that it draws the reader back to the original. And this is true, if the reader reads the original language. But few will, and *en face* only benefits those who can read it but not very well. And it makes translation too much about language and too little about literature. Therefore, it's great for language classes—for a pedagogical intent—but not for literature. Or as John Frederick Nims wrote, "The original is an experience. The translation, different but analogous, is an experience—but the two experiences cannot well be enjoyed together."*

But more than all of these considerations, enjoying the decision-making process, the journey, the sights, leads to the best results. The obstacles and pains are easy to enumerate, but the joys can be known only by taking an adventure yourself. No postcard or home video will do the trick. William Weaver told me, "It's the wrestling and pinning the text to the floor. It's that marvelous feeling when you say, Yes, now that sentence is right. Now I've done it. It doesn't always happen, and sometimes you do a lot of treading water. You say, Okay, I'll put this down and then when I come back I'll make it nice, I'll make it right. And then sometimes it comes right the first time. Either way is fun. Looking at a sentence you don't like, that hasn't come right, and pummeling it until you get it into shape, is very satisfactory."

This is really what it all comes down to, why intelligent, creative people who could be doing something else put up with all the elusive prepositions, the twisted sentence structures, the unyielding simplicities, the tightrope balancings, the unforgiving critics and unrecognizing readers. Because translating's a great joy.

Bettering

BESIDES THE JOYS AND THE SHARING, the major incentive to translate classic works is to do it better than others have. To get it
right, to do it more faithfully, to share your interpretation of it, to
keep it alive with updated language, to make it a truly great work,
to make it a truly contemporary work, to expose it for what it is,
to make it grander or bring it down to earth—there are so many
reasons why each translator feels a work is worth translating yet
again. And as an editor of translations, some of them second translations of major twentieth-century works, I feel the same way: I
think it can be done better and I turn to a translator I think can
do it better.

In talking about his early translation of Sophocles' *Antigone*,
done with Dudley Fitts, Robert Fitzgerald spoke of the "over-
powering sense that justice had not been done to the poetry of
Sophocles and that something approaching justice might not be so
difficult in view of the abysmal quality to our ears of what existed.
. . . We were dissatisfied on [Sophocles'] behalf. . ."*

The long work most often translated into English is Homer's
Iliad. Many works are translated anew by each generation, but
translating the *Iliad* was so popular among the Victorians, it was
being translated by a number of people at the same time. And
there have been three new translations published in the 1990s. In
fact, its popularity for us is so great it's been translated into English
over ten times as often as into French. From Chapman's *Iliad* of
1579, known to most of us primarily via Keats's poem "On First
Looking Into Chapman's Homer," to the latest, Stanley Lombardo's
Iliad in GI uniform (1997), a large number of famous writers,
lesser known poets, dons and schoolmasters have had a go at doing

Homer and bringing him to the masses. And they've done it successfully, at least the bringing to the masses.

Nearly every *Iliad* translator feels his (I couldn't find a published English translation by a woman) translation is more faithful, modern, or right than the others, just as Keats felt about one he read, "Yet did I never breathe its pure serene / Till I heard Chapman speak out loud and bold." In the introduction to William Benjamin Smith and Walter Miller's 1944 translation of the *Iliad* into dactylic hexameters (that is, each line has six feet of three syllables, with the stress on the first syllable of each foot), Smith wrote, "The present translation of the *Iliad* is, as far as I can discover, the first attempt to reproduce in English Homer's great epic line for line in the meter of the original." In other words, they were being more formally faithful or authentic than the dozens of translators that went before them. And since the dactyl is not intrinsic to English, the fact that no one else had tried it should only come as a mild surprise: it doesn't read very well.

But several translators have been formally faithful enough to translate the *Iliad* in hexameters, which makes for longer, more prosaic lines than the usual five-footed, ten-or-so-syllabled pentameter line. Iambic hexameter was considered by the Victorian poet and essayist Matthew Arnold to be the most appropriate form, because it was most faithful to the original form without going against the grain of English. Richmond Lattimore's popular 1951 translation used six feet, and Robert Fagles' 1990 translation is loosely based on a meter of six feet.

In their 1950 translation, American translators Alston Hurd Chase and William G. Perry, Jr. also felt they were doing the appropriate thing: "In order to derive from a reading or two something of that profound experience which an understanding of the *Iliad* brought to previous generations, the modern reader needs a translation which should try to interpret it as faithfully as possible in a style appropriate to his own day." Chase and Perry's style was neither hexameters nor pentameters, neither dactyls nor iambs, but prose. As the classicist W. H. D. Rouse said in the introduction to his 1938 prose translation, "This book . . . is a translation into plain English of the plain story of Homer." Appealing to the modern American taste for plainness is no different from what Alexander Pope was doing in 1718: writing heroic couplets, that is, rhymed pairs of iambic pentameter lines, because they were the preferred grand style of his time. The novel is our grand style today. And it certainly *is* hard to understand, not to mention get through, an epic poem when one is not used to reading poetry at all. Poetry is a language of its own, and if you don't speak it, its meaning is left obscure, like classical music.

Poetry also requires re-reading. No single reading of any translation of the *Iliad* is going to be enough to get it. It should be read several times in one's life, even if in the same translation, but preferably in multiple translations so that the experience changes a little, so that you can experience more aspects of the original as they have been chosen over others by various translators. I read it first in Lattimore's translation in high school, then in Fitzgerald's, which came out when I was in college (I had the great joy of hearing him read from it then, and this will make me forever prejudiced toward his translations, because I can still hear him reciting the words), and most recently I've dipped into Fagles' and Pope's, which of all the translations is, I feel, the greatest work of literature in its own right, and is happily back in print. I will most likely never read the *Iliad* in prose, and neither will you, but then we're not the audience the prose translations were written for. However, there are prose translations which are more artistically rendered than most poetry translations, even contemporary ones such as Lattimore and Rack. You'll see for yourself below.

Almost every translator of Homer wants to be faithful to him, but it's hard to be faithful when there is so much disagreement over what sort of poet he was. Was he noble or popular? Was he plain or archaic, direct or fanciful, natural or artificial? Differences of opinion show how each period views what is ancient, but there are also differing views within the same period. Francis Newman was the sort of Romantic Victorian classicist who saw the ancients as pure and popular, men of the people. Matthew Arnold, who argued with Newman about translating Homer, was a more modern-leaning, yet still Romantic, Victorian poet who saw in Homer a fellow spirit, a noble, modern poet. They both wanted fidelity, but to completely different conceptions of the original. This is yet another reason why fidelity is wanting as an approach to translation.

Robert Fitzgerald similarly saw in Homer a modern poet, but an even more modern one: "as Homer went along with his tale, he could and did invent new ways of handling episodes and passages that made each performance, in some way, a new thing. Do you see how this fact liberates, to a certain extent, the translator? . . . for that imagination no text, no text sacred or otherwise, existed . . . free improvisation was part of the essence of each performance. Therefore, what is known as freedom in translation would be nearer to what the original performer expected of a translator than it might be in the case of someone who had . . . labored over every line. . . . [Homer's] art was comparable to the art of the great musical virtuoso who can improvise."* Where Newman saw an archaic figure whose archaism must be preserved, and Arnold saw a poet whose meter, simplicity, and nobility must be preserved, Fitzgerald saw an improviser, a jazz writer, whose spirit of freedom must be preserved. Robert Fagles, similarly modern, has taken Fitzgerald's view a step further to greater formal freedom.

The decision of whether to render Homer as a contemporary poet or to reproduce the oldness of his work in the form of archaic language is somewhat similar to the major debate in jurisprudence between those who want to interpret the Constitution in terms of contemporary needs and sensibilities and those who want to preserve "its original intent." What Justice Brennan said about the Constitution in a 1985 speech could just as easily have been said about Homer: "We current Justices read the Constitution in the only way that we can: as twentieth-century Americans. The genius of the Constitution rests not in any static meaning it might have had in a world that is dead and gone, but in the adaptability of its great principles to cope with current problems and current needs." The latest *Iliad* translator, Stanley Lombardo, would definitely agree.

In the most unusual approach to translating the *Iliad*, the contemporary Briton Christopher Logue has been taking this approach one step further in a series of poems that adapt separate books of the *Iliad* with no attempt to preserve order, meaning, or even inclusion of all parts. What he is after is a contemporary expression of the poem's essence. As he said in the introduction to his first volume, the *Patrocleia of Homer* (1963), he translated "in the belief that no sort of fancy translationese should be allowed to muffle the impact of the original." Or as Christopher Middleton has said, "I must say that when I first read it I was alerted to all sorts of possibilities in the English language and all sorts of realities of Greek sensibility that I'd not felt very strongly before. It was an exciting experience. . . . I felt it was going to the core of the kind of shining, subtle and supple, muscular Greek sensibility of Archilocus or of Euripides."* George Steiner has referred to the "presentness" of Logue's translations, that is, the way he brings the ancient work into the present.

There are other reasons to take on Homer than to do it better, more faithfully, more contemporary, or for a different audience. For one thing, there's the joy of the activity and of giving one's own rendering—just like playing a Beethoven piano concerto a way no one has quite done before. But sometimes, the reason is simply fulfilling a commission from a publisher who wants a piece of a sizeable market for which no author has to be paid a royalty.

Here is an extensive but not complete selection of translations of a short passage from the *Iliad* (most notable of those translations missing here are early ones that can only be found in rare books libraries I don't have access to, and a number of mediocre-to-bad Victorian translations). The passage is from Book I. It is Achilles speaking to Agamemnon after Agamemnon has commanded Achilles to give up his woman to him. Rather than having a

confusing number of different spellings of Achilles, I have changed
the spellings so that there are only two, the three-syllable Achilles
and the four-syllable Achilleus.

A. H., 1581, ballad (tetrameter/trimeter on each line)

> Achilles straight full restless yet, him the speech he took,
> "I were (quoth he) a coward lewd, if I agreed to brook
> Thy governance, after thy will I ruled will be no more,
> For no obedience look of me, others command therefore,

From the French, modern spelling

George Chapman, 1598, rhymed hexameter couplets

> . . . Thetis' son prevented him, and said:
> "Fearful and vile I might be thought, if the exactions laid
> By all means on me I should bear. Others command to
>   this,
> Thou shalt not me; or if you thou dost, far my free
>   spirit is
> From serving thy command. . . .

Chapman was a major playwright and poet of the time, considered by
some to be "the rival poet" in Shakespeare's Sonnets. This is from a
modern spelling edition.

Thomas Hobbes, 1675, rhymed iambic pentameter

> Then interrupting him, Achilles said,
> I were a wretch and nothing worth indeed,
> If I whatever you command obey'd.
> I will no more to what you say take heed.

Yes, this is the same Hobbes who wrote *Leviathan*, a major work of
political philosophy. This translation was a work of his old age, after the
failure of his now famous work. The simplicity of the language is amazing
for the time, but the syntax is forced in order to rhyme.

John Dryden, 1700, heroic couplets (rhymed iambic pentameter pairs of lines)

> Achilles cut him short; and thus reply'd:
> My worth allow'd in words, is in effect deny'd,
> For who but a poltron possess'd with fear
> Such haughty insolence can tamely bear?
> Command thy slaves: my freeborn soul disdains
> A tyrant's curb, and restiff breaks the reins.

Dryden translated the whole of the *Aeneid* and *Odyssey*, but only translated the first book of the *Iliad*, at the end of his life. He was the leading poet of his generation, did a great deal of translation, and was also an important playwright.

Alexander Pope, 1715, heroic couplets

> Here on the monarch's speech Achilles broke,
> And furious, thus, interrupting spoke.
> Tyrant, I will deserve thy galling shame,
> To live thy slave, and still to serve in vain,
> Should I submit to each unjust decree:
> Command thy vassals, but command not me.

The *Iliad* was Pope's only major translation; he collaborated on the *Odyssey*. A follower of Dryden in the use of heroic couplets, Pope was also the leading literary figure of his generation. Read this excerpt again, if you already haven't. Note the amount, the complexity, and the effects of its alliteration (for example, the sarcasm that goes with the letter "v", used six times in this excerpt, four times in a single line). Note how the stilted syntax gives the language power rather than Hobbes' awkwardness. Note how effectively Pope places his stresses, so that the first word spoken to Agamemnon is an attention-getting trochee ("Tyrant"), and especially how the last three stresses of the last line of this excerpt fall on the last four syllables and the last three words, putting the line severely out of balance, slowing it down and creating the effect of powerful, antagonistic, self-centered speech.

William Cowper, 1791, unrhymed iambic pentameter (blank verse)

> Whom thus Achilles interrupted fierce.
> "Could I be found so abject as to take
> The measure of my doings at thy lips,

Well might they call me coward through the camp,
A vassal, and a fellow of no worth.
Give law to others. Think not to control
Me, subject to thy proud commands no more.

This poet, who aimed to free English verse from the elegance of the Augustans, was the first to bring Homer into the predominant English poetic form, blank verse. Note how the Romantic poets were the first to ignore Homer: there wasn't to be another translation of the *Iliad* by a poet until 1870, no translation of it at all for fifty years, and no attempt to translate it by any major poet for the next two hundred years.

S. Brandreth, 1846, blank verse

To whom Achilles interrupting said;
"I base indeed, and worthless should be call'd,
Did I each work, thou badest me, undertake.
Enjoin these things to others, and no more
Bid me; for thee I think not to obey.

William Munford, 1846, blank verse

Him interrupting, fierce Achilles then,
Indignantly, exclaim'd: truly the name
Of a dastard mean and base were justly mine,
Should I unlimited submission yield
To thy proud dictates! Others so command,
Not me; for I no farther will submit.

W. G. T. Bartel, 1854, heroic couplets

"Hilding and base should I be clep'd I trou,
Yielding to thee in all things speakest thou.
Though others rule, think not my chief to be.
No more I'll yield to thee.

Even more archaizing than the more famous Newman, Bartel's first line sounds like parodic nonsense verse.

Francis W. Newman, 1856, ballad

> Then quickly catching up his word,   divine Achilles
> answer'd:
> "For cowardly in truth might I   and worthless be
> reputed,
> If every matter I should yield   to thee, what e'er thou
> biddest.
> Be thy enactments now imposed   on others: for
> hereafter
> To me give no commands: for I   mean to obey no
> longer.

Newman is the only modern to attempt Homer in the traditional ballad form; his goal was to make Homer seem a man of the people, with a heavily Victorian use of archaic language. It was very controversial, especially because of Matthew Arnold's vociferous opposition, but the principal problem here, as you can see, is that Newman's verse is clumsy. The classicist had no ear.

Theodore Alois Buckley, 1856, prose

> But him noble Achilles interruptingly answered: "Yea, forsooth, I may be called a coward and a man of no worth, if now I yield to thee in every thing, whatever thou mayest say. Enjoin these things to other men; but dictate not to me, for I think that I shall no longer obey thee.

The first prose translation I could find, but still preserving the archaic qualities that characterize so many Victorian verse translations. Apparently, he was aiming to replicate Sir Walter Scott the novelist at the same time Newman was aiming to replicate Scott the poet.

X.Y.Z. (W. Purton), 1862, heroic couplets

> Hereon him straight cut short Achilles bold: —
> "I'll give you leave to call me coward, fool,
> The longer I submit to be your tool:
> Give your commands to others; don't tell me,
> If you expect that they should honor thee.

Edward, Earl of Derby, 1864, blank verse

> To whom Achilles, interrupting, thus:
> "Coward and slave indeed I might be deemed,
> Did I submit to make thy will my law;
> To others thou command; but not to me
> To dictate, for I follow thee no more.

Philip Stanhope Worsley, 1865, Spenserian stanza (don't ask)

> Then brave Achilleus with this word broke in:
> "Now, if I all things yield to thy mere clamor and din,
> Call me a poor weak fool, a man of nought.
> Others may tremble at thy will, not I. . . .

In another attempt to find a suitable heroic form for Homer, Worsley turned to the complex stanza used by Edmund Spenser in writing the epic *Fairie Queene* (1589-1596).

Edwin W. Simcox, 1865, very loose hexameters

> Then, his speech interrupting, thus answered noble
>   Achilleus:
> "Well should I, henceforth, merit the worthless name of
>   a coward,
> If in a single thing I obey thee whatever thou sayest.
> Lay thy behest on others, of me thou shalt never be
>   master;
> For from this hour I will never obey thy word nor
>   commandment.

In an 1861 essay, Matthew Arnold insisted that translators preserve Homer's hexameters. Simcox and many others in the 1860s, and even in following decades, were inspired by this essay. As you can see, the lines are long and prosaic, and in most hands, including Simcox's, they are heavily padded with superfluous words and phrases.

Charles Stuart Calverley, 1866, blank verse

> Then words of warning great Achilles spake.
> "Call me a coward and a thing of naught,
> If I yield all at every word of thine.

Talk thus to others—dictate not to me:
For I shall hearken to thy words no more.

Calverley was best known as a parodist and wit. This is a work of his youth.

Sir John F. W. Herschel, 1866, loose hexameters

Him interrupting, thus broke in the godlike Achilles:
"Base, indeed, should I be, and deserve the name of a
    coward
Were I to yield me a slave to whate'er thy caprices may
    dictate.
Issue thy orders to others! Command not me! For
    henceforward
Thee and thy cause I disown and spurn the control of a
    tyrant.

Herschel was a famous astronomer. This is a work of his old age.

John Stuart Blackie, 1866, loose rhymed hexameter couplets

To whom, with rapid word abrupt, Achilles made reply:
A dastard and a slave, a mean unvalued wight were I,
If I should quake at every breath thy high-blown whim
    may vent.
Seek other warriors to command: thou shall not cross my
    bent
So soon. I was not born to sink that thou mightst learn
    to float.

I couldn't find anything about this Scot, but he definitely could handle hexameters, even if his rhymes are forced.

William Cullen Bryant, 1870, blank verse

Hereat the great Achilles, breaking in,
Answered: "Yea, how might I deserve the name
Of coward and of wretch, should I submit
In all things to thy bidding. Such command
lay thou on others, not on me; nor think
I shall obey thee longer. . . .

The first major American translation I could find. Note how much more plain it is than its British contemporaries. Bryant was an important poet of the time.

Andrew Lang, Walter Leaf, and Ernest Myers, 1883, prose

> Then goodly Achilles brake in on him and answered: "Yea, for I should be called coward and man of nought, if I yield to thee in every matter, howso e'er thou bid. To others give thou thy orders, not to me. [Play master; for thee I deem that I shall no more obey].

A popular prose translation by three Cambridge dons. Lang had already co-translated the *Odyssey* and was an expert on Homer, a well-regarded poet and novelist, an anthropologist and an historian.

Arthur S. Way, 1886, loose hexameter couplets

> Brake forth Achilles the godlike, in mid-speech taking the
>   king:
> "Good sooth, and a byword were I for a dastard and
>   niddering
> If in all things to thee I should cringe, whatsoever thy
>   word may be!
> Unto others give such like commands, but not—for thou
>   shalt not—to me
> Give the word, an thou wilt: 'tis not I that will longer
>   brook thy behest.

This Australian translation shows how bad a combination of hexameters and rhyming can be.

Samuel Butler, 1898, prose

> Achilles interrupted him. "I should be a mean coward," he cried, "were I to give in to you in all things. Order other people about, not me, for I shall obey no longer.

Best known for his novels *The Way of All Flesh* and *Erewhon*, Butler translated both the *Odyssey* and the *Iliad* in his later years. He maintained that the *Odyssey* was written by a woman.

Edgar Alfred Tibbetts, 1907, hexameter couplets

> Then, interrupting quickly, divine Achilles cried:
> "Timid and worthless, truly, would I by men be named,
> If in all things I yielded to what your pride proclaimed;
> Enforce your will on others, you shall not rule o'er me,
> No more to you, I pledge you, shall my obedience be.

A workmanlike American attempt at making rhymed hexameters work.

Sir William Marris, 1934, blank verse

> Then answered great Achilles, breaking in:
> "Coward and abject I might well be called
> If on each point, what e'er thou sayest, I should
> Give way to thee. Go and dictate to others;
> Give me no orders, for I tell thee, I
> Will none of it! . . .

This was published in a mass edition by Oxford University Press. It's hard to imagine Achilles saying, "I will none of it!" But seeing this makes it clearer why even Marris stuck with old-fashioned language and syntax; modern English doesn't have much room for the heroic.

W. H. D. Rouse, 1938, prose

> Achilles interposed, and said:
> "Yes, for I should be called coward and outcast, if I yield to you in everything you choose to say. Lay your commands on others, don't order me about, for I do not think I shall obey you any more.

Here, for the first time, the *Iliad* is presented as a modern novel. The language is relatively formal (however, note "don't order me about"), but not archaic. This was a very popular translation.

William Benjamin Smith and Walter Miller, 1944, loose dactylic hexameters

> Brake in upon him with answer, at that word, goodly
>   Achilles:
> "Yea, for a coward in truth I were called, a contemptible
>   craven,
> Were I submissive in ev'ry affair unto thee as thou sayest.

> Give unto others indeed thine orders—not to Achilles.
> Play thou captain: methinks it is I no longer obey thee.

Yes, Americans were still trying to find heroism in hexameters and archaic language during the war years. The authors pushed this as the first translation to use authentic Homeric hexameters, using a dactylic rather than iambic foot. Too bad they were so bad at it.

E. V. Rieu, 1950, prose

> Here the noble Achilles broke in on the King: "A pretty nincompoop and craven I shall be called if I yield to you on every point, no matter what you say. Command the rest, not me. I have done with obedience to you.

This is, I believe, the best-selling *Iliad* of all time, having sold over two-and-a-half million copies, although it is not too different from Rouse's 1938 translation. It is still in print, in an edition revised by Rieu's son.

I. A. Richards, 1950, prose (abridged)

> Then Achilles cried out: "Yes, and may I be named a coward
> if I give way and do everything you tell me to do. You may
> give your orders to others. . . .

I was astonished to discover that this literary critic, poet, and founder of the theory of semantics had done an abridged prose translation of the *Iliad*. It was part of his interest in pushing Basic English, with a vocabulary of 850 words, meant for teaching English to foreign students and creating an international language. He also translated Plato's *Republic* into Basic English.

Richmond Lattimore, 1951, loose hexameters

> Then looking at him darkly brilliant Achilleus answered
>   him:
> "So must I be called of no account and a coward
> if I must carry out every order you may happen to give
>   me.
> Tell other men to do these things, give me no more
> commands, since I for my part have no intention to obey
>   you.

Probably the last hexameter translation for a long time. Lattimore, a classicist, handled the long lines skillfully, but his verse is still rather clumsy and prosaic, not superior to the better prose translations.

Robert Graves, 1959, prose

> Achilles interrupted. "That was exactly what they have done! If I stayed silent, everyone would call me a coward and accuse me of always yielding to your demands. Trample on whom you please, but not on Achilles, son of Peleus, for his engagement is at an end.

This well-known poet and novelist certainly brought more style and life to his prose than the other prose translators did. But it is hard not to smile when Achilles says of himself, in the third person, as if he were a singer giving notice to a theater owner, that his "engagement is at an end."

Robert Fitzgerald, 1974, blank verse

> Achilleus interrupted:
> > "What a poltroon,
> how lily-livered I should be called, if I
> knuckled under to all you do or say!
> Give your commands to someone else, not me!

This is not one of Fitzgerald's best passages. The only reason I can think of for him using the word "poltroon" is that he was doing homage to John Dryden, the last translator to use this word. The meaning of the word is perfectly appropriate, but it clashes with the more modern colloquialisms "lily-livered" and "knuckled under." In any event, this is the first truly modern verse *Iliad:* simple, colloquial, and (although it's hard to see here) beautifully rendered by a poet-translator rather than a classicist.

Martin Hammond, 1987, prose

> Godlike Achilleus made abrupt answer: 'Coward and nobody would be my name, if I defer to you in everything you care to say. Others can take these commands of yours, but do not give your orders to me, because I doubt I shall obey you now.

Hammond shows in this passage that classics dons today can write prose every bit as bad as the poetry they wrote in the nineteenth century.

Robert Fagles, 1990, free verse loosely based on hexameters

"Yes!"—blazing Achilles broke in quickly—
"What a worthless, burnt-out coward I'd be called
if I would submit to you and all your orders,
whatever you blurt out. Fling them at others,
don't give me commands!
Never again, *I* trust, will Achilles yield to *you*.

This is the current generation's *Iliad*, by a classics professor and experienced translator of classics, as well as a contemporary poet. It certainly follows Fitzgerald's example, but is more free and more contemporary in its language (note, for example, the generational jump from "lily-livered" to "burnt-out," and the childish attitude given to Achilles in the last line of this passage by the use of italics).

Michael Rack, 1994, blank verse

But illustrious Achilles cut him off:
"They'd call me a coward, good for nothing,
If I yielded to everything you say.
You can order them around, but not me—
I'll never obey your orders again.

This verse translation is so simple, it seems written in Basic English. It is like the flattest contemporary poetry.

Stanley Lombardo, 1997, free verse

And Achilles, breaking in on him:
"Ha.—Think of the names people would call me
If I bowed and scraped every time you opened your
        mouth.
Try that on somebody else, but not on me.

I've got to hand it to Lombardo: he's the only one to have realized the translator could drop Achilles' imagined name-calling and let the reader (along with Agamemnon) imagine what the names might be. Poetry doesn't get more prosaic, but Lombardo's goals are so clear and unpretentious—he's dressing Homer up à la World War II—the form is appropriate.

And last but not least here are a few unrelated lines from Christopher Logue, who has not translated the passage I selected. But first, the same lines from the prose translation of E. V. Rieu:

> Prince Achilles tried himself in the armour to see if it fitted and allowed his splendid limbs free movement. It felt as light as a pair of wings and lifted him up.

> Achilles stands; he stretches; turns on his heel;
> Punches the sunlight, bends, then—jumps! . . .
> And lets the world turn fractionally beneath his feet.

Well, what can we learn from all these translations? That there are many ways to hit a Homer, or at least many different historical periods to do it in. Viewed from a future in which none but the most recent seems like Homer to us, few of them seem to have actually bettered their predecessors. Many are different, some radically so, that is, the first prose translations, the first translations in particular verse forms, the first translations to use straightforward syntax. But most of these translations are marked by timidity, particularly with respect to making Homer sound heroic or epic in new ways. Formal verse forms and psuedo-Elizabethan language seemed to be enough for most translators. Some tried to be creative by using an odd form such as the Spenserian stanza or dactylic hexameters, but most chose their form because it was the current form of choice. This is even true of the most recent translations.

I don't mean to malign these translators. One of the things we learn from these translations is that translations reflect their period more than the period's great works—even when the translations themselves are great. They reflect their period in terms of common poetic forms, but they also reflect how their period views works of the past, the level of respect, the perception of how to express things like nobility and anger when they aren't those of a contemporary person (it's easy to draw a contemporary character being angry, and even in historical novels it is easier to use modern forms; there aren't the same sort of expectations and worries about getting it right). It is one thing to impose your interpretation on a work; it is another to both ignore the original verse form *and* choose a form that is not currently in use or recognized as appropriate for the particular type of work. Lattimore used a verse form—hexameters—not currently in favor, but he did it because the original was in hexameters. And his hexameters are certainly more modern than the Victorians'. Fitzgerald was a little more radical in using blank verse, but it's a free blank verse, and iambic pentameter remains the essential English verse form; even if most poets don't use it very often, it's often there beneath the surface. It will take a greater revolution than free verse to rip iambic pentameter out of the depths of English-language psyches.

When one considers that translations of classics are not only relatively conservative, as far as poetry goes, but that they are often the best selling books of poetry (Pope's *Iliad* allowed him to buy a house), it's easy to see why they have such a powerful and conservative, often reactionary, effect on poetry. A major Homer translation, for example, can give aid and comfort to those who are still doing what the translator is doing; it allows them to preserve forms simply by the fact that their work will, to Homer readers, sound more grand and satisfying, more right. And this effect will last until the next major translation comes along, and often much longer. Fagles' free verse translations came long after the general acceptance of free verse, but it will, simply by its existence and its wide readership among poets as well as readers of poetry, make free verse a bit stronger than it otherwise would have been.

For those who are truly taken with the idea of reading various translations of classical works, Penguin has an excellent new series of historical collections of translations, versions, and works inspired by the poetry of writers that includes, so far, Virgil, Horace, Homer, Martial, and the Psalmists. We are in the midst of one of many classics revivals. Ours, however, is different in one important sense: intellectuals generally turned to the classics to subvert the status quo, to find excuses for change. Today, it is merely another way in which to ground the identity of some portion of the populace, that is, of humanists repelled by the materialism, ideologies, and anti-intellectuality of their times.

It will be interesting to see the form the next major *Iliad* takes. However, it is very possible that the next *Iliad* will be less a matter of form than of person. Modern English-language *Iliad* translators have been exclusively aging white men (a rare exception historically is Alexander Pope, who started translating the *Iliad* in his 20s). It's high time for a woman or a person of color to try their hand at it, although it is also very possible that such a translator would approach the work not only with no strong feelings of fidelity, but with a feeling of antagonism, and that it would not come out as a work of translation at all, but would move toward something more like what the Caribbean writer Derek Walcott did with the *Odyssey* or what Christopher Logue has been doing with the *Iliad*. My guess is that the Fitzgerald and Fagles translations are still perceived as modern enough (and saleable enough) that a major trade publisher would take on the project only if something very different were proposed.

But whatever the next *Iliad* turns out to be, it is very likely that its translator or adapter will consider his or her approach better or, at least, more appropriate than what has been done over the last few hundred years. And that a hundred years later, it won't seem right at all.

It's Even Good for You

I HOPE THE LAST CHAPTER gave you some perspective on how translation changes over the centuries. We learn in school how literature changes, but where can one learn about the history of translation? Even more important, where can one learn that the history of translation *is* the history of literature, that in many ways it better reflects the history of literature because it consists of fewer individualistic works that are ahead of or simply outside the literary tradition? And where can one learn how the art of literary translation is done and practice it under the supervision of an experienced practitioner?

It will come as no surprise that there are not a lot of places to do this—although more than there used to be—and that most literary translators are largely self-taught or have learned informally at the feet of experienced translators or editors who have critiqued their work.

But it should be more of a surprise. Translation is a fascinating intellectual activity, a wonderful art, and a great writing exercise. All the other arts, both performing and creative, are taught at universities, conservatories, and other institutions of learning across the country. This is, however, a relatively recent development. In the past, most arts education was private, often through apprenticeship, or in specialized schools, and most writers, like translators today, were self-taught. But these days, teaching the arts is big business. Every community in America seems to have a multiplicity of schools, university programs, and organizations that teach everything from basket-weaving to film-making. There are many degree programs in every art, creative and performing, graduate and undergraduate. A large proportion of artists keep solvent by teaching their art. No more taking in students; artists have jobs, regular salaries, sometimes health benefits. But literary translation has remained on the outskirts of this arts explosion.

There are few acknowledged masters young would-be's flock to study with. There are no conservatories, few nationally or even locally recognized programs, not much in the way of schools or circles of translators, no regional or ethnic styles, few publications (and none that is recognized as the industry, or art, must-read), one national organization and pieces of two others, one-and-a-half regular conferences a year (plus a few scholarly symposia), and a few awards, although mostly for the translation of particular languages into English, funded by foreign governments out to spread their cultures (ours spreads like a weed with its own built-in fertilizer).

And role models are hard to find, because they're hard to see or hear. We can't go into a bookstore and ask for a translator's work or find it alphabetically listed under the translator's name, listen to a translator's work (there are only a tiny number of trans-lations on tape and, of this small number, only a small proportion are performed by the translator), or see the translator himself performing in public. His actual performance takes the form of a creative work, but it's someone else's creative work. His creativity takes the form of a performance, but it's not one we can see. Or at least we haven't learned how to look for it yet.

It's hard to be attracted to an art that's so confusing and hard to notice. "Its very elusiveness as a field of study and examination has always left it in the shadows," Gregory Rabassa has noted.* And in these shadows, the study of literary translation is unprofes-sional and rare, and there aren't many young people seeking out what is available. Why?

In academia, the professors who are literary translators are rarely professors of translation the way writers are professors of creative writing or architects have chairs at architecture schools. Yes, there are more positions and more money to be made in architecture than in translating, but there's not a lot more money to be made in poetry, and yet there are many positions for the teaching of poetry to students who will never make a penny at it.

But poetry is important. Professors teach and criticize poetry. There are famous poets. There are even, occasionally, wealthy ones. And more to the point, poetry is pure self-expression, the next best thing to being rich. And you don't even have to go to the trouble of learning prosody anymore. Why would anyone choose to study translation over poetry when they would have to learn a foreign language, fight over every word, depend on reference books, and not even say anything original or slough off a bit of angst? No, if there's not much to gain, better all the difficulty come from the pain of opening oneself up than from the pain of opening up our language and culture.

Okay, okay, I'm being censorious. And lack of demand is only one of the factors that makes translation something that's not widely taught. There's also the attitude of American academia to translation, which has done a great deal to keep demand for translation courses low. American academics have traditionally been opposed to teaching literature in translation, not to mention translation itself. In foreign literature programs, professors' first allegiance is to the foreign language, and they feel it is their responsibility to get students to appreciate their language's culture from within, that is, from learning the language and then reading the literature in its original state. And they see English as the enemy, something to be avoided, to be kept out of class, something read only by lazy students. Helen Lane, one of the few contemporary full-time translators (from Spanish), told an ALTA audience that in her language studies in school she was taught that "you look at the world through a language as if that language were a prison. It took me a long time to realize that for me, at least, my language was more of a window; we can look *through* it as well."

When language professors talk about translation, their tendency is to talk about what a translation lacks, about what the students are missing by reading a translation. Of course, students *are* missing something, but they would be missing a lot more if they couldn't read the book at all. When you're a person whose career is focused on a particular language and culture, it's hard to recognize that few people will ever learn your language well enough to be able to truly appreciate the greatest works written in it.

Translation *is* sometimes taught in language programs, more often, in fact, than anywhere else. However, when it is, it generally focuses more on the original language than on English; it's a way of better learning the foreign language, an enjoyable exercise, or a useful language-related skill. In the study of classical languages, translation has always been a principal way of learning the language. Because of this focus on the original language, translation is presented as something linguistic, word oriented. It's all about fidelity, getting the meaning of the words right, reproducing forms rather than interpreting or creating something beautiful or equivalent in English. It's not that this approach isn't useful, but it's not about translation, about art, about enriching English culture; it's an exercise to help understand the original better. It's about learning a foreign language. However, it did at least get all educated English-speakers to translate, and some of them found they enjoyed it, and kept on doing it. Now, with so few studying classical languages, there is no introduction at all to translation.

There are many other reasons for the paucity of classes and programs in literary translation. One is that the decline of language requirements means that there is not a large pool of students who could even consider such a course. Another is that professors do not generally translate themselves and therefore do not recognize the value of translation for the study of literature, for a young writer's development, or as a valuable intellectual and artistic discipline in its own right. Yet another reason is that the growth of multiculturalism has changed the former academic focus on language differences to a focus on differences of ethnicity, race, gender, class, and sexual orientation. This focus generally involves content-oriented issues, which are not of much concern in translation classes. Writers used to turn to foreign literature, that is, to literature in other languages, to make contact with the Other, to get out of themselves. Now they can do it without leaving English and even without reading translations. As Robert Pinsky told me,

"At this particular moment, the idea of the Other may be preoccupied with other Others."

In addition to finding new sorts of Others in our own literature and language, multicultural studies have turned many students in on themselves as much as creative writing classes do. One can now focus one's literary studies on the writing of people like oneself. And people like oneself generally speak the same language. Even when they're foreign, their likeness comes through very well in translation. One does not feel the urge to learn another language in order to get in touch with a Japanese woman, an Austrian Jew, or a gay Brazilian. Not the way Pound was drawn to the imagism of Chinese poetry, or the early German Romantics were drawn to the power of Shakespeare. Yes, they were all looking for themselves, but for themselves as artists, not as people.

Another reason for the paucity of translation courses is the problem of figuring out where they belong. Language departments, as I've already said, are most interested in their students learning a foreign language. Comparative literature departments are interested in playing critical games with texts, and tend not to see translation as another critical game (some have begun to recently, but what they do involves looking at translations in class rather than actually doing them). English departments focus on English-language literatures, which don't need to be translated (and few of their professors are translators). Creative writing programs are interested in creativity, in self-expression, and therefore rarely spawn other-expressive translation classes. Yet because multilingual translation courses use the workshop format employed by most creative writing courses, translation courses do tend to end up in creative writing departments anyway, even if their professors come from elsewhere. Or they end up being interdisciplinary, neither here nor there.

In short, there are many interests that militate against the teaching of translation in universities, and few interests that favor it, despite the value of studying translation. And what is that value? There is simply no better way to learn to write in English or to learn to interpret, that is, to criticize literature. Also, as classicists have understood for centuries, it's not a bad way to improve one's knowledge of a foreign language.

The process of studying translation is especially valuable for aspiring writers. Back in 1743, the German translator Johann Christoph Gotsched wrote, "Translation is precisely what the copying of a given model is to a beginner in the art of painting. . . . While they copy the design and the nuances and the full painting, they observe with great acumen every detail of the original artist's art and skill, the sum total of their example's beauty and perfection. They also make up a hundred little rules for themselves while they are working. They commit to memory a hundred technical tricks and advantages that are not immediately known to all and that they would have never discovered by themselves."* Ezra Pound told the nineteen-year-old poet-and—translator-to-be W. S. Merwin, "If you're going to be a poet, you should take it seriously and write every day. But you can't write every day; at your age, you think you have a subject, but you don't have anything to write about. What you do that will teach you more about writing than anything else is translation."* Translating gives young writers a way to write without expressing themselves, allowing them to focus on stylistic matters at the feet of literary masters. It's even better than copying, because it requires invention and interpretation as well, and the translation student can use old or contemporary forms, or can try both.

Translation courses also show young writers that the choices that make up their translations—as well as their writing—are an alternate form of self-expression. How one approaches the translation of a literary work says just as much about a person as how they have their characters act, just the way a musician approaches a composition says as much about him as a composition he writes. Even their choices of foreign authors express either translators' affinities or their desire to come into contact with writers whose visions and styles differ from theirs or from what they want theirs to be. Young writers can learn from translating that the voice they are seeking to establish has an aesthetic aspect that often gets confused with or lost behind the personal aspect. As Serge Gavronsky told me, "The difference between the same poem translated by two people is exactly their breadth line, their familiarity with language, their ability to decipher, decode, re-encode." It is not what we usually refer to when we speak of a writer's voice, and it does not reflect the writer's biography in the sense we usually think of this. But these aspects of voice are central to any writer's voice and are perhaps the most important part of his biography, more important than his relationships with his parents or his lovers.

And by coming into such intimate contact with others' works and by going through the process, a young writer's creative work can be affected by translation in much the way John Felstiner described it happening to Celan: "Sometimes you can see him as a poet, and at the same time or even years earlier, as a translator working with a similar word that sparked for him and jumped the gap between his own poetry and his own translations. This is where the two processes interact."* Richard Wilbur said much the same thing about his experiences: "the finding of words for some of Molière's or Racine's characters or emotions in English is going to make possible some transference to your own work. It's going to make it easier for you to make sounds of a similar kind in your own work." And can anyone believe that translating Kafka's "The Metamorphosis" as a young man had no effect on Jorge Luis Borges' writing?

Translation stretches a young writer's resources. As Christopher Middleton has said, "in all translating of poetry, you've got to extend your own linguistic resources beyond their normal limits so that you reach out with both hands and touch the original. . . . What you're really doing is exploring new possibilities."* Or as Frederic Will wrote, "Translation rubbed my nose in important matters out beyond me."* Will also wrote about what he calls "the paradox of selfhood" in terms of Ezra Pound's early translations: "Has he been a victim of the paradox of selfhood, that it is closest to us when we have reached farthest? Not simply; he has been finding his own analogues, and learning his own tone from hearing it on other people's lips."* Or as Richard Sieburth put it, translation is "a Hegelian motion of the spirit needing to alienate itself before it can return back to itself." It is a quest, like that of Telemachus, on which one grows and becomes more oneself, one's adult self. And it is also a quest by which one's native literature matures and finds itself. "This insinuation of self into otherness is the final secret of the translator's craft," George Steiner wrote.*

Yes, a young writer can find his tone by immersing himself in another English-language writer, but that writer's major antecedents are generally the same people the young writer has read or, if the other writer is long dead, his writing has already had its effects on the more modern authors the young writer has been reading. In other words, most English-language writers are part of our familiar tradition, and their style is one that feels comfortable or is, at least, an extension of what we know. Foreign-language writers are further from us, at least stylistically. They challenge us and stretch us in ways English-language writers cannot. And bringing these writers into English, trying to find equivalences, is the best way for a young writer to involve himself with these challenging aspects and to see how they can merge with his own writing. And there is nothing more exciting than finding in another language someone we identify with or whose work we want to assimilate, and then to actually write that writer's work, not just copy it, but actually write it. This is where writers have a great advantage over painters: they have the opportunity to both copy and create—to perform.

Reading itself is a participatory act: you go out to an author, share his vision, add it, in some ways, to yours. Translation is doubly participatory: the translator participates both as reader and as writer. The sharing and the adding are amplified.

But even without this coming into contact with Otherness, this stretching of oneself as a reader in order to find oneself as a writer, translation is simply a good exercise, a discipline for developing as a writer. As Robert Pinsky put it, echoing Ezra Pound, "the subject can't wobble around." And as Richard Sieburth told me, translation is "writing in its purest form, to the extent that it is virtually contentless . . . writing stripped to its barest and most essential gestures. Which is why, in the Renaissance, translation was seen as absolutely vital to the study of rhetoric and to the study of language learning, just to educate people to a sensitivity for purely linguistic structure."

Rhetoric. Such an old-fashioned word. The effectiveness of writing, the appropriateness of a form to express a poetic argument. Words and sounds being where they are for a reason. A movement and purpose to writing. One can write without really thinking about any of these matters, and one can criticize a work without considering its rhetoric. One can focus on imagery or symbols or whatever. One can look at a pattern that goes across a range of poems. Translation makes you focus on one poem at a time, and it forces you to think about things you would not otherwise consider. It puts you in the writer's seat. Why is one line in the poem longer than the rest? Did the author do this on purpose—must this extra length be preserved—or was it random, just something the poet happened to do? Does the last word of the poem have to remain the last word of the translation? How important is it? How is it led up to? In other words, what was the writer's poetic argument? What were his goals, what effects was he hoping to have on the reader, consciously or unconsciously? Every writer can learn from asking such questions, from becoming more conscious of his choices.

I have a very strong opinion on the matter of translation workshops. I should say up front that I'm not much of a believer in creative writing programs, especially at the undergraduate level. I think undergraduates should focus on reading. Without a solid reading background and a true appreciation of what one is reading, writing is little more than a form of therapy, of getting things off one's chest. It's great to practice, of course, but one doesn't need to take courses to practice. That's what late nights are for.

Having said this, I think that translation workshops are indispensable to anyone who wants to be a creative writer. They have all the benefits of a creative writing workshop with none of its negatives. They are not a form of therapy; they are not about getting things off one's chest, but rather about adding things to one's chest of treasures. They are not only about writing, but also, like the rest of one's literature courses, only better perhaps, about reading, reading very, very carefully. The translation student can't just throw something off late the night before it's due. He's got to choose something, read it again and again, make sense of it, and only then begin writing. Translation workshops are never gut courses.

In addition, it's much easier for a young writer to handle criticism about his translations than about what's coming from his feelings and ideas. Translating feels more impersonal—there's a natural distance from it because it's not only yours—and therefore teachers and fellow students don't have to hold back as much. Discussions can be livelier and yet cause less pain. And speaking of criticism, professors might be interested to know that someone as astute as Rainer Maria Rilke once wrote, "Translation is the purest procedure by which the poetic skill can be recognized."* In other words, translation is easier to grade than creative writing.

Since any opposition to undergraduate creative writing programs will not cause a scratch, not to mention a dent, in such well dug-in institutions, one thing that can actually be done is to push for more translation workshops, and to make them either mandatory or very highly recommended for all students majoring or minoring in creative writing. At Boston University, for example, the Translation Seminar counts for the creative writing program's language requirement and is therefore especially attractive to language-shy students who would never think of taking a translation workshop. Such encouragement, and even propaganda on the part of translation teachers and creative writing teachers who recognize the value of translation, is necessary to override creative writing students' fear of anything having to do with foreign languages.

We can't imagine a composer who hasn't played an instrument, who hasn't performed others' compositions. We can't imagine a playwright who hasn't acted or directed, who hasn't performed others' plays. Then why is it that so few aspiring writers are advised or taught how to perform others' works by translating them? Is it simply because writers don't consider translation a performing art?

Or is it that students no longer have the language background considered essential to do translation? My answer to this would be that, like most courses, translation workshops are not primarily intended to put out professionals. They don't require fluency. They are meant to teach essential skills, to show new approaches to literature, to expand students' resources. And the fact is that many professional translators weren't fluent in a language when they were in college; they either lived abroad later or were so entranced with translation that they set out to become fluent. Beware: the joys of translation can lead to changes in one's life that go beyond one's writing.

How is a translation workshop run? Let me describe the one I took with Edmund Keeley, a translator of modern Greek poetry and one of the first to teach translation workshops (at the University of Iowa in 1964, just before the National Translation Center was founded at the University of Texas in 1965). The course started out with some readings in the history and theory of translation, and in the first few classes Keeley introduced us to such things as the changeability of translations (historically), fidelity and freedom, and a lot of the other topics that appear in this book. The first assignments were exercises that divorced translation from language: translations of a bit of Homer, a bit of *Beowulf*, and a bit of *The Song of Songs*, based on multiple translations rather than on the original. This is an example of something language departments wouldn't consider, but which is very important to students first encountering translation: showing that it is about English and about literature, not about foreign languages.

Then, while still reading about translation (the readings ended about midway through the semester) students began to choose poems to translate from the languages they read. Professor Keeley imposed two requirements: one, that the work be a poem or prose poem only (this requirement is unusual, but I think it's wise, because translation problems are magnified and concentrated in poetry; in most prose, one can go whole paragraphs, even pages, without any serious issues to discuss); and two, that there be at least one published translation of the poem, and that it or they be xeroxed and presented with the student's translation. The purpose for this second requirement is to focus discussion on the differences in form and interpretation between the student's and the other translations. The student can thus explain his choices in the context of another translator's choices rather than the original, which most other students in the class would not understand. This allows for easy class discussion of translations from any language, and again it takes the emphasis away from the foreign language, even though it is sometimes referred to in a student's explanations. One might think a student would change his decisions after reading another, professional translation, and I'm sure this happens sometimes—I know it did with me on occasion. But in every instance, the student had major disagreements with the published translation. This was never a problem.

Although I've been emphasizing how translation workshops need to put the foreign language in a secondary position, a student must know a foreign language to participate, but only well enough to be able to read it with the help of a dictionary. He will make mistakes, misunderstand expressions, and miss references and allusions, but he will still learn how to translate and he can still do a creditable, if not professional job. Mistakes aren't so terrible, especially for beginners. In any event, the principal language problems in translation workshops involve English, that is, students' inability to write well and carefully.

Students' problems with writing English involve general thinking about and knowledge of style, which is central to the translation of poetry and literary prose. "I think," Rosanna Warren told me, "that our civilization as a whole tends not to respect language much. English or foreign. Because they do not respect English, they do not think very carefully. I see it in the quality of the prose that I read in the newspapers and in essays by professors. Thinking about style does not seem to be uppermost in their minds. It's about delivering some kind of information and arguments, a more utilitarian attitude toward language." Philip Lopate recently wrote, "It is as if poets were ashamed of their art's linguistic nature and were always wishing it could arrive at a nonverbal state. This prejudice against the verbal . . . is one of the factors that gives American poetry today an anti-intellectual cast."* This is the environment students have been growing up in, and it is an even more serious problem than the decline of language studies.

In 1996, I worked with a number of young translators who chose or were assigned selections from an anthology of fiction by younger Czech writers. All of them were fluent in Czech, had lived in the Czech Republic, and had studied the language and literature in universities here and abroad. Most of them were either graduate students or professors in Slavic Languages and Literature. Literature was their life. All but one of them was a native English speaker. Yet most of them had a limited grasp of writing literary prose. They had problems with English syntax and other grammatical matters, they had problems choosing a right word (not just one that best captured the original's meaning, but one that worked in the context of the English sentence they had chosen) and, most seriously, they did not have a good ear. This is, as I said at the beginning of this book, a matter of youth, of lack of experience. But I also think it is a matter of education, of the decline in the study of prosody and rhetoric and grammar, of the decline in the study of pre-twentieth-century literature and in the study of poetry relative to prose. And, as Warren said, of the increasingly utilitarian attitude of humanities professors toward literature, in other words, their focus on content over style. One can gain a lot more from literary experience when one is inclined, and educated, to appreciate all aspects of that experience. These young translators all seemed to be very well read, but I don't think they were looking for the kinds of things that help develop one's ear, one's judgment. And this was as true of those who were academically oriented as it was of those who were more literarily oriented, who were doing their own creative writing.

Ironically, one of the reasons young poets are not developing an ear for poetry is that a large proportion of the poets who are "in" are foreign poets, poets read in translation. Robert Pinsky, who teaches poetry workshops, told me: "It's particularly remarkable when you realize that young poets are so international and catholic in their tastes. I think the most influential poets for me were American and English poets; I think the most influential poets for people in their twenties now certainly include Rilke, Neruda, Lorca, Mandelstam, perhaps Akhmatova. . . . one thing one can say about being influenced by work in translation is that it will enrich the imagination, it will enrich the mind, it will enrich the cultural outlook, but it cannot enrich the experience of form; it cannot enrich the sound, the vocal, the physical or bodily aspect of your writing. You may learn about rhythm from translating Whitman into your own idiom, or translating Stevens into your own English, but you can't learn about the sounds of English from reading Cavafy in translation. . . . I know that I have more than once shocked some student by mentioning that Rilke and Cavafy were formal poets; they wrote in rhyme and meter. Astonishing! Because the translations aren't. So you read the Bly Rilke and you say, he was rather more like Yeats in form."

One of the great paradoxes of translation is that although the translator's work primarily involves form, in so much contemporary translation it is the content that is the focus and it is the content, therefore, which comes through best. And it is the content of such translations that usually attracts younger readers.

The most important part of the translation workshop is the discussion. It differs from discussions in writing workshops in two important ways: (i) the work is not strictly that of the student presenting; it's a collaboration with the original author, and therefore the student has some distance from it and is less likely to be defensive; and (ii) students can ignore the content of the work. Who cares if it's a love poem, a political diatribe, or nonsense verse. Who even cares how good it is, beyond a point? The questions are, why did the translator make the decisions he made, and what are the alternatives he had to choose from? Of course, this is part of what a writer has to talk about in a writing workshop, but here it is all there is. The discussion is focused on a few important issues with respect to each translation. The translator is the one who recognizes them, raises them, and explains his decisions. Then other students suggest alternatives. Rosanna Warren told me how eye-opening this process is: "One thing that surprises me is that young writers, graduate students in the Creative Writing program, who think seriously about writing and think of themselves as writers and spend a lot of their time reading and hoping and dreaming about being writers, are extraordinarily naive about the act of translation and what the act of translation tells us about style and stylistic choices. They think that there's one right translation. When you start taking one line apart and showing all the different ways it could come, and what would be brought out and expressed by a different set of pressures, they're quite shaken. And then it goes and makes them think about their own writing."

Sometimes it's just about finding the right word. William Weaver gave me the following example: "The other day in class, a Russian girl had translated this piece by Chekhov, and she said, 'The roast was producing a smell.' This was supposed to be attractive. And the whole class went, 'Aroma, scent, perfume, stink'—we got into every conceivable word that could mean smell and tried to hear the differences between them. And that's what the class does all the time, and actually they rather enjoy it. It makes them think about the words they use every day."

But the discussions go well past words into formal aspects, including the importance of the author's choices, as I discussed above. By the time a student has finished presenting his translation and responding to questions and comments, everyone comes to know the poem in great detail, especially its essence, that is, what absolutely has to be preserved in it. Thus, one learns a great deal not only from one's own translation exercises, but from presenting one's decisions, from questioning and commenting on others' decisions, and from going through everyone's thought processes, including the authors'. It's a very intense literary learning experience, the most intense I've ever had in a communal form.

Translating is not only good for a young writer's writing, it's also good for a young critic's criticizing. As I said above, translation is about both reading and writing all at once, and there is no closer reading than a translation. As John Felstiner has said, comparing criticism and translation, "It's the difference between talking the talk and walking the walk. The translator walks the walk." Literary criticism is essentially the close reading of a literary work, and among the many schools of criticism that have been spawned in this century, translation is one that is especially practical, because it develops skills that can be employed with any theory.

At an ALTA Conference, Dennis Kratz, a professor at the University of Texas, Dallas, read from an editorial on the crisis in literary criticism which ran in the *Chronicle of Higher Education:*

> The traditional critical style that we practice with such facility does not lend itself to the expression of authentic responses to texts. Lacking a language to express my complex response, I resorted to the familiar, disingenuous language of my profession, a language that banished all evidence of my emotional response and suggested a mastery and understanding of the text that I now know is false. I suggest that we need to develop a critical method that allows us to write sensitively, tentatively, and respectfully, that more faithfully represents our position as students of the text, not masters.

Kratz's response to these thoughtful words was, "Such an idiom perhaps already exists, such a model of thinking about texts and beyond texts about other minds, other peoples already exists, and that idiom . . . is translation." Or as the translator Michael Hamburger has written, translation is "a form of study, a way of getting into the very pulse and muscle of another poet's work without dissection or analysis."*

But, as Richard Sieburth told me, "In academia, one shitty article in *PMLA* is heavier on the scales than seven years devoted to a poet like Hölderlin." Why is translation only now starting to be accepted as an alternative form of criticism to the theories critics generally use? Well, it's not a theory, but an approach, and it's hardly original. No one can really take credit for translation; it's been done for thousands of years. It won't make anyone's career. In fact, it could be argued that translating undermines theory, because any process like translation, when presented as an alternative to theory, calls into question the whole concept of approaching literature via theories. Think about it: why approach something via a theory when you can approach it via an approach, when you can cut the distance between yourself and your ideas on the one hand and the literary work on the other, when you can create not a critical work, but a literary work, *the* literary work itself?

Another problem with teaching translation as criticism appears when it's time to criticize the results. The act might be extremely useful to a student, but the result is harder to talk about, and grade, than an essay. There isn't a good vocabulary or standards for critiquing it, especially its interpretive as opposed to artistic aspects.

I see translation as an alternative and underrated form of criticism much in the way I think parody is. John Felstiner wrote that in both of these, "criticial and creative activity converge," that both are forms of "engaged literary interpretation."* And he told me, "you might think of translation as a kind of parody . . . the source in both cases is a piece of writing, let's say a poem, but the result, whether a parody or a translation, is that one remove, which in the case of translation is not meant to be laughable, though it isn't always meant to be laughable in the case of parody. . . . Parody has long been seen as a quintessential kind of criticism . . . and translation is a quintessential form of criticism, even more pure in a way than parody, because parody must depart from the original, whereas translation tries not to." Like translation, parody also approaches a work more in terms of its form than its content. But good parody also comments on the author's vision and focuses on rather than copies or tries to hide its faults and quirks. Parody also leads to a work that stands on its own, that often tells a different story and always has a different point. But parody is even less appreciated than translation, both as an artform and as a form of criticism. But that's another book.

It's interesting how much the post-structuralist theorists talk about "translation." They have made it a metaphor for all reading, for the fact that every act that involves literature involves the interpretation and redoing of what's already there. So everything's translation, which means that translation is nothing special. Translation becomes even less than what it was, only a tiny subset of something with the same name. Even in Susan Bassnett and André Lefevere's introduction to Edwin Gentzler's *Contemporary Translation Theories*, they spoke of translation as a paradigm of literature: "the study of the manipulative processes of literature as exemplified by translation can help us towards a greater awareness of the world in which we live."* I think there are a lot of better ways to become aware of worldly manipulation, but not many better ways of becoming aware of literature. But when literature is nothing but a subset of translation, it's all the same, and the world, the content, becomes the central concern. Thus, the critical value of translation itself is of little meaning in the world of theory. Or is it threatening to the foundations of contemporary literary theory?

I agree with John Felstiner when he wrote, "translation presents not merely a paradigm but the utmost case of engaged literary interpretation."* Suzanne Jill Levine wrote, "What struck me almost immediately about [my] early translation experiences was how much richer the process was than the final product. Writing about translation made me even more keenly aware that the reader could gain a more intimate knowledge of the literary work . . . if only he or she knew how translation decisions were made, and how possible choices were finally set aside for what were considered better solutions."*

Ezra Pound also considered translation to be a form of teaching. He complimented Laurence Binyon's Dante translation for how much light it shed on Dante. He sought with his Cavalcanti translations to "'drive the reader's perception' far under the surface of the original. . . . Pound's point is that the translator has to lead the reader round the poem and all its ramifications, even those the poet was unaware of."*

A translation workshop is not the only way to use translations to more intimately approach literary works. Another way is to discuss translations in literature classes that use them. For example, a professor can discuss why he chose a particular translation over other available translations. Or a professor can hand out multiple translations of a central sentence or paragraph as part of a discussion about its meaning or effect. This could start students talking about why one translator's interpretation or the other is more accurate, interesting, or complete. Such a discussion would be more concrete than the consideration of what a variety of critics have said. It would also show students that translation is more than copying into another language.

Richard Sieburth told me, "Pedagogically, I think translation is one of the great tools for teaching. Teaching Rimbaud, I will say, here's Pound's version, here's Lowell's version, here are some other versions. This is a way of talking about Rimbaud, because you become attentive to the original text in a wholly different way than if they're not reading contrastively or diacritically."

Margaret Sayers Peden wrote:*

> Reading nine translations of sonnet 145 [by Sor Juana Inés de la Cruz], we have seen the poem de-structed, and observed the failures and successes of its reconstruction. Those failures and successes reveal to us the strengths and weaknesses of the original poem as well. . . . What we may not have seen, were it not for the magnifying lens the translations focus upon the poem, are lines where the poem itself is 'soft.' . . . Sor Juana's eye is fixed on *nada*. She is marking time in the five lines preceding the final line, letting rhyme and rhythm and repetition bear her toward the culmination of the poem. The seemingly sound architecture of the sestet is actually trompe l'oeil.

Douglas Hofstadter had a nice metaphor for using, in this case, two translations to better understand the original. He compared it to "the nautical notion of triangulation, in which having two different landmarks to sight on a coast allows you to pinpoint just where at sea you are."*

Rainer Schulte, a professor at the University of Texas, Dallas and the English-language leader in the use of multiple translations as a way of studying literature, wrote in the introduction to his and John Biguenet's excellent anthology *The Craft of Translation:* "the translation process affirms the 'how' and not the 'what' of reading and understanding. If one asks, 'what does something mean,' one expects a statementlike answer. If one asks the question, 'how does something come to mean,' avenues are opened that lead to the exploration of the complexities inherent in a text."

But translations are not explored very often in this way. When they teach a book, professors do not tend to look carefully at a variety of translations. "[M]ost academics are virtually indifferent to literary quality in the translations they assign for student use," Burton Raffel has written.* Exploring translations requires a lot of work of a type not normally considered central to critical inquiry. And if professors do do the work, what then? Choose the "best" translation, the most "faithful" translation, the one students will be most likely to read (prose or prosaic poetry), the one students will be most likely to identify with (usually the most recent, but not necessarily: they might want the distance an older translation gives to a classic work)? Lawrence Venuti is skeptical of the motives of even those who do look at available translations: "The professor who has read each of the fifteen translations will finally pick the translation that approximates not the foreign text but the professor's understanding of the foreign text. Although the rationale is that it's more faithful."

Second, professors often choose a translation for reasons that have nothing to do with translation itself. The principal criterion professors have mentioned to me is the price of the translation: they will generally choose a cheap, mass-market paperback over a more expensive trade paperback or hardcover edition. They feel they are doing their students a favor, and monetarily they are. But considering that each student is already paying more for each of his classes than the cost of the average hardback, it doesn't appear that expense is the first thing on a student's mind. Assuming they are not simply paying for a degree, education appears to be the first priority. One wonders why professors, whose every decision is oriented toward the teaching of literature, would orient themselves toward bargains only in the case of translations. It shows how little value they give to translation, and how little they are interested even in determining the relative value of translations they teach.

The other principal consideration is the material—essays, introductions —that accompanies and elucidates the text; unfortunately, teaching editions usually contain old and often poor translations, because all the money is spent getting rights to or commissioning the essays. Burton Raffel has written, "Hosts of students who have had to struggle through, say, Dorothy Sayers's execrable rendering of Dante, or Elinor Marx Aveling's ghastly butchering of Flaubert's *Madame Bovary*, or any prose translation of *Beowulf*, regularly find themselves bored, irritated, and worst of all on the basis of these mis-translations are unable either to understand or to feel any sympathy with the critical and other judgment proferred by their teachers."*

The poet-translator John Frederick Nims shows how difficult it can be to teach poor translations: "Such and such a poet, I might find myself saying [in the classroom], wrote sharply, colloquially; his lyrics were simple, sensuous, passionate, as in the poem on the page before us—but the class would already be looking at the page with deepening skepticism. Colloquial? simple? this unnatural word order, these expressions archaic centuries ago? And the limp rhythms? Or no rhythm at all?"*

So the ramifications of not taking translation seriously can be serious. Here I will hand the floor over to Lawrence Venuti and share what he told me about what he considers the scandal of repressing the discussion of translation in the classroom. "Comp. Lit. programs are reading translations, but translation is invisible. . . . the MLA series of books—there are over fifty of them now, they're called *Approaches to Teaching World Literature*—are case books based on a particular text. . . . These originate with a survey that attempts to get a cross-section of opinions about existing materials. But one of the crazy things about this, of course, is that in the section of the book that talks about pedagogical techniques, rarely is the issue of translation raised . . . the one on Dante is an essay by someone who teaches at the University of Toronto and uses Dorothy Sayers' translation. It finally comes down to the fact that it's in poetry, but how Dorothy Sayers inscribed an interpretation of the text, did the work of a translator, or the kind of English she wrote in and why that was important for a particular passage in Dante, or does it matter that she was translating between the wars in Oxford literary culture and reading Charles Williams' interpretation of Dante—none of this comes in. So the whole issue of translation is really repressed in the classroom. . . . The problem is that academics who are *doomed* to reading translations in the classroom don't know how to read translations as translations."

I asked Venuti, 'What do you do?' He responded, "Partly it means putting students in the place of the translator, and showing them what seems like *the* translation—or it doesn't even seem like a translation: you read Dorothy Sayers and you think this is Dante. You have to make them aware that Dorothy Sayers chose these words to render these Italian words, and that other possibilities are available. That's the first step. That's a basic one: you can do that without necessarily teaching foreign languages or relying on students' foreign languages; the teacher will have to do that work." The next step is to use translations to better understand and appreciate the original.

But there is a downside to literature professors being concerned about translation. Frederic Will wrote, "As a teacher I dealt so long, hardly realizing it, with pallidly textureless versions of originals, especially of original Greek and Latin Classics, that I came to overvalue the dramatic or attention-getting translation."* And Breon Mitchell told me, "The only problem with using translation in the classroom, particularly for a group that doesn't know the original language, is that once they begin to realize how much is in the original language that has to be in some sense either lost or choices have to be made, to a certain extent it can undermine their enjoyment of the translation, or reading anything in translation. They think, 'I was reading this and enjoying it in English; I now feel like every sentence is just one-tenth of what that sentence must be in the original.' As a language teacher, that's what I like to awaken in students: the sense of how much they miss in translation. But as a translator, I don't want them to feel they're missing so much that there's no point in reading translations."

I have found this to be a serious problem for people for whom translation is not invisible, but who do not really understand it. For example, in an Internet discussion about Latin American literature, the bilingual participants who mentioned the issue of translation agreed that English translations were terrible. But their criteria were very unsophisticated: the translations either didn't feel the same or they had found many "errors." Of course, English cannot feel the same as Spanish, and of course in any translation there will be either mistakes or different interpretations of what words mean in context. I found that several of the people in the discussion group generalized their feelings into the belief that everything is lost in translation, that translations are pale shadows of originals. There is no way around this except to deepen people's understanding of the art of literary translation. Teaching the art of translation and teaching about literary translation are, as I have tried to show, important to the education of readers and writers. Even, I feel, essential. But as with anything, quick references or discussions by those who do not themselves understand it are often worse than no reference at all.

I started this chapter talking about the lack of demand for translation courses. I would now like to look further not only at students' interest in translation, but also at the generations of younger poets who graduated in the 70s, 80s, and 90s and who do much less translation than earlier generations. In a period when translation workshops do exist at several major universities, when translation is the darling of literary theorists (at least in name), when poetry in translation is as popular with younger poets as it has been in centuries (and they are more likely to have studied their literature in translation), when the status of translators is being discussed and actually acted upon (translators are more likely to be mentioned, or at least named, in reviews than at any time this century, and their names are more likely to appear on jackets, covers, and title pages), why is it that younger writers are not showing more interest?

The decline in translation by younger poets is an especially painful thing for Eliot Weinberger. He told me, "If you look at American poetry up to 1970, it is very difficult to think of a poet who did not translate. I once made a list. Most of the major poets in the century, and most of the minor poets too, did at least one book-length translation of somebody, and practically everybody else—there are only one or two exceptions—translated at least some poems. And also up to 1970 you had many novelists who translated poetry, too. John Dos Passos was a wonderful translator, Hemingway translated poetry, even Fitzgerald translated Rimbaud. Now it is completely unimaginable. Updike has done a couple of translations, but he's also a poet of sorts. After 1970—the explosion of the creative writing school—poets are no longer translating. So you have this terrible situation—if you just look at Latin-American poetry: in the 1960s you had poets from all across the spectrum of American poetry, from all the possible poetry camps, translating Latin-American poetry. You had people like Mark Strand and Philip Levine at one end, to people like Nathaniel Tarn, Clayton Eschelman, Paul Blackburn, Denise Levertov, all translating Latin-American poetry. Since that time, there's no one, other than Eschelman, who's continued to work on César Vallejo; there are no translations by poets of Latin-American poetry . . . after the generation of Paz—Paz, Nicanor Parra, Ernesto Cardenal is a little bit younger. You had Ferlinghetti translating Cardenal, Ginsberg translating Parra, Robert Bly, James Wright, it's incredible the number of American poets translating Latin Americans. After this, there are practically no translations of anyone younger [by poets rather than Spanish professors]. And so the field, if you want to call it a field, is down to very few people. There's hardly anybody left. Alastair Reid still does it, I still do it; it's quite shocking actually."

Why has this happened? First I will re-enumerate some of the reasons I mentioned in terms of the paucity of translation workshops. Younger writers—and I'm talking about writers under fifty—are less likely than their elders to know a foreign language. Younger writers are less likely than their elders to be interested in form, to be caught up in the idea of capturing a writer's style in English. Writing is more utilitarian for them, a means to an end; they are more likely to be interested in being confessional, in being realistic or lyrical, or in dealing with issues of ethnicity, race, gender, class, or sexual orientation. They are writing about the world, and if they want to deal with foreign aspects of it, they can simply travel and write about foreign countries themselves. When writing stems to a great extent from a love of language, writers are naturally attracted to learning languages and translation seems like a natural part of one's literary work. But when expression is central, there seems no reason to learn other languages, and translation is not a consideration, except occasionally in collaboration with a linguist.

In this context, one major thing has changed about translation: it used to be considered radical, a way of injecting foreign notions into the domestic debate, an avant garde act. This is still a principal interest of such translation theorists as Lawrence Venuti: shaking up our literary culture. Some historical examples of translation shaking up literary cultures include Johann Heinrich Voss's translations of Homer making the hexameter the dominant meter in German Romantic poetry, Octavien de St. Gelais' translations of Ovid bringing into French poetry the alternation of masculine and feminine rhymes, and Jesuit translators' moralizing versions of foreign picaresque novels leading to the popularity of the bildungsroman in Germany.* These may not sound as exciting as current ways of shaking up our culture, such as writing about gay love or showing how awful life is for the underclass or for alienated youth, but to those who care about form, they are major, radical events. On the other hand, the literature with which today's culture-shaking works are being expressed is generally not very radical. And that is because most young writers are not seeking to shake up literature; they are seeking to shake up people, to be heard, to reach an audience. When you seek to shake up literature, you seek to shake up readers. When you seek to shake up people, you end up appealing to those who are similar or sympathetic to what you're doing. Few readers of gay love poetry will reject graphic depictions of sex, but many readers of translations of heavily stylized German poetry will reject it.

In short, the younger generation of successful writers is relatively conservative. Many have jobs in academia, careers to preserve, audiences to captivate. Seeding English with unusual foreign writing simply doesn't fit in. It doesn't help them get or keep a job at a university, it doesn't help their reputation (unless the original writer is already famous, which explains the involvement of some younger writers in such special projects as the collaborative Dante and *After Ovid*, neither of which required knowledge of the original's language), and it doesn't add to their audience. As Weinberger told me, "It's a very xenophobic moment, and I think it's tied to the birth of the creative writing school, because then poets all went to the academy, they became much more involved with departmental politics, with careers, the explosion of poetry readings, that sort of thing."

Pound was the model for earlier generations of American poets. As Richard Sieburth told me, "To be a poet was to go learn Provençal, and Italian for Dante, and Chinese, and French for Rimbaud, and you learned the classics at school and that was what you built on, that was the model. It's like the shift in Comp. Lit. that's taken place from a discipline defined by people who work with different national literatures or languages to an interdisciplinarity. To do literature *and* anthropology, literature *and* film, literature *and* philosophy. More and more all in English. That's the shift from a linguistically-based notion of difference to a discipline-based notion." Sieburth doesn't feel this is necessarily a terrible thing, but it is a major shift, and this shift is clearly having an effect on the amount of translation being done both by younger writers and professors, and by their students.

But what bothers me most about the younger generations of writers (and since I'm only forty-three myself, I'm including my own generation) is what Weinberger refers to as the lessening of the sense of community service among poets. When poets of earlier generations did readings, they read their own work, but also the work of other poets, often in translation. They shared what they loved. Today, it is rare to hear established poets reading other poets' works, in translation or not, outside of a special forum where everyone is assigned or asked to choose another writer to read from. And there really isn't much demand for this. The community obligations younger poets are asked to fulfill involve teaching aspiring poets, doing readings, backing causes.

Finally, the work of younger writers tends to be even more self-absorbed than that of earlier generations. The lyrical and confessional have been with us for a couple hundred years, but never before have there been so many other ways of looking into ourselves, so many genres that center around coming to terms with how what we are and where we've been has determined who we are. Rosanna Warren told me with respect to the work of younger writers (and she's the same age as me), "It's incredibly self-absorbed work; so much of contemporary American writing, fiction and poetry, is . . . not exactly autistic; it runs around in little circles of personal anecdote and doesn't seem to be able to envision larger structures. Of course, this isn't true across the board; there is a lot of interesting and wonderful writing going on, and I think partly why it's wonderful and interesting is that it has challenged itself with otherness, thematically and structurally. As you can see from my voice, I get rather impatient with literature as self-expression that I think we've been *condemned* to now. . . . I think that anything that makes us aware that we are only alive through continual inhalation of other works is good. A civilization dies from sealing off its windows and air-vents."

I think this need to connect with other cultures is responsible for the growth of English-language novels that take place abroad or deal with historical situations, curious characters, found diaries, great events. It's a way of bringing in the foreign while still creating, while still presenting the work as one's own rather than as simply a translation. It might require a great deal of research, but it involves recreating the world, not a work of literature. I think both writers and readers find this preferable, and that this takes some of the pressure off the need to translate.

So here I am writing a book about literary translation at a time when fewer writers are writing them, fewer publishers are publishing them, and fewer readers are reading them. This is not the end of the world. It is a great thing that English-language literature is attracting so many new voices with so many new, important concerns. It is, depending on your viewpoint, a fortunate or imperialistic thing that most Americans don't need to know a foreign language. It is a questionable thing that creative writing has joined the other arts as something to learn in school, and that this has given so many writers the opportunity to make a living teaching what they do. For me, however, the most painful thing is the growing narcissism of our writers and readers. Literature is not about writing *what* you know, but *how* you know. Literature is not about the most powerful woman of color in the country recommending books almost exclusively by and about women and people of color. Literature is not about "about"; that's what commercial fiction is for. When literature *is* about "about," there isn't much of a place for translations of anything but well-known authors, mysteries and other genre books, political writing, memoirs and eyewitness reports, and other books that appeal to particular, well-defined audiences.

No Translator Is an Island

SO FAR IN THIS BOOK, the literary translator has been pretty much alone with the original work, reference books, and a computer screen. He doesn't have an audience out there, a group or troupe or orchestra, not even anyone dressing him, putting on his makeup, or helping him set up his equipment.

But the translator is usually not completely alone up on his non-stage. In many cases, translation is collaborative, either between a writer and a linguist, two translators, or a writer and the author. If the original author is alive, he can be a resource, a pain in the ass, a friend, sometimes a lover, on occasion even oneself. And then there is the publishing house, or at least an editor (the host of other people—in promotion, sales, design, production, and finance—couldn't care less about translators). Because translation is the loneliest performing art, the translator is usually happy to be able to work with interested authors and editors, but there are times when the translator would be better off even more alone than he is.

Collaboration

Collaboration between a writer and a linguist, usually between a poet who doesn't know the original language and someone, usually an academic, who does, is one of the most controversial sorts of literary translation. But in many ways, it's a microcosm of the whole, because the argument against it is essentially, "It doesn't work." And yet it does. Just like translation.

Like everything, collaboration has a continuum all its own. At one end is the linguistically ignorant writer working with a trot, or literal, word-for-word translation of a poem by someone (usually referred to as an "informant," as if there's some sort of crime going on) who is not present or not knowledgeable enough to help any further. A step down the continuum, the ignorant writer works with an informant who is not very literarily knowledgeable, but helps with language matters. Then come some mixed situations: the partially knowledgeable writer and the partially literary inform- ant, the monoglot writer and the literary informant. As we move down the continuum we encounter more knowledgeable inform- ants, who provide all sorts of literary and background information, and increasingly bilingual writers as well. At the far end of the continuum is the collaboration between two equals, both of whom know the foreign language but write in English. Collaboration is more controversial the more ignorant the participants are of each other's field.

At the mutually ignorant end of the continuum, the working relationship is, as Burton Raffel described it, "as symbiotic as the fungus and alga which, jointly, constitute the compound plant we know as lichen."* In working on a volume of Vietnamese poetry in translation, Raffel "felt acutely uncomfortable—perhaps 'tres- passer' would be a more accurate word than 'transient traveler' —and was continually worried that what [he] was doing was neither appropriate nor legitimate."* Despite his concerns, he concluded that "the inherent inequality of this sort of translation is also an essential ingredient for its success."*

How does this sort of collaboration work? It was probably best described by the Chinese translator Lin Shu, as translated and then commented on by Arthur Waley: "'I once went into retreat, shut- ting myself up in one room for weeks on end. All day the people of the house passed to and fro outside, and although I could not see them I was soon able to distinguish their footsteps and know infallibly who was passing my door. I have a number of friends who from time to time bring me Western books. I cannot read any Western language, but these friends translate them aloud to me and I have come to be able to distinguish between the different styles of writing as surely as I recognized the footsteps of the people in my house.'"

"[A]s he more or less confesses in his analogy," Waley wrote, "[Lin Shu] is rather in the position of a blind man at a picture gallery, whose friends are able to tell him everything about the pictures except what they actually look like."*

Lin Shu depended almost exclusively on intuition. D. S. Carne-Ross, who hired poets who knew no Greek to translate from the *Iliad* for a BBC radio project, wrote, "If a man is a poet, and the right kind of poet for the job in hand, he can *guess* what the original is like from a crib."* Ezra Pound was credited with great instincts, even departing from the trots he was given in ways that corrected mistakes in them. In fact, it is Pound's foray into this sort of collaboration that made it respectable.

It's the joy of intuiting literature one cannot actually grasp that attracts poets to translate from languages they don't know. Working from what are essentially clues about something one can't see is both an exciting idea and produces exciting results, at least in the right hands.

What exactly does an informant do? Some of them just provide literal trots, but most go further. For example, Clarence Brown, a professor of Russian literature at Princeton, collaborated with W. S. Merwin on translating the Russian poetry of Osip Mandelstam. Brown wrote, "I developed a habit of preparing worksheets on each poem. These included, along with notes on every aspect of the poem that struck me, notations of variant readings, semantic nuances of the diction, peculiarities of the prosody, and so on, a plain English translation often with numerous alternative translations. . . . In the intervening couple of years we have, with a pleasure that I trust was mutual, debated the early results, sometimes syllable by syllable, often by painstaking corespondence and more often still by personal meetings in Princeton and London."*

Richard Wilbur collaborated a bit differently with Max Hayward in translating the poetry of another Russian poet, Andrei Voznesensky: "I spent, oh, a couple of days sitting and drinking scotch with Max Hayward while we talked over three poems only of Voznesensky's. He read over the poems to me in Russian, and he gave me, with admirable restraint, strictly prosaic translations of them, not pushing me toward one or another word choice, and I asked him questions about the appropriateness of the meters to the subject, and I asked questions about the individual Russian words—what their flavors were, whether they were high or low—that sort of thing. I took notes all the time about what he told me. By the time I was through, I really had done about as much thinking (though not in the same order) as I would do in producing a poem of my own."*

This sort of collaboration is a way for excellent poets to turn foreign poetry into excellent English poetry. But it just doesn't seem right. If translation is about understanding, interpreting, recreating an experience, how can someone who doesn't understand and who cannot recreate an experience he's never had, how can someone like that translate? Is intuition based on even extensive indirect input really enough?

One of the main reasons skilled poets are asked to translate poetry from languages they don't know is that most people feel it takes a poet to translate poetry, that only a first-rate poet can write a first-rate poem. But it's not that simple. Octavio Paz has written, "In theory, only poets should translate poetry; in practice, poets are rarely good translators. They almost invariably use the foreign poem as a point of departure toward their own. A good translator moves in the opposite direction: his intended destination is a poem analogous although not identical to the original poem. He moves away from the poem only to follow it more closely. . . . The reason many poets are unable to translate poetry is not purely psychological, although egoism has a part in it, but functional: poetic translation . . . is a procedure analogous to poetic creation, but it unfolds in the opposite direction."*

In other words, collaborating poets often produce great results, but they are rarely translations in the same sense as those done by translators. A verb form of this sort of work was taken from the name of the most successful of these contemporary collaborators, W. S. Merwin: to merwinize, that is, to take foreign poetry and write it over in one's own voice. In his history of translation Louis G. Kelly practically dismisses the far end of the collaboration continuum: "From the end of the nineteenth century it has become common to translate poetry in rare languages from English cribs. . . . the essential act here is not one of translation, but one of literary creation from an unpolished original. . . . it is more in the nature of a thorough-going revision, whether it belongs in this book is a moot point."*

One of the most interesting criticisms of the ignorant end of the collaboration continuum comes from poet-translator John Frederick Nims: "When the language is unknown, no amount of discussion will help very much. Recently it was my good fortune to have as my dinner companion a Japanese lady; we talked . . . for perhaps an hour about Basho's famous haiku . . . She told me it 'meant': An old pond—/frog jumped in:/water's sound.' Then she tried to show me why this is the most celebrated of all haiku. I understood every word she said, yet had almost no idea what she was getting at. 'But you'd have to live in Japan!' she laughed, finally. . . . Obviously I am not ready to translate this poem, and probably never will be. . . . certainly handsome poems have been produced in this second-hand fashion. As handsome children have been produced by artificial insemination—but surely something human has been lost in the process?"*

Understanding, affinity, immersion in the specific linguistic characteristics of the original—these are all missing from the ignorant end of the collaborative continuum. Yet Auden felt that collaboration was the best way to translate, because when you can't read the original, it can't get in the way.* But this is a poet's attitude, not a translator's.

In an essay, Michael Gormon asked whether a poet who does not know the original language can capture poetry as described by Edwin Arlington Robinson: "Poetry is a language that tells us, through a more or less emotional reaction, something that cannot be said." Gormon commented, "Can any translator, not a native speaker, capture that elusive gleam?"*

The collaborative poet can hear the original's echo, but he

can't hear the original sound that produced it, even if he can listen to someone reading it. A sound sounds different to people with different levels of experience and understanding. A jazz solo is meaningless to someone who doesn't know jazz. It can't be judged, and it can't really be heard. But this doesn't mean the echo isn't beautiful itself; in fact, in the right hands the odds are high that it will be as sharp and beautiful as the original sound. It just won't be the same sort of equivalent. I've found that sometimes the best reading is in a foreign language I can't quite grasp. It's like the beauty of a river valley seen from a ridge through a deep morning fog; sometimes what at first appears to be a lush assemblage of fresh images turns out to be just a rotting pile of old chestnuts. Sometimes it's best to admire from a distance, not to go near enough to see clearly.

Collaboration is yet another wonderful way to approach literature. There's a magic to the re-creation of something whose creation a poet can imagine, perhaps even experience at some level, but whose full reality the poet cannot ever know.

The most customary form of collaboration, especially in prose translation, is between husband and wife, both of whom know both languages but at different skill levels. The norm is a foreign wife and an Anglo husband, but many couples, such as the Muirs, best known for their Kafka translations, were both native English speakers. The most prominent couple today is Richard Pevear and Larissa Volokhonsky, who live outside of Paris while translating classic Russian literature, especially Dostoevsky's novels, into English. Volokhonsky left Russia in 1972; she majored in English there. Pevear was a poet who had done a variety of translation projects, including a play by Sophocles, poetry by Yves Bonnefoy, and Italian fiction. When the two began translating together, he knew very little Russian. Pevear described the way the couple works together: "My wife does a completely literal version in pencil and she comments all over it. What I get from her is wild, but that's what's good about it. And then I start typing. And I look at all the other translations to guide myself, because if I worked just from her sheets, I wouldn't have any idea what was going on. And then, after I type it, I read through it and ask all kinds of questions. And then my wife goes through it, answering my questions and also comparing with the original and asking her own questions. And then we go through it together and decide what to do with all these marks. And I write in our decisions and then produce a theoretically final draft, which I type up and then we go through that. We do a rereading of that, aloud while my wife follows in the Russian. . . . We're lucky that we're happily married; it could be disaster. The fact that we're married gives us a very strong intuition of each other's mind, so we work very economically, very quickly. . . . She's very strict with me. She won't let me get away with anything. If I can't think of how to do something and I say to myself, Well, that's good enough, she always finds it and says, This isn't good enough."

But not all couples work on fiction, and sometimes it's the husband who's foreign. I only had to travel down the road I live off of to find such an odd couple, Barbara and Benjamin Harshav. He's Israeli (although born in Europe), she's American, and together they translate poetry from Hebrew and Yiddish. "When we met," Benjamin told me, "I was starting to work on translations of American Yiddish poetry, and I needed a native speaker and a native ear. And that is how we collaborated. And then we got trapped into marriage, too. It's a very intimate and close collaboration.

"I don't know how to say which words did who. We sit at a computer together. Bobbi types and I look at the original. I think the results are very good because I know very intimately the original language and all the connotations, and Bobbi has a very rich English, which you can see in her translations of fiction [which she does alone]. So she formulates the English text. . . . By doing it together, we exhaust both sides of the possibilities. And then we individually reread it and edit or ask questions. It goes through several stages. But the first, most intensive translation is intimately done together."

"Sometimes," Barbara added, "it's almost uncanny that we'll both come up with the same exact word at the same moment, and sometimes it's not a very common word. Or turn of phrase. It's just a matter of closeness. It's been like this from the beginning."

Ah, intimacy again. Translation seems to be all about intimacy. To have two intuitions working their magic on a single work at the same time, that sort of triangle of intimacy might be even more exciting than the collaboration between a lyricist and composer, where the third side of the triangle is missing.

At the far end of the collaboration continuum is the situation where there are two equally skilled translators working together. This is a relatively unusual situation, especially outside of couples. But it was very successful for Edmund Keeley and Philip Sherrard, translators of modern Greek poetry. The first thing they did together was an anthology of work by six poets; here they simply split up the poets, so it was more an editorial than a translation collaboration. But the second time they worked together, they built on this foundation to translate the poetry of George Seferis, whom both of them knew personally and poetically. They divided up the poems arbitrarily, except for those they had already translated separately, either for the anthology or otherwise. They did first drafts separately, mailed them to each other, commented on them, did second drafts based on the comments, and then got together. Keeley wrote, "[I]n the summers, we . . . would sit down at a table with Parnassus in the distance across the gulf to read the draft translations aloud to each other and work on them intensely until they sounded right. We did not much discuss what 'right' meant, except to agree that any idioms too specifically British or American should be avoided, along with all archaisms, inversions, personal idiosyncrasies, and rhetorical flourishes that might make Seferis sound less frugal, less demotic and contemporary than he sounded in Greek. . . . At this stage of the collaboration there were disagreements, compromises, a sometimes haunting sense of

inadequacy that would push us to debate the sound of a phrase
or line even after heading out to sea in a casual matching sidestroke
during the heat of the afternoon or during the evening's bout with
densely resinated wine at the local taverna. But by the end of the
summer sessions it was no longer easy to know who had done the
first draft of what poem, and by the time the book went to press
. . . impossible—to my ear at least."*

Another type of collaboration between equals involves different specialists, none of whom is a poet. This is typical in scriptures
translation and other areas where expertise is considered more
important than literary ability. But Stanislaw Baranczak has seen it
with contemporary poetry as well. He told me, "The Japanese have
a very elaborate way of translating [Seamus] Heaney's poetry. They
think there are so many cultural differences between their experience and Heaney's—Catholicism, Irish history, etc.—they do it as
a sort of foursome. Four different Japanese translators collaborate
on the project: one of them specializes in Catholicism, another in
the history of Ireland, another in animals, etc."

Collective translations, that is, translations created by a
number of people working together, have led to such books as the
Septuagint (the first Greek translation of the Old Testament), the
King James Version, the Chinese translations of the Hindu scriptures, and the work of the translation factories of King Alonzo of
Spain. In fact, nearly all scripture translations are collective either
in the sense of people working together or in the sense of building
on earlier translations. That is certainly true of English-language
translations, which build on William Tyndale's translation of the
New Testament and parts of the Old Testament (much of the King
James Version was taken out of Tyndale), which itself was based
on Erasmus's edition of the Septuagint, Erasmus's Latin translation,
Luther's German translation, and the Vulgate, St. Jerome's fourth-
century Latin translation, which was actually a collective work
itself. The Septuagint was said to have been translated by seventy-
two men working separately for seventy-two days, all creating
exactly the same translation. Divine fidelity.

No one is against the idea of collaboration between or among equals. If the collaboration works, it should make the results better rather than more questionable. But most translators don't collaborate even in this way. First of all, it means less money, because the already measly sum has to be divided; this explains why so many teams are married couples: all the money stays in the household. Second, translators see themelves more as writers than as performers. Performers naturally collaborate; even one-man shows involve others. Translators tend to be more like writers and other creative artists, who prefer no one around when they create. Perhaps translators would be more inclined to collaborate if they began to see themselves as performers. The essence of performance is collaboration, working together, playing off each other, responding to each other, fighting your way to the best result (or often spoiling the pot). I think that one of the reasons translation is not as well as recognized as it should be is that the translator is too isolated to perform at a peak level. He usually has no director or conductor, no co-star or accompaniment, and his editor is usually of little help. It's the rare performer who can be great alone.

Working With Authors

When it comes to working with authors, the biggest difference for a translator is between working with a living author and working with a dead author. On the one hand, a living author can answer questions. Richard Howard told me, "When [authors] die, it's very difficult. When Roland Barthes died, it was really terrible, because I was quite accustomed to calling him up and saying, 'Where did this quote from Hobbes come from? What is it?' And he would tell me. It was very helpful." On the other hand, there is usually a lot more serious criticism available about dead authors, so one can often gather a lot more ideas to help interpret a dead author's work than one can get from a living author and his reviewers. On yet another hand, living authors can be useless, difficult, demanding, or unreasonable. Richard Howard continued: "I like having a living author. Although sometimes it's painful . . . Authors can be very captious."

Most authors are no more than cooperative. They believe in Milan Kundera's words much more than he himself does: "The writer who determines to supervise the translations of his books finds himself chasing after hordes of words like a shepherd after a flock of wild sheep—a sorry figure to himself, a laughable one to others."* They have better things to do with their time than look over their translators' shoulders, especially popular writers whose works are translated into many languages. Robert Pinsky told me, "I've looked at [the Italian translations of my poetry] and I thought they were pretty good, but I haven't wanted to study them or make suggestions. . . . I don't want to become, even by one percent, the author of a poem in Italian."

For most writers lucky enough to be translated widely, it means extra royalties, more readers, and not much more than that. Most translators, too, do not really want to spend their time bugging authors; they figure things out the best they can and leave it at that. Especially outside of the U.S., in those parts of the world where translation is not done by professors and others with time on their hands, the name of the low-paying game is, get it done and move on to the next book. But American translators, who are more likely to have the time, the fastidiousness, and an income, are more likely to be in touch with their authors. And there are overseas grants that bring author and translator together. One of my translators was given a grant by the city of Munich to meet there with her author. Can anyone imagine the city of Atlanta arranging such a thing? The only place I know that does this in the U.S. is the University of New Orleans, which invites French poets over to work with their translators.

The author's ignorance of the translator's language is a major factor limiting his involvement. Unfortunately for American translators, the language they translate into is the most popular second language in the world, and so most foreign authors speak it, to some extent, and therefore are at least capable of looking at manuscripts of English translations of their works. Our translators are, therefore, much less protected than translators into less well-known languages, which includes all of them. But despite mixed feelings and experiences, nearly all of the translators I spoke with prefer to work with living authors and do turn to them with questions.

The word translators use most often to describe working with authors is "fun." For example, Breon Mitchell told me, "I like to work with them, get to know them. You know what that's like: it's fun. And when you have a problem and you say, 'Look at this sentence, this little phrase, it doesn't work, you can't fit it in there, it louses everything up': the living author can leave it out, change the sentence. It happens again and again, because for the author the text is a living text; they don't mind changing it, it's theirs. . . . If I could talk to Franz Kafka and I could say to him, 'I'm having problems working Frau Grubach in,' and if he could just say, 'Don't worry about it, Breon, put her name in later, it doesn't matter that much, I can take it out of the German, it makes no real difference to me,' then I would feel comforted." Mitchell talks with Kafka in his mind, but that is a far cry from talking to the author in person and getting his consent. Or even his opposition.

Suzanne Jill Levine appears to have had more fun working with her authors than any other translator. The authors she wrote about in her book *The Subversive Scribe* are Latin Americans Guillermo Cabrera Infante, Manuel Puig, and Severo Sarduy. They differ from the usual author in that they have not been concerned about the translator profaning their sacred text, because they saw themselves as profane, as parodic, as taking their own freedoms.

Some authors have institutionalized their relationships with translators, have found a way to originate and formulate the fun. Umberto Eco, for example, writes up instructions to his translators. Those for *Foucault's Pendulum* were thirty-one pages, plus copies of quoted texts, an engraving of a character's apartment, and other illuminating or curious extras. His English-language translator, William Weaver, wrote, "I was slightly miffed to find that some of my brilliant (I thought) solutions had been anticipated by the wily author. But, of course, Um. offers countless really useful ideas, so I keep the instructions at my right hand, adding to the clutter, and obstructing the 'mouse.' . . . Eco's instructions are fun to read, but not always useful. Does he really expect anyone to realize that Soapes is an anagram of Pessoa? I suspect that in drawing up the instructions, he was often just enjoying himself."*

Günter Grass goes one step further: each time he has a book ready to be translated, he brings together all of his translators and he spends several days talking about the book and answering translators' questions. Such an international meeting can be held without any interpreters, of course, because everyone speaks German. It creates the closest thing one can get to a community in the lonely business of literary translation. However, such an affair is possible only with popular writers, whose many publishers are willing to purchase rights and select translators in advance, in order to get the book out as quickly as possible. It is more typical that this situation occurs with a very popular American work, by Stephen King or Danielle Steel, than with one of the high-falutin' writers whose works appear in English. But somehow, I can't see a popular American writer calling his translators together.

Eliot Weinberger has had an exceptionally positive experience with his principal, and much older, author, Octavio Paz. Weinberger has been translating Paz since the age of seventeen. "I've essentially grown up with Paz. It's very unusual between translator and translated, in that we've never had a fight. It's especially unusual when the foreign author knows English very well . . . I've always sent him drafts of the translation, he writes comments, and we go back and forth, we debate things, but in the end he always gives me the last word, because he knows that I know English better than he does.

"At the last reading we did, at the Metropolitan Museum, Paz was saying—we were talking about my translations—and he was quoting Valéry, who said when he read the Spanish translations of his own poems, 'I just love myself in Spanish.' And Octavio said, 'You know when I read my poems in English, I just love myself in English.'"

The author-translator relationship isn't always just a one-way affair, with the author commenting on the translator's work. The translator is, after all, a careful reader and critic of the works he translates. Weinberger told me that sometimes, "when I was translating poems that hadn't been published in Spanish in book form, he would see the translations and decide that there was something wrong with his poem, and he would change something in the original. . . . I find in my own writing, if there's something that's particularly weak in the writing, some point or stylistic matter, it becomes magnified by the translation. . . . Sometimes the translator cleans it up, but you notice it and you realize you have to do something about the original." James Joyce is said to have done this with his Italian translator.*

Translation is a form of friendship, because it is essentially the translator's sharing what he loves with others. This sharing can form the basis for a true friendship between translator and author. Although Gregory Rabassa is often identified with Gabriel García Márquez, whose early novels he translated, Rabassa was closest to the Argentinian novelist Julio Cortázar, who was eight years his senior: "He was the one I think I was closest to, of all the writers. As a person. He would come see us every time he was in New York. We'd stay up all night listening to jazz records. He was a beautiful person. Children could smell him as a kindred soul. My daughter—she was a little girl then, without saying anything—knew there was some kind of electricity in the man. And you could see in the stories, what he was was a seven-year-old child. He had the mind of a child, but he also had seventy years of adult experience to feed that mind. He was a great person."

Or there's William Weaver's relationship with Giorgio Bassani, best known as the author of The Garden of the Finzi-Continis: "I translated all of Bassani's fiction . . . Bassani's someone I've known since I first arrived in Italy. I met him when I was about twenty-three or twenty-four; long before I became his translator we were friends, his family, too. Through him I got to know Ferrara. But I started translating his books before I'd ever been to Ferrara. I used to translate with a touring-club map of Ferrara open on my desk.

Then I spent a memorable few days there with him and with my editor, Helen Wolff, and his French publisher and Giorgio Mondadori. He laid on everything: we had a trip to the mouth of the Po, where we ate eel on a houseboat, and then we went to the Abbey of Pomposa, and we went to a friend's house in the old part of Ferrara, where there were medieval frescoes that had been discovered on the living room wall. There they were. We went all through the ghetto and through the cemetery, and had dinner at his family's house, with his mother, which was the house in the movie *The Garden of the Finzi-Continis*, the house where the boy who's called Giorgio is having dinner with his family. That was the room; we sat at the table. It's been a long relationship; I saw him just the other day."

A long-term friendship such as this is a wonderful bonus in a long-term translator-author collaboration, but the relationship can be even more intimate. British translator, poet, and publisher Anthony Rudolf became involved with two women whose work he translated. In one case, the translation came first; in the other, it came after the relationship had begun. But he told me, "when you translate a poet that you know, you are in a very intimate relationship, and I won't say the erotics—it's not a sexual thing—although if you're heterosexual and you're translating the work of a female person . . . it may not be that you're having an erotic relationship, but you might be, and it's actually much more interesting if you're not. If you're translating a poet that you're having a real-life love affair with, that's almost banal. But the erotics of translating someone you're not having a love affair with is kind of between the lines . . . much more interesting because more fantastic, more fantasy, than the other kind."

But there is another sort of affair one can have with an author. Rudolf's first love, translation-speaking, was the French poet Yves Bonnefoy: "I don't think I'm mythologizing too much, but with the great turning points in one's life one does mythologize. That's what they're about. I was at Cambridge in the early sixties, and I found myself, partly by accident, partly by design, associating with student poets or at least students studying English. I was studying modern languages. I was not myself writing, and I was jealous of these friends; one part of me wanted to be a poet or whatever. . . . I went into a bookshop in Cambridge and picked off the shelf a book by a poet called Yves Bonnefoy, and I was transfixed and transported and trans-whatever-other-words, trans*lated*—I've never said that in earlier versions of the myth—into somebody else. I knew at that moment that I would have a life in writing, in some form or other. All the kind of vague things became more focused. I bought the book . . . and when I got back to my room I thought, I'm supposed to know French, I want to be a poet, obviously I'm going to translate these; that's the obvious thing to do. And I translated some of the poems. I thought of myself as being a translator . . . Forever it was that book on that occasion which triggered it. I sent them to Bonnefoy and he replied with a very favorable letter. . . . That kick-started me, and I began also trying to write. . . .

"When I first translated another poet than Bonnefoy, it was kind of like adultery, like I was married to him almost; it was this commitment, it was this fidelity . . . and it occurred to me that he might even mind, which was ludicrous, it was a projection. It can happen, but in his case certainly not: other people were translating him."

Relations with authors do not always involve smooth sailing, however. According to Harry Zohn, Ralph Manheim, the German-into-English translator of such writers as Günter Grass, once said, "To translate is to invite trouble." As someone who collected reviews of his translations as evidence of how poorly translations are reviewed, Manheim was most likely looking for trouble. But many translators haven't had to look far to find it when it comes to authors.

Harry Zohn, himself a translator from German, had problems with Brigitte B. Fischer, whose autobiography he translated. She had lived in the U.S. for a decade, and so insisted on seeing a draft of Zohn's translation, on which she made some useful, some harmless, and many absurd recommended changes. "After more than a year of this sort of thing," Zohn wrote, "I grew tired of giving her English lessons in return for demeaning cavils and subtle insults. . . . My patience finally gave out and I asked her to stop inflicting her 'Emigranto' on me. . . . Since I have come to feel that a translator's primary loyalty is not to the author but to his/her book, I spent many hours making sure that Brigitte Fischer's book . . . did not suffer because of what may charitably be described as authorial failings."*

The quality of any translator's relationships with authors varies greatly. Arthur Goldhammer told me, "As in any other human relationship, it's a matter of chemistry. Sometimes it clicks and you can develop a friendship . . . and that's wonderful, you have real collaboration. In other cases, you hit upon an author who considers himself a master and the translator a kind of valet, and that's very unpleasant for the translator. Sometimes there can be a real clash of styles and personalities, and there's no way to resolve it except to insist, and then the author may say, 'Well, I insist on *my* way,' and the question has to be resolved by a third party, usually the American publisher, who will either say, 'I have complete confidence in this translator' or 'The author's word goes.'"

Working out disagreements with the author is always a difficult thing, because it is the playing out in real life of the translator's internal conflict between the feeling of fidelity and the desire for creative interpretation. When respect is not mutual, that is, when either the translator does not respect the author's writing or the author's knowledge of English, or when the author does not respect the particular translator's writing or translators in general, there can be problems. And the greater the difference between what they think they know and what they actually know, the greater such problems can be.

Relationships between translators and living authors are not, however, the sort of submissive-dominant relationships they might very well be. So much of the concept of fidelity is tied up with revering and respecting the original, but the author, no matter how great, is not a work of art, but a person. He might be a person with a big ego, he might be demanding, rude, controlling, but he is nearly always someone who can be negotiated with, cajoled, enlightened, even put in his place. And he is often someone who really doesn't care, who doesn't have the time to worry about translations, who sees the matter less in terms of personal fidelity than in terms of doing a creditable job in a timely manner. He might not respect translators as fellow artists, but at least he sees them as useful craftspeople. And he leaves them alone.

Self-Translation

There is no more intimate or problematic relationship between translator and author than what occurs in self-translation. Few writers are capable of doing it well—which doesn't always stop overinflated egos who don't trust anyone else with their master-pieces, at least in the languages they know—but there are some famous and even some very successful instances. To English-language readers, the best known and regarded self-translator is Samuel Beckett, an Irishman who lived in Paris and wrote most of his work originally in French. He is that extremely rare writer who actually translated into his first language, because he had chosen to write in his adopted tongue. Why? "French is a good, clean language," he said. And as David Ball, a translator and professor of French Literature at Smith, told me, "He didn't want the conno-tations and multiple meanings that English has. He wanted to pare things down."

The self-translator feels that he can't trust anyone else to get it right, that he is better off doing translation all by himself. And in addition, the self-translator must feel that translating into this other language of his is equally or more important, because he must sacrifice the time and energy that might have gone into writ-ing more works. Or, of course, he might simply enjoy the play of rewriting, recasting, reading and interpreting what he has written.

After all, many writers keep writing the same book again and again anyway.

What's wonderful about self-translation is that it allows the translator to take any liberties he feels like taking. Beckett certainly did this. Michael Hamburger has said: "[Authors] take liberties that another translator ought not to take and that only the author has the right to do when translating. . . . they are rewriting them according to the laws and needs of the other language, which are different."* In other words, there are no ethical issues in this sort of self-translation, except perhaps in terms of the reader: the reader should be alerted that he is reading a translation, and that the author has made many changes to the original in bringing his work into English. And if the author has made substantial changes to the original, if the author has done a *version* rather than a *translation*, the author should allow his work to be translated by someone else. But would anyone prefer an authentic *translation* to an authentic author's own *version*? We might often like the way someone other than the songwriter performs his song, but we feel differently about authors as opposed to translators.

Self-translation takes translation back to the Renaissance, when most translations were free versions, when fidelity to content was not of much concern. It is translation at its most free. But that does not mean it is also translation at its best. The self-translator has some advantages and some disadvantages. One advantage is that he knows what he meant, or at least what he thinks he meant, by everything in the original. He also knows about, or has researched, what he wrote, so that he need do no further research for the translation, at least if he is truly bilingual. Otherwise, he might to have to look up some terminology or ask for advice. The self-translator is free to choose any dialect, even any location for the work to take place, so that dialect is generally not so difficult for him to deal with. In fact, he doesn't *have* to get into many quandaries at all, because the solution he chooses is right, even if it's not the best or the most creative.

Here is where the self-translator is at a disadvantage: the difficulties of translation, like the difficulties of original creation, are what makes the good translator create something special. Freedom isn't always the best muse for artistic inspiration. The self-translator can be lazy. His big problem-solving, creative energies have already been expended. He knows what he wanted to say, he's said it, and now it's a matter of copying it out, of doing what many people think translators do. Or if copying doesn't work in a particular context, redoing it, coming up with something else. The self-translator doesn't have to interpret, and is often too close to the original to do so.

Thus for truly first-rate self-translation, it takes an exceptionally anal or highly responsible (to his audience as well as to his fame) writer who's truly bilingual and doesn't feel any frustration that he's not working on another original. A first-rate translator is already all of these, and generally doesn't feel any frustration at all.

One example of a self-translator who uses his freedom constructively is Stanislaw Baranczak. But then he is primarily a translator. Here's an example he gave me of how he uses his freedom: "In Polish I used 'Simon and Garfunkel,' for one reason: it rhymed with a Polish word. A translator other than myself would feel obliged to retain Garfunkel in English too. This is what the author says in the text. In English I had a different rhyme: I used 'Peter, Paul and Mary,' because Mary rhymed."

Hugh Kenner has written about one of Samuel Beckett's self-translations, "From beginning to end, *How It Is* ["Translated from the French by the author"] is *Comment C'est* less translated into English than re-experienced in English drop by drop, with the unique authority of a great stylist equally master of both tongues and making each tongue do what it has never done before. Perhaps so much thought has never gone, twice over, into the disposition of such common words."* Beckett had all the tools, every word meant a great deal to him, and English was actually *more* important to him than French, because it was his mother tongue and because it provided a larger, more important audience, too. Beckett chose French for the resources the language provided him, not for the readers it gave him. He had everything going for him, including the fact that he did a good deal of regular translation as well.

Another Nobel Prize-winning self-translator, Joseph Brodsky, has not received such high marks for his English-language versions of his Russian poetry, although Jonathan Galassi told me, "They don't sound like what an American or English person would write; there's a feel that this is something that has been wrenched out of one language into another, and I think he wants that sense of uncomfortableness." But then Brodsky was translating into his second language.

Although it is rare to make very large changes in a self-translation, a good deal of rewriting generally goes with the territory, much as it does when the author goes over someone else's translation. As Vassilis Alexakis, who translates his own work between Greek and French, has said, "When you see your text through the prism of another language, you can see its weaknesses and correct them."* Kundera worked on the French version of *Immortality* after sending the first, Czech version off to the printer. Working on the French version led him to keep reworking the Czech version. Then the English translation was made from the edited Czech version after the French version was in production, and Kundera made changes to the English version as well.

Working with Editors

Both translators and editors work on authors' manuscripts with the goal of publication; they are both intermediaries between the author and his public. So relations between translators and editors should be unusually smooth. Jonathan Galassi, an editor of literary translations at Farrar, Straus & Giroux, told me, "I often feel that when you're working with a translator, you're collaborating together in getting the author out." But then, he's a translator, too.

One thing about the translator's situation that greatly differs from that of the editor is that the translator does not only work

on the author's manuscript, he creates one of his own. The translator is the monkey in the middle, with loyalties divided not only
between languages and cultures, but also between author and
publisher. And there are many factors that can be involved in this,
and can affect which way the translator leans.

First, a little background about editors. There are essentially
two types of editor at American book publishers: acquisition editors
and copy, or line, editors. Copy editors are the ones who go over
manuscripts with fine-tooth combs. They do what most people
imagine editors to be doing when they're not out at fancy restau-
rants with famous authors. But actually, these days most copy
editors don't even work at publishing houses; they do their work
freelance at home, have no expense accounts, and rarely meet
unknown authors, not to mention famous ones. Most translators
find copy editors helpful, and when they know the foreign
language, copy editors can be very helpful. But some can be pains
in the butt.

Acquisition editors deal with people more than with words.
They are the ones who "acquire" books, that is, haggle with literary
agents over the amount to pay the authors they want to publish
or already have in their stable. They have expense accounts and
do occasionally get to go out with famous authors. Most of them
lack the time or skills to deal much with manuscripts, but the best
editors of translations have the skills and make the time.

A. Leslie Willson, a translator and editor of translations, once
described the ideal editor of translations to a congress of American
translators (I have edited this editor by reorganizing his paragraphs
so that they lead to an ending he placed early in his talk): "[The
editor has] a responsible role, for he owes his allegiance to a triad
of deserving entities: to the eventual reader of his product, to the
integrity of the translator, and to the reputation of the author. . . .
He must surmount the barriers and sidestep the pitfalls erected and
laid by a host of persons otherwise involved: his own publisher, a
foreign publisher, assorted literary agents perhaps, and a printer
bent on destroying the enlightening or entertaining experience he
plans to bring to readers. The editor of literary translations is

perhaps above all a mediator—preferably a dedicated and resourceful one—but he must also *ideally* be an interpreter of texts, a
superb linguist in as many languages as he must review. He must
be incredibly well read, and, not least, he must be sensible. . . .

"The editor must meticulously compare the translation with
the original work. Every editor should have, must have, cannot act
effectively without, one foremost rule: Never accept a translation
unskeptically. . . . He must have a sense of style as well as that
increasing rarity, common sense. He must realize that a sentence
syntactically confused and awkward is amazingly often not a reflection of the author's style but a grievous misreading or misunderstanding by the translator. . . . When an editor meets a translation,
he must be ready to make use of the three-letter-word: *Why?* He
must wonder *why* a translator has chosen one rendition of a word
or a phrase over another; he must ask himself *why* a translator has
chosen to change a tense or omit a passage or truncate a sentence.
Is what results still a true rendering of the spirit and meaning of
the original text? . . .

"An editor trains and retrains translators, happily informing
and improving himself, if he is fortunate. An editor must be yielding in his symbiotic relationship with a translator, but he must also
be firm when he is convinced that his vision and his understanding
exceed that of the translator temporarily in his care. . . . An editor
is in a way a translator himself, or the translator raised to the
second power. He must deal with the translator in a diplomatic
way, reasoning with him, perhaps laughing with him at risible
blunders, cajoling him, and congratulating him. . . . He is initiator,
receptor, director, accomplice, beseecher, evaluator, disciplinarian,
exhorter, researcher, interpreter, and perhaps first and foremost he
is a reader himself. . . .

"Does such a paragon exist? Probably not."*

I share Willson's ideal image of the editor of literary translations. It is what I strive for. It's almost frightening to see how
much stress, like me, he puts on common sense, or what I call
"good judgment": judgment in dealing with people, judgment in
dealing with words, judgment in interpreting literature. Diplomacy,

taste, understanding—they're all variations on good judgment, what lies behind all the decisions a translator has to make. And they're every bit as important to the editor as they are to the translator.

My judgment and intuition have grown a great deal since I started editing translations. Although I am far from fluent in Czech, when I read English translations of Czech I have a sense of what the Czech is and where the translator might have slipped a bit making the leap into English. Sometimes it's as simple as a translator having flipped an accent mark in his mind, so that the word seems to mean something completely different, and the translator has made sense of it anyway, because he's on automatic, instantly making sense of whatever he thinks he's reading. Sometimes the translator has taken a word or phrase to have one of its possible meanings, and I feel the author meant it to have another of the meanings. I also have a much better sense of when the author's voice hasn't been captured, when the author's sort of logic or rhetoric is departed from in a translation. I can see a sentence or phrase and realize that it is, in the Czech, a repetition, or near repetition, of something that is not similarly repeated in the English, not with the same words. This sort of intuition is, ideally, what every translator has, but the translator often gets too close to the work, or falls in love with his words, or simply works on it over a much longer period of time, and therefore cannot as easily see inconsistencies and things that don't ring quite true.

In addition to editing manuscripts, editors interact with translators in a number of ways, and nearly always from a position of power. The editor is generally the only representative of the publishing house with whom the translator deals. The editor chooses which translations are to be published, which translators get to work on them (and which ones don't), and how much and how translators are to be paid. The editor does not always have all the power himself—often he is stuck following his company's policies on pay and credit, for example; and sometimes he has to go along with the author in disputes or even in the choice of translator. But compared to the translator, the editor is in the seat of power.

This power can be used in ways that make translators wish the editor were less involved. William Weaver has said that "some editors regard manuscripts—and not just translations, I'm afraid—as raw material which is shaped into an exquisite vase by the editor."* Terrible things have happened to fiction in translation, even at major literary houses. In literature translated from Czech alone, there are several instances. There is the infamous switching around of chapters by the first British publishers of Milan Kundera's first novel, *The Joke* (Kundera blames this act on the translator, but such decisions are generally made by editors; it is the rare translator who even suggests such a thing). An entire section of a hundred pages was cut from William Harkins' translation of Eduard Bass's *Umberto's Circus* by Farrar, Straus. And even more seriously, both the British and American editions of Karel Čapek's *R.U.R. (Rossum's Universal Robots)* were not translations of the play as written by Čapek, but were rather British and American adaptations, with characters combined, major speeches cut, etc. It's normal for each director of a play to make cuts and adapt a play to its actors and audience, but it is not normal to publish and republish such adaptations, unless, of course, it's just a translation of a work by a foreigner.

In general, however, most translators and editors work hard and together to protect the integrity of a work. But sometimes it's those editors who care most about a work's integrity who cause the most trouble for translators, because they have a clear idea of what they want in a translation, and that idea does not always coincide with the translator's idea. A significant recent example of this involved the new translation of Kafka's *The Trial.* The acquiring editor was Fred Jordan at Pantheon, an imprint of Random House. Jordan's first language is German, so he was in a position to know the Kafka original and to admire it even more than those who only know it only in the Muirs' translation. Jordan first hired another translator for the job and then rejected the completed translation. Then, Breon Mitchell told ALTA, "[Jordan] asked me if I would translate a sample of ten pages, and I said sure. I translated those ten pages and sent them into him. I translated them quickly, but the way I would translate Kafka. . . . He said, 'This is not quite what I want. What I want is a translation that is very literal, very close to the original. In fact, I'd like you to translate Kafka as if you were translating the Bible.' Every word would be sacred, every word would be translated with an English equivalent, and there would be no English word for which there was not a German. I understood what he meant; I have that sort of reverence for Kafka, like a sacred text. I would love to be able to do that, but I said, 'I don't think that can be done effectively. I don't think that will sound right.' He said, 'Well, give it a try.' I did it, and I sent in the most literal translation imaginable, thinking this will show him what it looks like. I get a fax back, and indeed he said, 'This is too literal.' He said, 'Could you give me a version, could you do me the same ten pages halfway in between?' I said to him, 'Why don't *you* translate it? After all, you know exactly what you want . . . make it your project.' He said, 'I don't have any time, and I'm convinced you can do it.' So I did something halfway in between, and he liked it. The only problem was, I didn't, but he liked it and we signed a contract . . . I submitted the manuscript to them two years ago. He looked at it and said it was just what he wanted. He liked it and felt it would be a strong translation that would make an impact. And I said, 'I would like, if I could, to go over it one more time, maybe loosen it up a little bit here and there,' my theory being that once I showed him I was willing to do the whole thing, then I could do it the way I wanted to and he wouldn't notice. So he said, 'Go ahead, do your revisions.' And over the next three weeks, over Christmas, I did about sixty pages the way I wanted to do it. And I sent those sixty pages to him in January, and I got a letter back from him saying that he was no longer editor."

I could go on with dozens of stories like this, and much worse. I'm sure my translators have felt this way, too, because I get very involved with the translations I publish, I read the languages, and I have my own ideas about how the translations should be done.

As with authors, there are advantages and disadvantages to working with a hands-on editor.

One of an acquisition editor's most important jobs regarding the publication of a translation is choosing the translator. I asked Peter Glassgold, an old-style editor with the small literary house New Directions who for ten years chaired American PEN's Translation Committee, how he goes about it, especially when he doesn't know the original language. "From a publisher's point of view, you want a competent translation. You want an experienced translator who knows what a finished manuscript is, who goes about his work in a professional manner. If they have name recognition as writers and/or translators, all for the better, although that's not the primary point."

Jonathan Galassi told me, "The first requirement of a great translator is that they be a really good writer of English. And then they need to know the culture and language and author and all that. But if they can't write, they can know all that stuff and it'll be lousy. Lots of translators are that: very learned, very sensitive, very meticulous—they just can't write."

Most editors will ask for samples from potential translators, especially if they're not familiar with their work. Drenka Willen, an editor at Harcourt, Brace, told me she asks for "a few pages, between five and ten. We usually ask two or three people when we need a new translator. And then compare them and choose what we think is best. We receive letters from people who want to translate, and we get recommendations. And even when someone is recommended highly, we still ask for a sample translation." Editors with mutual respect also compare notes about translators.

What does she look for in samples? "Obviously for accuracy, but also for a certain style and readability. It has to read well in English—very important—but not lose character, and that's not always easy." Can it be *too* smooth? I ask. "Yes, sometimes that happens, but not very often. More often it's too literal, awkward. One can go right back to the original language by reading the

English version; then we know that it's wrong. It simply won't work. Sometimes we get a good sample translation, but the end result is not so good. We work on it. Sometimes we return it to be redone; we can see that it's a first draft. . . . More often than not, what one gets the second time around is not really that much better; then we simply have to work on it ourselves."

Editors are in the hot seat when it comes to paying translators. Like everyone else, translators would like to be paid better. Generally, they are paid a piecemeal rate, so many dollars per thousand words. There is no official "going rate," but the norm for an experienced translator doing work for a commercial publisher is somewhere around $75 per 1,000 words, or about $8,000 for a 300-page novel, which, depending on the level of difficulty and the amount of research and consultation with the author and with editors, represents about six months' labor. But translators are paid anything from $300 to $30,000 for a book; fees lean toward the low rather than the high end of this scale.

Since there's no hope of a regular salary or union wages for their performances, translators generally want a piece of the action, in other words, royalties, a percentage of the cover price of every book of theirs that is sold, instead of the one-time payment, or "fee" they usually get. It would still be the great exception for royalties, which for translators are only one to two percent of the list price of a book, to amount to more than what they are being paid now. But at least, like authors, the translator could dream. One of their books might make it, and they might get one or two percent of the millions that followed the film or the Nobel Prize or inclusion in one or another canon. Harry Zohn calls it "bestseller insurance." Richard and Clara Winston had it, he has written, and it kicked in at around 35,000 copies, but "only a handful of the more than 150 books they translated from the German achieved that status"*

The best situation for a translator is when the original is a classic work in the public domain. In such an instance, since there is no author to pay advances and royalties to, publishers are more likely to offer the translator royalties, and larger ones, as much as ten percent.

Gregory Rabassa, who primarily translates living authors, told me, "I like to put [a royalty] in the contract, but I've come to the conclusion that it's prestige, because an advance will never melt away. I look at my royalty notices: I'm a hundred-and-fifty dollars closer to getting royalties, but still four or five thousand to go. Unless it's a bestseller. García Márquez was before the royalties."

But with royalties, publishers can win out if the translator, because he wants to be treated more like a writer, accepts royalties in exchange for less money up front. Harry Zohn had this sort of experience: "I foolishly agreed to work for royalties only. The publisher said, 'Oh, we can sell 10,000 copies easily.' Well, they sold less than 3,000. So I got a fraction of what I was supposed to get . . . I would never agree to only royalties, because then you're dependent on the publisher's good graces, whether they want to promote it or not."

An advance against royalties that is less than the usual piece-meal rate is a risk any publisher should be happy to take, because when they do well with a book, they're happy to share the wealth. The big concern is losing money on translations, not making money and giving some of it away. But being paid as a piece worker, by the word, feels terrible to many translators, even though, after all, actors and musicians are paid by the performance. In other words, translators hate being paid piecemeal because they identify with authors rather than with other performing artists. But translators don't really want to be treated like authors and paid little more to translate a five-hundred-page book than one that's two hundred pages. The best thing would be for the translator to get an advance the size of the regular piecework fee, plus a royalty just in case the book turns out to be successful.

Yet, despite the fact that royalties are a harmless thing to offer a translator, most publishers don't offer them, and most translators don't ask for them. William Weaver told me, "I remember the first time I decided I wanted a royalty; I thought Blanche Knopf

[Alfred's wife] was going to have a heart attack. This was long ago. Actually Helen Wolff [at Harcourt, Brace], who wasn't exactly Miss Cornucopia when it came to handing out money, did give a royalty and didn't fuss too much, because usually it was a totally token idea." But the royalties finally did pay off when *The Name of the Rose* became a bestseller; they paid for Weaver's co-op apartment.

One of the best things that can come from a translator's relationship with an author is that if the author becomes well known and says he will only work with one particular translator, that translator is given a great deal of leverage and can get a good deal for himself. Sometimes authors will even determine the percentage of royalties that will go to the translator. But this doesn't happen often.

Publishers hate to talk about translators' fees, partly because they vary so widely, they don't want translators to know how much they're paying the translators of the few popular foreign authors; partly because the figures are embarrassingly low.

Susan Harris, the managing editor at Northwestern University Press, spoke about the subject at an ALTA panel: "One wonders: if a trade house finds itself unable to publish translations, for cost reasons, effectively, then how can an academic press do so. And interestingly, the very stringent restriction within which university presses have been forced to work in the last decade, to publish their conventional list, are what has enabled us to move into fiction: we've been able to modify our contractual arrangement, not necessarily to the advantage of the translator, I'm afraid, but we have been able to rework the way we calculate and establish how our translators are compensated, to remove the particular encumbrance from the cost of the book itself." As the panel's moderator, French-into-English translator David Kornacker, said later, "I love Susan's long circumlocution for saying, 'We'll publish but we won't pay you anything.' Not a whole lot. It limits the number of people who can afford to translate, if they don't have some other source of income. And potentially it affects quality. I know that that's not always true, but it puts great pressure on quality."

Arthur Goldhammer, who primarily translates French scholarly works for university presses, told me, "Publishers, which are always trying to save money, will hire grad students or people who have some knowledge of the field and the language, and they feel that they can take a translation, and it may not be of the highest quality, and polish it up in the copy-editing process. This has two effects: it tends to devalue the professionalism of the field, and also to hold down the amount of money one can earn, because there's always this pressure from below. There are people who, while in grad school, are willing to do a translation for relatively little money, on which a professional couldn't live."

And this is what is happening. Grad students, young professors, and foreign natives who haven't lived very long in an English-speaking country are willing to accept the $500 or so that some university and other presses are offering for full-length translations. In one case, involving a very difficult contemporary novel, Northwestern University Press offered a young translator around $3 per thousand words, about 4% of the normal rate.

Not only do they pay too little, according to translators, publishers also don't give translators much up-front credit, and that's free. Editor Jonathan Galassi told me, "I believe in [putting the translator's name on the cover], speaking as a translator. It's not always possible, but I personally think it's the right thing to do. It has not been the tradition here, however. . . . Translators are an abused species: they don't get much credit, they don't get much money, and they're often fighting with publishers for more credit. That's why I feel that if you can't give the guys a lot of money, at least you can give them credit. Publishers don't like to put the translator's name on the cover because they think it makes the book look harder to swallow, and therefore it won't sell as well. I say, people who are going to buy a translated book, they know it's a translation."

Few translators' names appear on the front cover, or even on the back cover or jacket flaps of books, although a lot more do now than ten or twenty years ago. Some translators don't even get their name on the title page, but this situation, which used to be quite normal, is now very rare. When the translator is also the editor of the edition, say, of a volume of selected poems, or if he writes an introduction, especially if it's scholarly, there is a much greater chance the translator's name will appear on the cover. After all, editors' names nearly always do; editors don't seem to scare readers away. University presses are also generally better about putting the translator's name on the cover, because they know that a work's foreignness is more likely to *attract* their sort of reader than to scare them away.

One would think that one of the most effective ways translators could gain respect from editors and others in publishing would be for them to suggest the best books from their country of specialization, thereby giving editors who treat them well a jump on other editors. After all, translators read widely in their language, and editors respect their opinions enough to pay them to report on books recommended by agents, foreign publishers, and authors themselves. A book suggested by a translator even comes with its own excited, knowledgeable translator, saving the editor a search for an appropriate one who is free to work on it within a reasonable time. Yet the reality is that almost no fiction in translation is initiated by a translator.

Why? First, it's not the way editors do business. Most books published by commercial publishers come through a literary agent or, in the case of translations, through a foreign editor, rights manager, or government agency. These people try to save the editor the time of looking at, or sending out for evaluation, works they would not be interested in. Thus, if an editor does a lot of mysteries, they will send him mysteries. If he's into literary stuff, then they'll hold the mysteries and send him truly insoluble books.

Second, translators generally do not think in terms of markets, and editors think in terms of little else. Translators, who after all are usually professors, tend to recommend books that are difficult but "important," which is another way of saying "unsaleable." Often the recommended books are old and their authors dead, and most editors are looking for living authors, unless a dead one has suddenly been elected into the pantheon of literary gods.

Third, translators generally think in terms of books: "This is a book I'd love to translate." Editors tend to think in terms of authors: "This is an author there might be an audience for." When a translator approaches an editor with a book by a living author, it is often a book by an older writer, or a novel by an essayist, or a book that made a big splash among the literati of his country, but which is not the sort of thing the American literati are much interested in, say, a lesbian novel that shocked Latvians but would merely amuse Americans. In other words, one-book deals. Some of the more successful translators are those who sell a book to an editor not on its literary merits, but on the basis of its subject or political message. There is a clear market for this sort of book, and the author isn't as important, so it's a perfect "book" for an editor to pitch to his marketing department.

But in any case, the editor's prejudice is always in favor of tried-and-true writers, "writers on our list," to whom they feel some loyalty and in whose reputation their house has already invested money. A new book by a new author means a new investment of time, energy, and cash.

Even the "big-name" translators, such as William Weaver and Gregory Rabassa, have had little luck convincing their editors to publish books they love. Rabassa told me, "I can get publishers to read books. I can't get them to publish them, though. . . . However, I did get one author published: Dmitrio Aguilera-Malta, an Ecuadorean who was an old friend—my wife did her dissertation on him. I met him in Mexico, where he was living. . . . Then he came out with this nice novel, *Seven Serpents and Seven Moons*. I was interviewed by *The Wall Street Journal* about translation. They asked me, 'What are you working on now?' I said, 'A labor of love.' The article came out, and I got a call from the University of Texas Press; they were interested, and they published it. The irony is that one of the founders of the Socialist Party in Ecuador was published because of *The Wall Street Journal.*"

But note that it was a university press that published the book, and also note that the translator did not approach them. However, university and small presses *are* much more open to projects that come from authors and translators rather than from agents, not because they're nicer or smarter people so much as because they can't afford the sort of advances agents require. My press, for example, which has never taken a book from a literary agent, *has* published two books that two different translators very much wanted to translate. One was a novel by a long-dead member of the Czech canon, Karel Poláček, whose work had never appeared in English and which did not, as any editor would have predicted, find an American market. Monetarily, publishers are right not to listen to professors, but I'm glad I published the book. And there are several university presses that are actually dependent on translator-professors bringing them translations, the same way that critic-professors bring them their books of criticism.

Richard Howard, a professor only after making his reputation as a poet and translator, feels that one reason translators are not successful with projects they try to initiate is that they don't try hard enough. "You have to go into an office and dance on the table," he told me. "You can't expect someone to come to you and say, I long for you to translate some obscure thing . . . You have to go in with your own interest and your passion for it, and convince an editor to do it. And it can be done." I agree. In the eight years I've been an editor of translations, I've received very few professionally written submissions from translators, and almost no impassioned arguments. Translators, as a rule, simply do not know how to market their work, not only according to the norm, but even in a special, interesting way. And those who speak best or loudest—agents, foreign publishers, certain authors—usually win the contracts.

Copyright Laws

Behind much of the difficulties in relations translators have with
authors and publishers are the copyright laws and contractual
norms of our time. In the world today, the author has complete
ownership of his work, unless he sells all or part of the various
rights that make up what we call copyright. No translation can
legally be published without the author's permission and usually
without payment to the author of an advance against future
royalties. Typically, one publisher is given a monopoly on the right
to publish a literary work in each of the languages in which it
appears.

The author usually keeps the copyright in his work. The translator, on the other hand, rarely keeps the copyright in his work.
A translation is treated not as a performance, but rather as a separate literary work. But since the translator is recognized neither as
author nor performer, translation in America is generally considered
"work for hire," that is, work contracted out just as if the translator
were a copy editor or other freelancer. A musical performance, on
the other hand, is usually not a work-for-hire, and a recorded
performance can in turn be copyrighted by the musician or singer;
the performer has control over its subsequent sale. Because translators are not recognized as performing artists but as commissioned
workers, the publisher usually holds the copyright in a translation.
And even when the publisher does allow the copyright to be in
the translator's name, something translators are increasingly
requesting and getting, the contract between them puts all the
control over disposition of rights in the publisher's hands. And
when it comes to rights, the contractual arrangements matter much
more than whose name appears on the copyright page.

When a translated book goes out of print, the translator has
no right to go and find another publisher for it, although usually
the publisher will allow this. When a foreign author becomes a

success, the translator who helped make him a success has no right to translate the author's next book.

In continental Europe, the rights situation is even worse, because they take more seriously something known as *droit moral*, "moral rights," according to which an artist's creation is an extension of the artist, to the point that defaming a book is equivalent to defaming an author, and making changes to a book without the author's permission is illegal. This allows the creator absolute power over his creation, which includes control over translations. Even in the United States, translations can be rejected by the author or publisher and prevented from ever being published, although this rarely happens for other than reasons of quality, unless a good deal of money is involved. Things are different for other performers: a singer or actor can sing a song or appear in a play, and the composer or playwright can do little or nothing about it, except collect a fee for each performance (although money and fame can come into play here, as well).

Publishers can also keep other translators from interpreting a work, so that readers are limited to only one translation of even very famous poems. This happened to Rainer Maria Rilke. It was only when his work went into the public domain in 1976 that it began to be translated into English by so many different people. This monopoly situation can be especially serious when the one translation is a poor one.

David Kornacker told an ALTA audience, "Small presses do remarkable work in certain ways, but sometimes they will take a very important book and massacre it. And once it is out in their translation, under copyright, no one can do it, and in some ways its existence is worse than it not existing at all. In my own experience, I've seen that a few too many times." William Weaver has spoken about one of these times, in Italy: "When *Catcher in the Rye* was about to come out in America, a small publisher in Florence somehow bought the rights for very little . . . And since he was a stingy, or poor, publisher, he had the book translated by somebody who had spent a week in England or something. The translation was practically unreadable. And the book came and went absolutely unnoticed. . . . Years later, another publisher renegotiated the rights, got another translator, a real translator, to retranslate the book, and it was an immense success."*

Copyright laws became the norm and began to be enforced in the nineteenth century, around the time fidelity became the prevalent approach to translation in the West. Serge Gavronsky told me, "In the sixteenth century, everyone was doing imitations and signing their names to them. French poetry was enormously enriched by poets of the Pleiades who translated from the Latin and signed their names. Today that's plagiarism; it was then called culture. . . . That's the point of departure for French poetry: stealing."

Lawrence Venuti has been the principal exponent of one solution to this problem: putting translation rights into the public domain before other rights. In other words, the author and his descendants would continue to have full control over the publication of his book for fifty years after the author's death, but at an earlier time, say when the author dies, anyone could translate the work into any language any way they wanted, and pay nothing.

Frederic Will looks back to earlier conceptions of literature as a collective enterprise to support his ideal literary culture in which writers see themselves as contributing to the common good. Copyright law is a move "toward a world in which the writer—the artist in general—no longer works in terms of the whole purpose of his society, multiple as that has of course always been, but in terms of himself, his patron, his ideal for art, or, perhaps, simply in terms of the market. . . . a situation in which the artist simply had to look on his work as a private possession, a potential commodity. . . . Translation would best operate in a particular kind of social-cultural situation; a global one, a world situation in which efforts—economic, verbal, philosophical—would as a matter of course be pooled, in which achievements of value would not be moves in the strategy of competition but contributions to the general good; in which cultural convergence rather than cultural competition would be the norm."*

In a world where literature is considered part of a common pursuit, a common wealth, copyright would seem like a ridiculous, if not insidious thing, something that stood in the way of sharing, a property right in a community commons. But, of course, this sort of a world is a fantasy. There would be sharing, yes, but there would be a lot more copying, stealing, exploiting. Not that there isn't a lot of that already, but at least it is either illegal and the perpetrator can be sued, or the creator is compensated for his work's exploitation (e.g., almost any film version of a worthwhile novel). Also, in such an ideal world it would be hard to get anyone to invest in publishing anything (and therefore hard to get paid for writing), because most publishers thrive on the sale of rights. And nowhere is the sale of rights—especially foreign rights—more important than in the United States, home of commercial enter-tainment whose popularity is phenomenal all over the world. This is our greatest export business, and our media companies would fight to the death to oppose anything that would dilute their and their creators' property rights.

But it's a lovely vision—a world where literature is there to respond to, to play with, rather than to monopolize. If only such activity could be limited to people with taste, talent, and ethics. If only there were a community of people who would enjoy the responses and the play. No, I don't think we're going to go back to the Renaissance, literarily, for quite a while, especially since this only worked when the writers were wealthy or had patrons and therefore were not looking to make a living from foreign-language sales of their writing. However, there are many who feel that the Internet, where costs are as low as pay, is leading us into a different sort of common wealth.

No, better than trying to create a different sort of world, it might be better for translators to consider the alternative of being recognized as performing artists, with a performer's rights in their work. But this would require a new approach to copyright, because performance rights are set up now for recordings, and the more popular a song, the more often it's played and recorded, and the more the composer makes from his performance fees. Modern literary works, even if they were placed in the public domain, would not be translated often, and so under the current law involving performances it would be hard to remunerate writers of popular books more than writers of less popular books, when both have their works translated only once into English.

And would translators really like to open all works up to multiple translation, and would publishers be as willing to publish a translation or pay even as little as they do now if someone else could perform a competing version? Having the law recognize you for what you are doesn't guarantee a better situation. But as it is now, not being legally recognized as performing artists means being enslaved by the law and the contractual arrangements that have grown up around it. Because only a work's expression, not its content, is protected by copyright, copyright law can protect the author only by assuming the fidelity metaphor—that translation is a faithful re-enactment, a copying, of the original's expression. But the truth is, of course, that the translator preserves only the content and has to rework the expression. It is the legal restrictions of copyright law that place the translator in such a powerless position vis-à-vis author and publisher.

Love Is All There Is

IT SHOULD COME AS NO SURPRISE that translators and editors, although very much alike, have some of the same problems found in any manager-employee relationship, and that their complaints are rather similar: not enough money, not good enough, unequal power. It's also no surprise that they should have some of the same complaints found in any artist-director relationship: not enough credit, difficult to work with, unequal power. But unlike most employees, literary translators are highly skilled intellectuals, and they are neither employed on any regular basis, nor given benefits, job security, or regular pay. And although they're performers, they generally don't have agents watching out for their credit and their rights, nor are they themselves as sophisticated in a business sense as others who are treated like them, for example, freelance copy editors.

Beyond the legal situation and their freelance status, why are literary translators treated so badly? Why are they the low of the low both as employees and as performing artists? In short, why don't they get no respect?

I think the main reason is that there simply isn't much money in publishing literary translations. Much of what is true of the treatment of translators is also true of the treatment of unknown poets and literary novelists, except that translators, as non-creators, are one peg lower on the totem pole; at least poets are *poets*. Yet translators do have one advantage over such writers: translators might be paid little and by the word, but at least they're paid. Many poets get nothing or almost nothing for their work, because, frankly, it has no market value. Publishing poetry is a labor of love, and it is assumed that the poet has some other way to make a living. Unknown literary novelists, and even a lot of unknown commercial novelists, are given very small advances. The difference is that their ship might come in one day: a film might be made of one of their novels, their books might do well in translation, or they might actually become popular. The best that can come in for a translator is a boat.

Publishing literary translations, at least of writers who are not already famous, is no more a business than publishing poetry or putting on concerts of new music or producing experimental theater. No one involved expects to make too much money; there aren't even a handful of editors whose pay or position is based on the success of the translations they publish. And there are only a handful of people in the U.S. who make a living from literary translation, and it is usually a rather slim living, like the Winstons making a go of it together on a farm in Vermont. Jonathan Galassi told me, "I've never done translation for money myself, vocationally. I think that must be extremely difficult, frustrating, and embittering." Nearly all people who see themselves as translators have other forms of income, either a spouse or a real job, usually teaching, writing, editing, or doing more remunerative types of non-literary translation. And most people who do literary translation do not consider themselves translators; they see translation as something they do on the side, for fun, love, or an enjoyable way to make a little extra money over the summer.

People are working out of love all the way around, except at some of the commercial houses, where they dream of publishing the next *Name of the Rose* or another García Márquez. And almost never do. Translating fiction, then, is more like writing poetry than writing fiction; it's more like playing jazz than playing rock; more like acting in off-off-Broadway than acting on TV. The big difference is that there isn't much in the way of subsidies or positions. There are many fewer prizes, grants, communities, readings, classes, etc. than poets have. And with only a few exceptions, literary publishers receive much less grant money than theater companies.

On top of all this, everyone is happy to pay a premium to see an especially good string quartet or theater company, but no one is willing to pay a single penny extra not only for an especially good translator, but even for a translator at all. A publisher cannot charge significantly more for a translated novel than for one originally written in English. And if the book is especially long, the publisher cannot hope to recoup the extra per-word translation costs (if there's just an author involved, length only increases production costs, not what the author gets).

Translation is an art that is of little interest to grant givers, who support poets and prose writers alike, not to mention musicians, dancers, actors, and opera singers. And individuals don't see giving to literary presses as a typical way of supporting the arts. Translation is once again penalized because it falls in the middle: translators aren't creative artists, and arts organizations, grant givers, and possible patrons don't considered them performing artists either. And translators rarely rarely try to get them to. Translation as a scholarly, interpretive discipline is also not of interest to grant givers, except the NEH, because it is only recently beginning to be recognized as a legitimate scholarly activity, and even then only at some universities, and only in some departments.

America is odd in its treatment of translators. Throughout the industrialized world, the translation of literary works into and out of a country's language is heavily subsidized by government organizations—international, national, regional, and local. In the U.S., nearly all the subsidies there are come from countries such as Germany, France, Sweden, the Netherlands, even the Czech Republic now, which pay for translations *out* of their languages, sometimes the full cost of translation. And outside the U.S. and Britain, literary translation is for most translators just a job involving the rapid translation of commercial literature and nonfiction—self-help books, children's books, biographies, the whole range of writing. You're not paid much and you're expected to just churn out the words, but at least there's constant work and a lot of people doing it. Translation is a profession done by people educated for the job, as well as by young aspiring writers who can get at least a small regular income this way, while gaining valuable writing experience as well.

An important difference between here and abroad is that, although more quality literature is translated into languages other than English, the great majority of translated literature abroad consists of commercial fiction, and there's a lot more commercial nonfiction translated there as well. Here, few commercial books are translated, and our translators have the pleasure of working almost exclusively on first-rate fiction and nonfiction. The translation work done abroad is usually competent, sometimes awful, only sometimes at the level of ours, if for no other reason than most of what is translated does not require the skills and is not given the sort of dedication that our amateur, academically oriented translators bring to it.

In 1965, Hans Erich Nossack spoke to the International Congress of Literary Translators about the recent and "objectionable . . . practice of foreign publishers to seek to exploit the success of a book that has just become a 'bestseller' in the original language by insisting on an all too hasty translation. There have been a few cases in recent years in which the translations were so horrible that the original writers felt compelled to file legal suits to prevent a second printing of these thrown-together translations of their works."* This opinion was echoed by American writer Hans Koning in the pages of the PEN writers group newsletter. After looking carefully at translations of two of his novels into French and Dutch, he wrote, "The quality of the work was astoundingly low. . . . The translators were well-known; one had done several novels by Faulkner. . . . they committed errors that made nonsense of entire passages. . . . Puzzled with one Dutch translator's unfailing choice of *le mot injuste*, I found—after digging up my English-Dutch dictionary, a standard, commonly used one—that the translator had always selected the first meaning given, even if a dozen others were offered."* In other words, translation abroad is something that is done too often for the cash, with corners cut, little pride in the result, and little or no editing.

Here, where translation is more play than work, unless you're translating one of the few popular writers, such as Eco (Weaver once referred to his "murderous deadline"), you're given a lot of time to complete your translation—what's the rush? no one's out there waiting to buy out the first printing—and you're expected to do better work. Most of all, you get to translate mostly very good and often great stuff rather than American trash.

An amazing thing in this country of translation as play is that there are thousands of people out there translating entire books partly for the fun of it and the education, partly in the hope that someone somewhere will love it just as much, or at least think it will sell, and publish it. Most of these translations aren't up to American standards, but some of them are incredibly good. For example, when Peter Kussi and I started asking around for translations of works by Karel Čapek for our centennial Reader, we discovered some truly first-rate work that had already been done, most of it purely for love. One play had been commissioned, but the other plays and stories and essays were translated without any real hope of ever being published or staged. And there was enough excellent work to fill a sizeable volume.

Love, despite such stifling things as fidelity and submission, is what makes translation such a wonderful art to be involved with here in the U.S. As I've said too many times, but will still say again, of all the arts translation is the only one where there is no such thing as monetary success or real fame, except a moderate amount for translators of Homer and some other big-time classics.

Hans Erich Nossack talked about love in his 1965 talk: "It would be ideal . . . if every translator were in a position to love what he translates, if he had to translate only what appealed to him. We writers, who want to be translated, greatly depend upon this emotional, human element of translation. . . . the writing of a book is not only an intellectual process but also borders on a biological necessity for the author, and it is crucial that this be apparent in a vivid translation. . . . Of course, considering the current economic conditions of the literary marketplace, I know that the ideals I demand from a translator are utopian. But can a person exist without utopias?"*

I think the situation in America today is closer to being utopian, in this sense, than the situation anywhere else in the world. Yet things are bad for translation in America. The numbers are falling and the pay is not growing. There is a little more respect for translators, but most of it is token. The only real explosion in the translation world involves theory, and most translators have little interest in theory, some never read it at all, and most of those who do say their interest in theory is separate from their actual translation work.

Things are bad, but translators should remember how lucky they are to be doing what they love, and remember that no one else is making money off of it, except printers and paper manufacturers. Digging ditches might pay much better than literary translation, but it doesn't build up the same muscles. No translator likes hearing this, and from a publisher of all people, but for me, too, it is a matter of love and learning. I love working with people who love it as much as I do. I'm not exactly writing this book to make my fortune either, or even a living. That's what selling out is for, and there simply is no selling out in the field of literary translation, at least not in the U.S. The closest thing is technical translation—of journals, documents, instructions, and the like—which is hardly selling out, just good, honest work. Is there any other sort of artist in America who is unable to sell out, even if he wants to? If you didn't think translation was a singular art yet, I hope this convinces you.

The situation in translation today might mean that almost nobody can make a living as a full-time literary translator, but then almost nobody is making a living as a hack translator of genre literature either, something that would be very unattractive to nearly all the people who bemoan the situation as it is. If we were to suddenly become like the rest of the industrialized world and publish large quantities of literature from all over, mediocre and good and awful, the people who would benefit would not be the translators of today, but young graduate students and recent graduates of writing programs who had enough knowledge to do the job, the need for some extra cash, and the time and energy to knock off a quick three hundred pages, but who were not really capable of or interested in doing what today's translators would consider a good job. Then, eventually, a true profession might evolve.

Not that hack translating is a sin, any more than hack writing. Somebody's got to do it, if there's a demand for it. But it's not the same thing as the world of literary translation American translators know and love, any more than playing weddings is the same thing as playing serious jazz. Foreign literature is simply not popular in America, and popular literature is not too much fun for intellectuals to translate, although it does have its own joys and challenges.

If translators really care about making a little more money on the average translation, they might consider putting together some sort of share-the-wealth arrangement that would divvy up among the many the rewards that go to the few from translating classics and books that get made into films or are otherwise popular, usually for reasons other than the quality of the translation (although rarely with poor translations either). Some athletes have done this with the money that flows from television deals. Translators, most of whom are relatively liberal intellectuals, should be at least as socialist as athletes, shouldn't they?

How bad is the situation in the U.S.? Literary translation has definitely been in decline, at least from commercial houses. University presses are publishing more translations than ever, and translations from small presses seem to be holding their own, but this underlines the fact that the market is small and shrinking. According to Lawrence Venuti, British and American translations have constituted between 2% and 4% of total books since the 1950s, "not withstanding a marked surge during the early 1960s, when the number of translations ranged between 4% and 7% of the total." In 1965, there were substantially more translations in the United States than today or any time since then, over twice the translations published in 1955. In hard numbers, there were 276 literary translations published in 1956, and 562 in 1966, the latter out of 2,069 total translations. The highwater mark was 1970, when 2,500 book-length translations were published in the U.S., 756 of which were literature (including children's books), but by the 1980s the totals were down in the low 1,000s, and by 1984, the last year American statistics appeared in the UNESCO *Index translationum*, which is where my statistics come from, the number of literary translations was back down to 1956 levels: 289. For some context, here are the numbers of literary translations published in a number of other countries in 1986: West Germany - 5,045; Spain - 5,029; USSR - 3,536; Netherlands -2,326; Sweden - 1,351; Japan - 1,227; France - 786; Italy - 424; Poland - 410; Great Britain - 401; Norway - 359; Hungary - 358. We beat everyone to the moon, but everyone beats us to the literary world. Even the most literarily chauvinst country in the world, France, published three times the number of literary translations, and despite being famous for keeping out foreign goods, the Japanese published four times as many. Even the U.K. published many more than us for a much smaller English-speaking audience. As with films and pop music, we export a great deal more than we import.

Why has there been such a decline in the publication of literary translations by commercial houses in the U.S.? Before I consider the decline, I should first take a look at the heyday. Starting in the 1920s, America was fortunate to have had a number of immigrants for whom European high culture was the most important thing in the world. And those immigrants founded some of the most important literary publishers, such as Alfred A. Knopf, Farrar, Straus, and Pantheon. These publishers filled their lists with the leading writers of Europe, as well as some writers from Asia and South America. They did not do it to make their fortunes, or even for prestige, but because this is what they loved, this is what made them proud. Yes, I suppose I'm romanticizing a bit, but the important thing is that the last of these people are retiring from the publishing scene, and the houses they founded are now part of communications empires, even if the first two are still the publishers of some of the best foreign literature that appears in English.

The days of gentleman publishing are practically over. This world is dead, and not only are we losing our tradition of publishing fine literature in translation, we're also not shifting to a European breadth of translation. Not only has there been a decline in the number of book-length translations published each year in the U.S., the sales per book are not rising as competition for the serious reader eases. Publishers are right: readers have little interest in translations, except in big books such as those by Homer and Dante, Dostoevsky and Mann, García Márquez and Kundera. And a few literary mysteries, such as *Perfume*, books that are turned into somewhat popular films, such as *Like Water for Chocolate* and *The Lover*, and books that are both, such as *Smilla's Sense of Snow*. It's not hard to identify the contemporary foreign authors whose books sell well without a film involved: besides García Márquez and Kundera, there's Günter Grass, Umberto Eco, Isabel Allende (all of whom eventually did have films of their books made and distributed in the U.S.), and maybe the latest Nobel Prize winner. Dead poets sell far better than living ones, and who ever buys a translation of a contemporary play if it's not assigned for a course?

What's wrong with our readers? I've talked about this a little in terms of the decline of translation among younger poets. There is the effect of multiculturalism and other sorts of market-based literature, that is, literature aimed at particular constituencies. Fewer people are looking for Others, and when they are, they aren't looking to other languages for them; English has more and more of its own. We have Salman Rushdie, Derek Walcott, Arundhati Roy and others from the Subcontinent and Caribbean, we have Hispanic and Native American writers, we have South Africans and Nigerians, not to mention Australians, Irish, Scots, and Welsh. Oh yes, and even Canadians, at least the majority who write in English. If we want to read, for example, a great lesbian novelist, why do we have turn to Marguerite Yourcenar, even if she lived most of her adult life right here in the U.S.? She wrote in French; we have our own, and they market themselves better than she did. And they're what we expect. They don't challenge our assumptions. They're one of us. Also, as Lawrence Venuti told me, "One of the curious things about the PC response is that often what gets translated is realistic narrative or poetry that is very romantic in our terms and not experimental, in other words, can be easily assimilated to the values that have dominated Anglo-American culture since the early nineteenth century."

The reason for this is especially clear with Third World literature. Few Third World nations had a literary culture based on the novel; many didn't even write down their languages. Their sophisticated oral cultures were based on performance and can be better experienced in dance and music. So the novels we get from Third World writers are generally realistic narratives like most of our fiction, because these authors were educated in the West and are bringing our forms into their culture; literarily, for Americans, little of it is of much interest.

Ironically, much of the most important literature written in Third World languages is literature in translation. Swahili, for example, was given a literary language primarily via the translation of the great works of Western literature. Julius Nyerere, president of Tanzania and socialist critic of everything Western, translated Shakespeare into Swahili. The same thing happened with respect to modern Hebrew, another twentieth-century literary language. Modern Hebrew writers were also translators; translation was part of the same enterprise of creating a literary language. Even Vladimir Jabotinsky, the spiritual father of the Likud Party, translated, and he did not bring a war epic like the *Iliad* into Hebrew, but rather the Sherlock Holmes stories and the poetry of Edgar Allan Poe. No culture can create great writers at the snap of a finger, but the intelligentsia of any culture can enrich its literary language by translating the great writers of other languages. However, we cannot experience this creative renewal of other cultures' literature through translation; in fact, we can't experience other languages' translations at all unless we know the other language and its literary history. In this sense, translation is the most culture-restricted art there is, far more restricted—more impossible to get across frontiers—than poetry. Translation, one could say in turning around Frost's infamous dictum, is what gets lost.

English-speaking countries can afford to be lazy in their incorporation of other literary cultures, because we have such a great literary history. But the great periods of English literature have also been great periods of translation, and in its Elizabethan youth the English language and its literature were created and modernized in large part through translation. Shakespeare was, to some extent, the greatest Renaissance translator. The translation boom of the 1960s may be attributed to writers feeling that the English language and American culture needed to be renewed by outside stimuli. It is no accident that today's mediocre period of English-language literature coincides with the decline of translation and a looking inward, both in terms of language and in terms of readers' identities and interests. It might also be no accident that so many of our best English-language writers today come from foreign cultures, either first or second generation—Kazuo Ishiguro, Salman Rushdie, Philip Roth. As Charles Tomlinson, editor of *The Oxford Book of Verse in English*, wrote, "English poetry happens to be so rich because of what it managed to incorporate into itself."*

Another reason for our translation decline is America's preference for content over form. To those who love literature for its own sake, the content doesn't matter very much; it's the approach that counts. We lovers of form couldn't care less which gender(s) the love story we're reading is between, or among, or how it ends. Yet there aren't enough of us, and it's very hard to sell a book whose interest is formal rather than subject-oriented. And even with translations, as Lawrence Venuti told me, "if [a publisher] can't identify a market, in the way they can for an American book, then they don't translate."

Why? First of all, it's hard to describe a book that doesn't follow the rules, that comes up with a fresh approach. If it's fresh, how do you let people know it is, especially if you're the typical publisher's copywriter, who's barely out of college and doesn't even know what fresh is? Saying it's fresh isn't enough; every book is sold as fresh and unique and all those other words that are thrown around indiscriminately.

And that's what it comes down to: discrimination. Being intellectual, caring about literature for its own sake, is about being discriminatory, noting differences in approach, caring how something is done more than what it is in terms of plot and character. Peter Glassgold told me, "Americans seem to be ashamed of or devalue the development of intellectual prowess. Train the body at the gym, but to train the mind at the desk is something else again."

Jonathan Galassi told me that in translation, "the aim is transparency, to create a book that is like an American book but comes from somewhere else. . . . There's no hitch in reading it, it's written in a language that relates to our vernacular. And then through that language you learn about another sensibility, another world." This is what the great majority of American readers of literature in translation want: writing with no hitch in it, no difficulty, writing that allows you to learn about another land and culture. Translation as travel, exotic but easy to consume, Trans Lite, one might call it. There's nothing wrong with this, of course; when I was younger that was exactly why I read so much foreign literature: I wanted to learn. I wanted to grow. I longed for the exotic and the new. I still do.

But the fact is that literature is not the best way to learn about other lands and cultures, especially when the literature appears in our own culture's forms, that is, when the literature is familiar in form, realistic or magically realistic, bent on telling a story in a way we like our stories told. We don't listen to African drumming because it's familiar, but because it makes us feel so different. We don't watch an Indonesian shadow puppet play because it's familiar, but because it's so odd, theater completely unlike ours. We don't go to exhibits of pre-Columbian art because it looks like our paintings and sculptures, but because it reflects such a different approach to art and to the world. Then why do we want to read foreign mysteries or realistic political novels or women's novels set in Vietnam or watered-down magical realism that's so much like the magical realism being written right here? Why? Because there's no more enjoyable way to think we're learning about other cultures.

Lawrence Venuti considers this approach to literature narcissistic, "looking in foreign literatures and wanting to see your own taste, instead of approaching the translated text and looking for it to change your tastes in some way."

Even when a foreign author *is* special and challenging, he doesn't reflect his culture very well. All the Czech authors of the postwar era, for example, have not together sold as well in English as Milan Kundera, and he is the least Czech of them all. Eco is not very Italian, and Grass is not particularly German either. Their American readers are learning little about the national cultures, at least the literary cultures. But many readers of foreign literatures aren't really seeking the foreign culture, but rather information about the foreign land, about how others view the world, about their history and politics and problems, things that can better, but not so entertainingly, be provided by nonfiction. The problem literature has, compared to the other arts (except, to some extent, film), is that no one seeks information or knowledge from music or sculpture or dance; it is only the formal aspects of culture that we get from them. Literature stands alone in supplying both culture and information, and information wins out in America today, that and politics. Politics is on the wane, certainly, yet reviewers were still disappointed to find in my house's 1997 collection of fiction by younger Czech writers that there was no clear response to the new freedom and capitalism that came with the Velvet Revolution. As if the principal purpose of literature were to mirror current social realities.

It is commonly believed among publishers that readers do not want to work at their reading and do not like things to be any stranger than they have to be. Is this even true of the rare readers who read literature in translation? No, the die-hard literary crowd actually *likes* to read difficult, often even pretentiously difficult, writing, but that's a pretty small group in this day and age when New York intellectuals are rushing to confess that they don't enjoy reading anything too difficult, and when it's the rare reviewer who can understand a complex contemporary work, even one written originally in English. What's most important is the way commercial publishers look at the situation: there is a sizeable potential audience consisting primarily of people who at least occasionally read literature in translation, and it is this relatively sizeable group that makes the rare translation profitable. It consists of college-educated people who read primarily for escape, information, and self-help, who are not likely to read literature in translation unless it fits the sort of reading they do anyway: mysteries, women's novels, socially conscious tales, soft-core pornography, novels that have been made into arty films. It is these readers who are most easily put off by the difficult and strange, at least in contemporary fiction and poetry. When it comes to new translations of Dostoevsky or Rilke, they'll just pick up what's on the shelf, which is why with classics translators have more freedom, why this is where much of the most interesting translation is being done and where all sorts of publishers are concentrating much of their efforts. But for new work, smoothness and familiarity are the hallmarks of attracting, or at least not frightening away, the largest group of potential readers.

Why are educated, relatively adventurous audiences able to sit through challenging avant garde theater, performance art, new music, and the like, yet unwilling to sit through a challenging translation? It's about participation, I think, and work. In a live performance, the performers are doing the work and you can participate at any level you choose; you can let your mind wander off, or in and out; you can let the performance rush over you; you can even fall asleep, if you like. When you're reading a book, only part of the work has been done for you by the performing translator. There's a lot left for the reader to do, and if you let your mind wander then you're not reading at all; the book's still there waiting for you to turn the page. You can't not participate, you can't shun the work, you too have to perform. With a live performance, the less you pay attention, the less work it will have been. But a book, if you actually go through it cover to cover, the way you sit through an entire play or concert, is harder and harder the less you pay attention. There's the rub.

Even if an editor doesn't think of pandering to the big group of potential readers, even if he accepts the fact that few of these people will ever read the translations he publishes and when they do will generally be looking for something other than what he's concerned about as an editor, it's still hard for him to forget his responsibility to readers. They are, after all, the people he's working for, even if the people he's working *with* take emotional precedence. It's rude to force translations down readers' throats like medicine, to think that, for example, a translation that brings Kafka's (and German's) sentence structure into English will sell anyway and be good for them. It's a very difficult dilemma, this choice between satisfying the tastes of the few connoisseurs who like their translations strong and spicy or the many more potential readers who like their translations weak and bland. It's not like throwing a piece of new music into a conventional concert, or a theater company putting on a challenging version of Chekhov. Rarely does a work get more than one translator per generation, and with few exceptions a work is translated only once ever into any particular language. A challenging translation of Chekhov's stories may be the only one many people will ever see, at least at this stage in the appreciation of translation, and it might prevent people from reading any further.

This dilemma of choosing between conventional and more experimental approaches is not one I have yet been faced with, because I've worked only with moderate translators who want to capture the effects of the original as best they can, without giving much thought, if any, to freer, theoretical, or avant garde approaches to translation. The translators I've worked with have sought a faithful recreation of the original, never slavish, never literal, never following anybody's rules, but responding to and interpreting the original as best they can, pace by pace, inch by inch.

For my part, I have never expected or asked for anything different. Although I had already done a great deal of reading about translation, working on this book has made me much more conscious of and open to the full range of possibilities in translation. I would love to work with translators whose respect for the original leads them to take more risks and find more creative ways to capture certain effects that would otherwise be completely lost, but who are not necessarily more theoretical in their approach to translation—because I think there are few people who can pull off a first-rate translation based on theory. Lawrence Venuti is one contemporary exception; he manages to work into his translations an historical range of English usage which calls atention to the translation without ever feeling like translationese.

Theoretical approaches do make great experiments, but I think most experiments should be kept short, for example, some poems rather than a book of poetry, a couple of stories rather than a novel. In any event, taking a fresh approach to translation or to a particular work is not something you can impose on a translator, any more than you can on an author. You can encourage it, and I intend to in the future, but it has to be something the translator wants as much as you do. If the work is historical, I might repeat what Richard Sieburth told me: "It is much, much more difficult to teach students just how distant and different texts are than it is to teach them how much like us they are. It is much more interesting to teach Racine as something as far away as Noh drama, which it is, than to try to 'make it relevant,' . . . do modern dress versions. [Translation involves] the need to articulate a distance."

The leading bemoaner of decline in American translation is Eliot Weinberger. He told me that it became really clear to him when he was a judge for the PEN/Book-of-the-Month Club Translation Prize in 1994: "There were less than ten substantial books of poetry translations published in all of 1994. This includes all presses, even presses I'd never heard of. I racked my brains trying to think of something I didn't get. It's just astonishing. There's not a single small press that's consistently publishing [poetry] translations. . . . you have the university presses doing a scholarly edition with a lot of notes, mostly historical, and other than that it's very hard. If

I'm going to do a contemporary Latin-American poet, there's practically no place to go.

"I was talking the other day to Sam Hamill at Copper Canyon, one of the better presses for poetry, a place that does maybe one translation a year, and he told me he gets about forty good poetry translation manuscripts a year, that he could publish. Forty aren't even published a year, about ten are; so it gives you an idea of how many are floating around. . . . Yet the way poets get their reputations is by being translated. Paz, when he was first translated, was not a well-known poet; now he is, thanks to his translations that started in the fifties, and his books sell a lot. You can't keep that sort of thing going [if you don't translate new poets]."

Not everyone, however, agrees that the glass is nearly empty. Drenka Willen of Harcourt, Brace said, in reference to what Weinberger told me, "That sounds very positive to me. Eight? Excellent!"

Of course, I'm somewhere in between. I don't think eight is excellent. I also think the numbers are higher than this, but not substantially. And I think it's frightening. As Ernst Renan wrote, "A work that isn't translated is only half published." And when a work isn't translated into what is essentially the world language, the language read by the Nobel Prize committee, it's less than half published. Breon Mitchell told me, "for most German authors, being translated into English is a sign of breaking out of the level of being a national writer who just writes for German readers, into some international sphere. It's a major step." In fact, some authors don't make it in their own countries until they're translated and become popular overseas. William Faulkner was popular in French translation before he became fashionable back home, and the same thing happened more recently to Paul Auster.

A tiny number of poetry translations means that even the literary publishers with grants, sugar mommies, or wealthy owners don't think poetry in translation is of much value. It's not like they're making any money publishing what they're publishing now; why not poetry, why not translations? It means that the market—the insidious market-oriented concept known as the "niche"—has taken over, and that guts and taste have gone out the window. My small-press distributor has told me they do not want my press to publish poetry; its salesmen simply can't sell it, or don't want to make the effort (any more than readers do). Check the poetry section in your local bookstore, super or independent. It's terrible. It has the big names, the pop poets, maybe a few local poets and maybe a few translations (and maybe not the best) of a few big-name twentieth-century poets, such as Rilke and Pablo Neruda. Try to find Paz, a Nobel Prize winner, in anything but the best stores.

I'm guilty here, too, because my house has never published poetry (although we are, finally, this season; however, it's an expanded collection by Nobel Prize-winner Jaroslav Seifert; the only good English translation of his poetry was allowed to go out of print by a large house and would never have appeared, certainly not from a large house, without the prize). My defense is that I don't know poetry well enough and I don't know how to sell it. But although I do know fiction much better, I still don't know how to sell it, either. I don't think anyone knows how to sell serious fiction in translation, or even, for the most part, any good fiction that can't easily be pigeonholed. Or quality humor for that matter, my house's other specialty; that's at least as hard to sell as fiction in translation.

As I said earlier, the overall decline in the publication of book-length literary translations in the U.S. actually has more to do with the large houses than with publishers overall. University presses are publishing far more literary translations now than they did ten years ago, and small literary presses continue to publish pretty much the same small numbers. But with the commercial houses publishing more popular and classic translations, and small and university presses publishing more historical, trendy, and very difficult work, the nature of what is being published in translation has changed. And also, it has become harder recently for small presses to sell their books and to have their books reviewed. Many important university and small press poetry translations are not reviewed anywhere, and many translated novels are not reviewed in general review publications.

Peter Glassgold told me one of the principal reasons small and university presses tend to do more translations than bigger houses: "You can get better quality books for less money . . . When you're working on a very tight budget, this is a very good way to go."

But there are serious disadvantages to publishing books by these less expensive authors. First, you have to pay not only the author, but also the translator, and the total of these can be more than a small or university press pays for an English-language original. Which is the principal reason why small and university presses offer so little money to their translators, unless there is a grant involved.

Second, with literature in translation there aren't very many rights to sell. (Rights include foreign-language rights, paperback rights, film rights, and first serial, or excerpting, rights.) Films are jackpots for publishers of fiction, but few foreign books are made into English-language films, and foreign-language films based on novels are rarely given any substantial distribution in the United States. The big exceptions are also the most successful translations: for example, Umberto Eco's *The Name of the Rose*, Milan Kundera's *The Unbearable Lightness of Being*, and Laura Esquivel's *Like Water for Chocolate*. A publisher can hardly sell foreign rights in a book when they're buyers of foreign rights themselves. The principal rights that an American publisher of literature in translation can sell are also the only foreign rights they have to sell: British rights. And if you don't have reciprocal arrangements with a British publisher to publish each other's translations, then even these rights are difficult to sell, no matter the quality of the book. What such reciprocal arrangements do is spread the translator's fee between two houses, making translations easier to afford. But it has to go both ways or it only benefits the publisher that originally acquired the work, cutting his costs by getting a publisher to share them.

Even Jonathan Galassi, whose house places nearly all of its translations with a British house and which has had numerous successes with translations, told me, "Some of these projects are incredibly expensive and time-consuming. It's really a public service. That's the only reason it's being done." This is especially true when the translator does not do a good job, and a new translator or editor has to be brought in. Sometimes, as with *Smilla's Sense of Snow*, the British and American publishers (in this case Galassi's Farrar, Straus) publish different translations, because they do not agree about what is acceptable. Drenka Willen told me, "Occasionally we have trouble with British translators who seem to be less aware, in the sense that they translate into 'high English,' I'd call it, and sometimes a Polish schoolboy sounds like someone in a British public school. That simply doesn't work. . . . We try to use what I call 'standard English,' something that's respectable both here and there. In other words, it really shouldn't be too American or too English, something in between. . . . When the British translator refuses to have any changes made, then we simply bring out our own translation; we edit it. It increases the expenses, unfortunately, but we do it."

At the 1995 ALTA congress, translator Michael Henry Heim proposed an alternative way to look at literary translation that might make it appear more profitable to publishers. He spoke in terms of the "symbolic capital" of literary translations, as opposed to popular literature, which requires an enormous up-front investment in marketing. Heim said essentially this: Trendy books designed to make short-term profits will not stick around, and quality books that have no hope of making short-term profits may, if they are allowed to stay in print, make money over the long haul as slowly but surely selling "backlist" books, sold to people as they discover the writer (as the writer's work is published over the years) or sold for college courses, if the writer is recognized as important. "We are all suffering," he continued, "what I call the Eco Syndrome. *The Name of the Rose* made such a splash that many editors felt that their next translation had to do the same thing. That was a signal to over-package, over-advertise, over-tout a number of works that then fell flat, because they couldn't stand up to that treatment. That may have contributed to editors' queasy feelings when it comes to translations." And then Heim went on to talk about various ways to make the publication of translations more viable, primarily by saving costs, for example, by publishing translations in series that use uniform covers and then advertising the series rather than the separate titles.

He definitely has a point, but publishers are already doing a lot to lower translation costs. The principal cost-cutting device among commercial houses is extraordinarily simple: keep translations shorter. An unusal number of literary translations these days are 200 pages or less. This keeps the translator's fee down (to below $5,000), keeps the printing costs down, and yet you can still charge twenty dollars or more for it. University presses, which will charge as much as forty dollars for a translation, depending primarily on libraries for its hardcover sales, do not have to worry so much about length; and they pay their translators less anyway, on the whole.

Another principal form of savings is for publishers to focus on reprints of classics in translation. If the book is still under copyright, the advance to the author is small, and usually the translator receives nothing at all. If the book has gone into the public domain (that is, when the author has been dead for fifty years or more), there are no costs if the translation too is in the public domain, and if a new translation is done, only the translator gets paid, and the publisher has a book that comes with a name and an audience. As Luann Walther of Vintage Books, the trade paperback division of Random House, told the *New York Times*, "Classics are the safest translations for a publisher, because they are in the public domain and except for the most obscure ones, you know there is a market for them."*

All of these things are being done by all sorts of houses, but neither the number of translations nor the number of profitable translations seems to be going up; but a larger percentage of translations are classics, and the size of the losses is going down.

As painful as it is, as exploitative as publishers tend to be, the fact is that translators' services are not considered very valuable by our culture. Better than complaining about what they're paid and how little interest and respect publishers have for them, I think translators should (i) appreciate how lucky they are to be doing what they love and (ii) start working on ways to expand their audience by educating it about translation and giving themselves a public image. And this is the topic of my next, and last, chapter.

Performing Without a Stage

I RECENTLY SAW the journalist-novelist Pete Hamill on a C-Span2 writers panel saying that in order not to be affected by other writers' styles when he's working on a novel himself, he limits his reading to translations. Balzac, for instance.

None of the other writers on the panel disagreed or questioned this; in fact, they laughed heartily when he went on to paraphrase Frost's "Poetry is what gets lost in translation." They accepted what Hamill said despite the fact that Balzac's straightforward style is hardly poetry and comes through into English very well; that if he'd said Proust, he would have sounded ridiculous, because Proust's style, even in translation, could have a great effect on one's writing; and that if he really cared about not being affected by English style, Hamill would read books in a foreign language!

Did any of the authors or any members of the audience think for a second that instead of mentioning Balzac, since Hamill was referring to translations, it would have been more appropriate to have mentioned a translator such as William Weaver? No, I don't think so. And if he had mentioned Weaver instead, would it have been considered a condemnation of his work, that is, a statement that Weaver was incapable of writing in a style that might affect Hamill's, whether or not that style was actually the "same" as the original author's? If so, was it any more polite to say this about the numerous translators of Balzac's novels?

The fact is that even among writers who have been translated themselves, and in front of an audience of people exceptionally interested in literature, anyone can condemn translation and translators wholesale, and find overwhelming support. Translators might be the only minority group for whom the PC corps has not yet demanded respect.

I also recently watched Russian director Andrei Tarkovsky's 1983 film *Nostalgia*, in which there is a scene between the two protagonists, Andrei, a Russian poet visiting Italy, and Eugenia, his Italian translator. Eugenia tells Andrei that she has read the poetry of Arseny Tarkovsky, who happens to be the director's father. Here is how the conversation proceeds, at least in subtitles:

> Andrei - In Russian?
> Eugenia - No, in translation—quite a good one.
> Andrei - Throw it away.
> Eugenia - Why? The translator's a very good poet.
> Andrei - Poetry is untranslatable, like all art.
> Eugenia - You may be right that poetry is untranslatable,
> but what about music, for example?
> Andrei - (Sings)
> Eugenia - What do you mean by that?
> Andrei - It's a Russian song.
> Eugenia - But how could we have got to know Tolstoy,
> Pushkin, and so understand Russia?
> Andrei - None of you understands Russia.
> Eugenia - Nor you Italy then, if Dante, Petrarch, and
> Machiavelli don't help.
> Andrei - It's impossible for us poor devils.
> Eugenia - How can we get to understand each other?
> Andrei - By destroying frontiers.
> Eugenia - Which frontiers?
> Andrei - Between nations.

As in the film, where the problems are not between nations, but between people and within nations and individuals both, in translation the problems are not between languages, but between people and within individuals as well. The problem is that few people understand translation, and even fewer are able to appreciate it, to enjoy it as translation or to criticize it intelligently. But this doesn't stop them from belittling it. Writers belittle translation, professors belittle translation, publishers see it as little more than an expensive nuisance, readers and reviewers rarely see it at all, and when they do they tend to belittle it, as well.

There are so many ways to belittle translation and translations, and so few ways, it seems, to praise it. In Western culture, the wholesale condemnation of translation can be traced to the holiness of scriptures. The Jewish scriptures could not be translated; the word of God could not be handled, and dirtied, by human hands, no more than you could drag the Torah through mud. And once the Christian Bible was translated into Latin (by a saint, of course, and an especially ascetic one at that), it too could not be translated into filthy day-to-day tongues. When, to take a simplistic but, I think, useful historical overview, the Reformation led to the translation of the Bible (which became, ironically, the most translated book in the world), the Enlightenment relegated religion to an increasingly secondary status, and Romanticism made poetry sacred, the newly sacred replaced the Bible as something impossible, if not wrong, to transfer into other languages. The content could be brought over, certainly, but not the spirit, not the form. The result is that when people speak about translation, they generally focus on its limitations, on what it is incapable of doing, on how it destroys the original, on how poorly its amateur craftsmen do their work. There is a contradiction in condemning it at once as something impossible, as something incompetent, and as the simple transposition of words (that is, of meaning) from one language into another. These three situations could not coexist. Translators neither have their cake nor get to eat it; they're not even served.

And translators are usually condemned by people who don't understand what they're doing, who think their work is about languages and words. Arthur Schopenhauer wrote an essay in 1800 with the apt title "On Language and Words," in which he said, "A library of translations resembles a gallery with reproductions of paintings."* Of course it looks like copying to someone who doesn't see past the translator's palette!

And then there is the mocking. I've quoted some snide comments earlier in the book. Let me add, for the record, a few lines from Vladimir Nabokov:*

> What is a translation? On a platter
> A poet's pale and glaring head,
> A parrot's screech, a monkey's chatter,
> And profanation of the dead.

Can you imagine condemning acting wholesale? Or the playing of instruments? Or dancing? All of these consist of interpretive performances? What's so different about translation?

Well, what most distinguishes translation is ironically just what requires its existence: it is accessible only to those who speak the language it appears in. A Japanese actor can bring the gestures of an American actor back home with him. Think how many actors around the world have imitated Bogie. But who outside of English has ever imitated Pope's *Iliad*? A Ghanian drummer can bring the motions of an Afghani drummer home with him, but a Ghanian translator will not look to even the greatest Afghani translator for inspiration. An American writer can't read a Chinese translation, and even if he could, he wouldn't. But if he did, he'd be very unlikely to read the original too, to see what in fact the Chinese translator contributed to the gestures and motions of the prose. In short, translation is a dead end. It is a solution to what God did to man for building the tower of Babel, but it is nothing more than a solution, limited in time and space and language. Music, acting, and dance are universal and forever, even if tastes do change. One need only look at the current fad for early music to see over what large time spans music can make a comeback. How many people are reading Renaissance translations, other than Shakespeare's, which are not considered translations?

Closely related is the other major difference between translation and the other performing arts: translation can't be seen. Yes, we see the words and sentences, but we have no idea what is the translator's doing and what is the original, and so we tend to assume we are reading the original, that the style is the author's or, at least, as close as one can get to it in English. Few of us love a translation and then rush to buy another book by that translator, his translation of another author's work. No, we rush out to buy

another book by the author, and rarely concern ourselves with
whether it's the same translator or not. Hardly what we do with
actors and violinists.

Of course, this is less true with dead authors than it is with
living authors. New translators of Homer or Dostoevsky are the
only ones available for readings, interviews, and photo opps. As
Jonathan Galassi told me, "Robert Pinsky's the Vladimir Ashkenazy
of Dante right now, because Dante is not an author that you can
go interview. Pinsky is the author, in effect. It's like a new CD by
Ashkenazy; it's Pinsky's Dante, he's seen as an artist. Whereas
Edith Grossman doing Mario Vargas Llosa, Vargas Llosa is still
around and takes up most of the space." Pinksy's Dante increased
interest in his poetry because he was already a notable poet, but
how many people will, after reading Robert Fagles' *Odyssey*, go out
and read his Sophocles or even his own poetry, since he was not
already known as a poet? This is one advantage classical musicians
have: most of the composers they play are long dead.

The irony here is that although (and because) the translator
does not have a stage to perform on and, therefore, his performance cannot be seen, the performance is pure, direct, and complete: nothing comes between his performance and his audience,
not a camera or sound system or even the limits of the viewer's
particular seat. The audience doesn't see a film actor's performance, but rather his performance as seen from a particular point
of view at any moment, one angle at a time, in context or out of
context, close up or from far away, with all the sounds he makes,
some of them, or none of them (in fact, sometimes another voice
entirely). He might move or the camera might move. Any move
a translator seems to make is the translator's. A film actor's performance is edited by a director and an editor. Yes, editors do
make changes to translations, but they are generally minor and
done with the translator's approval. Few actors ever approve the
way their performances appear in the final cut. They have to direct
the movie to do that, and even still, the audience sees only those
parts of the performance that he as director chooses.

The musician's performance, when recorded and distributed to the public, is more pure and direct, affected only by acoustics, the sound system, the mixing, but it is not very complete, because it is usually only one part of the musician's interpretation process, one of many performances of that piece by that musician, one of many contexts that musician has performed and will perform it in, and one of many that a number of musicians, sometimes a countless number, will perform. Most translations are the only performance that will ever been done by that person, even by anyone in that language or at least, with only a very few exceptions, the only one of that generation.

If you don't like a musical performance, you can try somebody else's. If you don't like a translation, there's nowhere to turn and nothing to compare it to. It's frustrating, aggravating, an impossible situation to be in. No wonder it's condemned so much.

The place translation is condemned the most is in the pages of book reviews, the place where the translator's public image is formed and where people can most openly vent their feelings about translation. One of the favorite ways people have for venting their feelings is nitpicking. As D. J. R. Bruckner said in reviewing a translation, "the pleasure of going through any translation is to catch lapses."* John Hollander has written in response to this attitude, "It is only [in literary translation] that *correctness* seems today to matter so much."*

Sara Blackburn coined the now-accepted name for nitpicking critics, "Professor Horrendo." Gregory Rabassa, who popularized the name, has written of Professor Horrendo, "If there is a mistake or a slip, he will surely find it, and he is not above suggesting alternate possibilities, some of which are as cogent as that exasperating last entry on multiple-choice exams. . . . But it is his mood that offends, for in truth he is often right."* John Dryden was faced with his own Professor Horrendos: "'Tis a sign that malice is hard driven, when 'tis forced to lay hold on a word or syllable; to arraign a man is one thing, and to cavil at him is another."*

Since Catbird is not a university press, its literary books are not taken seriously enough by academics to have merited more than a few scholarly reviews. But one is enough to show what Professor Horrendo sounds like. Professor Peter Z. Schubert of the University of Alberta, one of Horrendo's many aliases, wrote in his review of William Harkins' translation of Vladimír Páral's *Catapult*, which appeared in the *Slavic and East European Journal*:*

> The translation certainly could be improved. It appears that the translator was hurried. Usually the meaning is not impaired by the frequent mistranslation of individual words like *hrud'* (chest) which becomes 'breasts,' and *lotky* (elbows) which become 'shoulders' (both on p. 7). Occasionally, the meaning is changed as when *dokud* (while) is translated as 'so far' (p. 3) and the past becomes the present; however, it never happens in any important passages. Other such examples are on p. 8 where 'he didn't like me' is transformed into 'I don't like him,' or, on p. 9 where 'pork-belly roast' changes into a 'roll' or, on p. 11 where 'enchanted' becomes 'bewitched.' At times a line is omitted, as, for instance, on p. 20. Moreover, there are changes in repeated renditions of the same situations, which implies a deviation from the intended monotony, and similarly, the baby talk is not consistent in the translation. Nevertheless, the first translation of a work by one of the foremost Czech writers is a definite contribution to the literary scene.

Not only do the little errors he points out not affect the value of the translation, as Horrendo admits, but also most of his nitpicks are wrong or at best give evidence of not understanding the translation process. For example, in his condemnation of "so far," the good professor failed to note that this was actually the translator's addition, not a mistranslation, and that the translator's combination of "so far" and "but" at the beginning of the sentence's two clauses gave the sentence the exact same effect and meaning, only not word for word. I won't bore you with counters to the other nitpicks, but just remember that any time you see a reviewer focusing on a translator's words, except to show consistently poor word choice throughout a book, you can be sure the reviewer does not understand translation.

I do want to give one more example that shows how a reviewer's lack of understanding of translation approaches can cause him to criticize a translation for exactly what makes it so special. Richard Pevear and Larissa Volokhonsky have been trying to make classic Russian literature seem new, fresh, funnier, more what they seem to Russian readers. One of the things they do is to create new, often delightful or moving English idioms to match Russian ones, rather than simply giving the meaning of or equivalents to those idioms, as earlier translations have done. In his *New York Times Book Review* look at Pevear and Volokhonsky's translation of Nikolai Gogol's *Dead Souls*, Ken Kalfus picked out for criticism the following phrase, "neither a good nor a bad being, but simply—a burner of the daylight." Kalfus commented on the phrase "burner of daylight" as follows: "The metaphor, far from simple, is quite opaque. It's refracted from Gogol's *koptitel neba*, the noun form of a common idiom that literally means 'to smoke the sky.' That is, it literally means nothing at all. . . . One has to consult David Magarshack's 1961 translation or the Oxford Russian-English dictionary to learn that Tentetnikov is simply an 'idler.'" As if translation should do no more than a dictionary, as if Pevear and Volokhonsky didn't know what the expression meant or that it was a common idiom. And what a flat translation Kalfus preferred to such a delightful phrase. Knowing a language but not understanding translation can be even worse than not knowing anything, because it gives the reviewer the illusion that he is qualified to criticize a translation.

Enough of this; it could go on forever. Horrendo feels nitpicking has to be done or he wouldn't be doing his job. However, saying anything interesting and valuable about a translation, trying to understand it on its own terms and to let readers know what the translator is doing and how much he has succeeded, is clearly not something he feels obliged to do. And this is exacerbated by the fact that so few translators are asked to review translations; this means that few reviewers are *capable* of reviewing the translation aspects of foreign works. It's as if a gardening expert rather than an historian of landscape architecture were assigned to review a book about Italian Renaissance landscape architecture. The gardening expert might know all the plants in the gardens, but he would likely have no knowledge from which to evaluate the author's discussion of their placement in the gardens. He could point out where the author got the species wrong, but not whether his theory of garden history had any validity.

A major book review editor, who asked not to be named (it should be noted for the record that the only person I talked with who asked not to be named was a newspaper editor), told me that it is not important to have a translator review a translation, and that there are more conflicts of interest between translators than there are between specialists in an academic field. Translators see each other as competitors and all know one another, especially at the top of the profession.

Well, it is hard for me to believe that there is any group as competitive as specialists in an academic field, and I don't know of any artists who are more supportive and less competitive than translators, especially at the top of the profession. Yes, there are few jobs available for most translators, but I don't know a top translator who doesn't have a backlog of translations, because they nearly always have other jobs, especially teaching and writing. With only a few exceptions, they do one or two translations a year. Professors are protective of their approaches and reputations, because they depend on grants and seek higher positions at better universities; translators have much less to be protective of or competitive about; they know that their reputations don't travel far, that all the fame they can accumulate won't get them more than a part-time position teaching a translation class, and that there's almost no grant money available to them. No, the fact is that the fame and academic status of the reviewer is important to book review editors. Only a handful of translators have either, and these few are extremely busy people.

And despite what the book review editor told me, translators from the same language do not tend to know each other very well, except in their role as professors in the same specialty area. Few Czech translators knew each other until I organized a conference at Columbia University a few years ago, and few of them stayed in touch afterward. When once I was calling to get a German translator for a job and each time I was rebuffed asked for other names, each had no more than a couple to offer. It's specialty editors like me who know the translators, not the translators themselves. I know all of the top Czech translators, and I know of no personal animosity between any of them. In part, this may be due to the fact that they don't have to review each other's work. As it is now, the biggest problem would be an unwillingness to harshly criticize each other.

But enough of this, as well. My point is that the problem is not so much Professor Horrendo Himself as it is book review editors turning to their usual stable of professors and writers—to gardening teachers and gardeners rather than landscape architects—to review translations.

Not only are most professors and writers unable to understand translation or what a particular translator is doing, for many of them translation itself is a threat. As Willard Trask, both professor and translator, has said, echoing the words of most foreign literature professors, "I wouldn't think of reading a translation from any language that I know." And "when I want to read some Indian scripture or other, I try to get one of those old translations that are practically trots, make no pretense at being literary . . . I'd prefer to fight with something like that instead of having someone else's 'beauty' to cope with!"*

Decade after decade, professors of foreign literatures have knocked into the minds of their students, who become the next generation of professors, that literature must be read in the original, that the translation process is a tragic one filled with loss and incompetence. How could it be otherwise? If the opposite were true—if translations were every bit as valuable as the original—then there would be no need for foreign literature professors. An Elizabethan scholar's words with respect to the translation of classics still rings true today: such translations profane "the secrets of Philosophy, which are esteemed only of the learned, and neglected of the multitude. And therefore, unmeet to be made common for every man."* So it takes a brave and thoughtful professor to praise a translation for anything more than existing, being smooth, and capturing as much as possible of the original.

As for American writers, well, translations are to them what foreign cars are to Detroit: competitive imports that might change what readers are looking for, might make American writers have to work harder and put out better products. This fear often makes them fail to understand, feel ambivalent about, or even attack foreign literature. An example of an author's attack on a foreigner's approach to literature is E. L. Doctorow's review of Michael Henry Heim's translation of Milan Kundera's *The Unbearable Lightness of Being*. [Please note the format I used to describe this book; it is the proper way to refer to any translated work; yet it is far from being the norm.] Doctorow, a Romantic realist, attacked Kundera for writing "disclaimed fiction" and doing violence to the "sanctity" of the story, in other words, for not being a card-carrying realist. Doctorow's only reference to the translator was as follows: "This is a kind of conceptualist fiction, a generic-brand, no-frills fiction, at least in Michael Henry Heim's translation."* He never comes back to his implied statement that perhaps Heim is to blame for Kundera's lack of frills, an implication that's especially humorous in light of Kundera's public condemnation of Heim's frilling up of his prose. I'm not saying that Doctorow's disdain for the translator is typical, although it is shared by many writers; but I do think that his treatment of foreign literature from the point of view of American realism is typical. Like Kundera's fiction, the Czech fiction I have published makes no attempt to create three-dimensional characters. To most American writers this is a sin, and a few have criticized my authors' artistic choice as if it were a failure. Czech translators wouldn't even think of making such a ridiculous criticism, first of all, because they can place books within the context of Czech literature and second, because they have no investment in realism or in any other form of literature.

If you really want a neutral but knowledgeable reviewer, you can always turn to a translator from another language, who will understand literature as much as the average professor or writer, and will also understand translation far better. Would any editor ask someone to review a play who had disdain for actors? Or didn't understand what they did? No, I don't think there is any reason in the world for book review editors not to ask translators to review translations as much as possible, except a general disdain for and distrust of translators, their lack of typical credentials (recent books out or full professorial positions), and the fact that their names are unknown to readers of reviews.

There are two other serious problems involved in the review of translations, problems even translators face. First of all, most book review editors don't want to take space away from telling the story and evaluating the work to give readers information about the translation that they certainly aren't demanding and feel they have no use for. Editors could solve the space problem by simply giving more space to translation reviews, but since foreign literature already has a *smaller* audience than domestic literature, why should it get *more* space? Second, there isn't much in the way of standards or a vocabulary for evaluating translations. Many book review editors feel that just one adjective or adverb is not enough, but no one has come up with a better way to critique a translation.

My response to the first problem is that since a lot more goes into the production of a translation than into the production of an English-language novel or book of poetry, more should go into its review, as well. Just as publishers still do put out translations, knowing that they will lose money on them, review editors should also give up a little extra space to them, give more consideration to the qualifications of those reviewing them, encourage their reviewers to give more thought to the quality and, more important, to the *qualities* of each translation, and even pay reviewers more in order to get them to read the original or at least read *part* of the original in order to see what the translation problems are, what approach the translator is taking and why. Not as a favor—just being good literary citizens—but because, first of all, translations are important additions to our literary culture. Even if their audience is small, it's an important audience that includes writers who matter and who depend on translations, who feed off of them and who need reviews to give them an idea where to find their sustenance. Second, there is no justification for condemning an entire art to obscurity just because of space considerations. Entertainment editors offer the space for criticisms of musicians and actors, as well as for those who design the sets, and sometimes those who do the lighting and sound; why can't book review editors offer space for criticisms of translators? One of the principal reasons there's so little interest in translators is that book reviews provide so little to spark such interest.

The second problem is the really tough one. If the qualities of translations are rarely written about or discussed, how can even a translator describe a translation, not to mention evaluate it? In some ways, translation is as difficult to grasp as quantum mechanics, which David Park has referred to as "a science of qualities, not of things."* Translation is an *art* of qualities and not of things. "To write about translation is to write about one of writing's most conscious operations, one that lays open the function of writing as a manipulation of words and not of realities,"* wrote E. Rodriguez Monegal. The only relevant realities for the reviewer to grasp on to are the original work and the translation. It is a purely literary reality, a reading and a writing, without characters, plot, images, visions, that is, without nearly all the things reviewers focus on. In fact, if you were to take a typical review of literature and take out of it everything that could not be said about a translation, you might be left with nothing more than the single adverb or adjective normally used to describe a translation.

Translation is pure post-modernism, derivativeness that has no pretensions about being original. It is an incredibly serious art, brim full of responsibilities, but having nothing to do with life, not to mention our lives, except for that aesthetic aspect we don't quite know how to describe. There's no identifying with characters or, even when the reviewer is an author himself, with the author of the translation. Non-translators can only identify with the translator as reader and as laborer. And it is the ability to see in this labor the translator's vision of his responsibilities, his approach to literature, his understanding of the original, and his competence, that is necessary to produce a valuable review of a translation.

But how can reviewers be expected to understand the qualities of something without a story or lines of its own? Without standards or vocabulary? It sounds more impossible than translation, and just as poorly paid. But it's terribly important to try. Translation may not be easy to criticize, but like a translator, the reviewer has obligations, and one of these is to try to determine and express a translation's qualities and lacks. As a start, one should completely put aside the translator's accuracy, unless it rises to the level of serious incompetence. It is rare for a translator to not know what the original means, in the dictionary sense; what is much more common is for a translator to not know how to express various types and levels of meaning, how to evaluate the relative importance of preserving them, and how to write English well. The translator's ability to read and write at a professional level is what reviewers should be looking for instead.

What makes a good translation? The common wisdom is that if it reads well in English, it's a good translation. This seems positive, but behind it is a double-negative view: a good translation is something that is not written in "translationese," that is, not in awkward, overly literal language that clearly shows the translator's incompetence. Nearly all inexperienced translators write translationese. It is the result of two things working together: the lack of an ear for English and the fear of being too free with, too unfaithful to, the original. Arthur Waley described it like this: "People . . . who write very well when expressing their own ideas tend (unless they have been to some extent schooled in translation) to lose all power of normal expression when faced with a foreign text."* The effect is much like what happens to non-writers who communicate well when they talk, but clamp up when they try to put their thoughts on paper.

The common wisdom is, if there aren't too many signs of translationese, it's a good translation. It's smooth, fluent, fluid, well turned. For most reviewers, as for most editors, this is enough.

Whether it does a good job of capturing the feeling of the original, of conveying its power or humor or particular sorts of beauty —well, how are most reviewers supposed to know! The short of it is that reviewers look at how well translators write, but not at how well they read. Yet it is this ability to read that differentiates the excellent translator from the merely competent one.

One important question for the reviewer to ask himself is, what does the book review's audience want to know about a translation? Under the present circumstances, readers show little interest in knowing more about a translation than whether it is good, bad, or middling. With the exception of classics, however, does such a barebone evaluation have much effect on whether a reader picks up a book or not? My guess is that, "A middling book in a middling translation" isn't going to attract a lot of readers. However, "a great book in a middling translation" will. Readers haven't been taught to expect any more than competence. How about "a great book in a lousy translation," but where the reviewer says "the original still shines through"? This probably wouldn't have too much effect on sales; if that's the only choice, readers will probably grit their teeth and try to look through the lousy but at least non-opaque translation. The important question is, would "a middling" or even "a lousy book in a great translation" make the book more saleable? Like a lousy movie with great performances from the actors. I think this might draw some readers if it were expressed well, but the fact is, this sort of conclusion is highly rare. If a book reads well and seems great, the reviewer assumes it was translated well and that the book too was great. If a middling book has a lot going for it, yet wasn't written very well, but the translation is great and so it reads much better in English, will any reviewer notice?

This question was asked in wonder by Joe Queenan in his review of Barbara Haveland's translation from the Danish of Peter Høeg's mystery novel *The Woman and the Ape*. In reference to Høeg's earlier mystery novel, *Smilla's Sense of Snow*, translated by Tiina Nunnally, Queenan wrote (without noting the change in translators, so that the compliment was directed to the wrong one) that it was "written in prose so nuanced that most practitioners of the [mystery] genre would, well murder to be able to put such words on the page. And this was prose that most of us were reading in translation. Raising the questions: Does John Grisham read better in Danish? Could a resourceful Dutch translator make Robert Ludlum's books seem intelligent?"* The answer most translators would have supplied is Yes, Grisham couldn't read half as badly in any other language, and Ludlum might seem more intelligent. But it is likely that Danish and Dutch readers, privy to American-style reviews, would never know how much credit is due to the translators for these improvements. In fact, some Danish reviewer might have asked the same question after reading a Grisham novel in translation.

Wouldn't it be exciting to read a review that said, "The book was awkward in the original, but the translation will knock you off your feet"? But it doesn't happen. What we get instead are reviews like Victor Brombert's of Geoffrey Strachan's translation of Andrei Makine's *Dreams of My Russian Summers:* "Makine's moving novel impressed me when I read it in the original French, and it has lost none of its qualities in Geoffrey Strachan's attentive translation."* Note the double negative "has lost none of," intended to be highly complimentary but actually showing how little this professor expects from a translation, and the word "attentive," which would be the faintest of praise to any other sort of performer.

Does it really matter who gets credit for the quality of a translated work of literature? I think it does. If it didn't matter who got credit for the quality of a performance, there wouldn't be so much talk about credit to directors and actors and screenwriters. Why would people credit actors with doing as much as possible with a lousy script, or directors for getting the most out of mediocre actors? People love to write and read this sort of thing, but it's almost unknown in the world of literary translation.

Enough of this negative stuff. It's time to ask what a good criticism of translation would look like. I've dug up a couple of examples, by translators of course. First, an excerpt from David Wevill's review of two translations of poetry by Yves Bonnefoy;

second, John Felstiner's critique of Angel Flores's early translations of Pablo Neruda's poetry.

> Partly [translating Bonnefoy] is difficult because the poetry is hypnotic and this hypnosis can affect the translator to the degree that he is no longer re-creating but merely obeying. Anthony Rudolf stays closer to the text in most particulars, but 'I dare now to meet you' for 'J'ose à présent te rencontrer' is awkward, and Kinnell's 'Now I dare meet you,' though it is an approach to the problem, sounds irresolute.
>
> This awkwardness seems to be the penalty Bonnefoy's poetry exacts, if the translator is to be faithful to his meaning. The words are there, and are deceptively simple. Follow them, and you have an approximation of the French original with all its fluid shifts and precise, stepping-stone progression toward a resolution which is never quite stated. To take liberties with Bonnefoy is to get among poison ivy pretty soon. . . . Bonnefoy is not yet willing to enter the world of real objects, and the English language cannot compete with French in the middle ground between living and dead. This is not a moral or aesthetic distinction but a problem of translation. Or perhaps they are the same.*

> . . . the transit from a Spanish to an English poem tends to stall midway, failing to reactivate Neruda's palpable surprises. What results is a hybrid idiom that flattens and rationalizes Neruda's strangest creations. . . . Flores goes word by word, not taking chances though Neruda did . . .
>
> Here it is the rhythm that must bring out Neruda's logic . . . so a plain rephrasing will not quite do. Given each phrase's tentative, protracted movement in Spanish, the translator can try a similarly groping rhythm in English.
>
> Por so, en lo inmóvil, deteniéndose, percibir,
> Flores: For that reason, stopping in the immovable to
>   perceive
> Felstiner: That's why, in what's immobile, holding still, to
>   perceive

> I have in fact learned from studying Flores and bene-
> fited from his initiative. With hindsight, of course, one
> can all too easily fault earlier practitioners or forget that
> one's improvements depend on their work in the first
> place. And possibly the early stage of translating a poet
> is inevitably marked by too much fealty."*

What distinguishes these passages is their understanding of the problems of translation. They not only describe the translators' weaknesses, but put them in a valuable context. They show what is lost and why. Felstiner brings to his criticism a belief in going beyond the preservation of meaning to capture the rhythm as well, because the rhythm is basic to the logic, as basic as it is, say, to Whitman's or Dickinson's. Both critics lead the reader to think about translation while at the same time thinking about and appreciating the original. Actually, because translation is itself interpretation, a good critic can do both at one time. Here, then, is the true solution to the space problem: recognizing translation for the interpretive performance it is and approaching the original through the translation. This is much easier to do with poetry, as in these two examples, but it can also be done with literary prose.

There *are* ways to intelligently and usefully review translations, to develop a language for reviewing them. It will take knowledge-able and capable reviewers, for the most part translators, and it will take book review editors who, even if they don't understand translation, recognize its existence as an art, its value as an inter-pretive approach, and the importance of its qualities beyond the double negative of not being incompetent. This is much easier to do with major poets, such as Bonnefoy and Pablo Neruda, whose work has been translated by several translators, but it can also be done with writers whose works are translated only once.

Translator organizations have, during recent years, worked hard to get book review editors to include the translator's name in each review and have their reviewers try to say something, even if only one adverb modifying "translated," and this is done far more today than before. But it's time for book review editors to think about what more they can do to actually recognize translation as an art that exists beyond translations of Homer and Dostoevsky, to give translators at least as much space as theater reviewers give the lead actors in a play. In their choice of reviewer and in what they expect from reviewers, offering more space and cash, they can do a lot more than this book in bringing the art of translation to the attention of literate Americans. They can start by insisting that no translated work is mentioned anywhere without the translator's name, and by facing the fact that they, along with publishers and translators themselves, are most responsible for the status quo, in which translators can look forward to being either belittled, faintly praised, or ignored.

Ignored. It could be argued that it's better to be recognized and misunderstood than to simply be ignored. I've been talking about reviewers who do give at least some space to the translation aspect of a translated work of literature, but in most cases nothing at all is said, or there's just that one adverb or adjective. Often there isn't much to be said, for example, where what's being translated is straightforward nonfiction or genre writing. However, most of the fiction and poetry translated into English is special: style is important, something new is done, and therefore a workmanlike effort is not sufficient to bring over those special aspects of the original that actually can be brought over.

For some hard statistics, here is how Catbird's translations have been reviewed. I broke the reviews down into length and amount of criticism. For length, the categories are short, medium, long, and prepublication (that is, short reviews intended strictly for libraries and bookstores, not for readers); for amount of criticism, the categories are nothing, one adverb or adjective, two to three words or phrases, and more than this. Here's how it looks:

Short - 6 nothing, 7 one, 1 two-three, 0 more
Medium - 8 nothing, 2 one, 0 two-three, 2 more
Long - 9 nothing, 3 one, 2 two-three, 2 more
Prepub. -17 nothing, 3 one, 1 two-three, 0 more

Total - 40 nothing, 15 one, 4 two-three, 4 more

Percentages - 63% nothing, 24% one, 6% two-three,
    6% more
Post-publication Percentages - 55% nothing, 29% one, 7%
    two-three, 9% more

To summarize, only about a third of the time (although nearly half
in post-publication reviews) did reviewers have anything to say
about the translation, and only one out of eight times (one out of
six post-publication) was it more than a single adverb or adjective.
Single words included fluent, fluid, ably, well, jauntily, stalwartly,
competent, deft, beautifully, and good. Two-to-three-words-or-
phrases included "skillful if at times too literal," "in Mr. Harkins'
supple translation, it's clear that Mr. Páral can write like an angel,"
and "smooth and colloquial." The four reviews that used more than
three descriptive words or terms included Professor Horrendo's
review in *Slavic and East European Journal*; a very long review in
The Nation by a British writer who was ecstatically happy to see
good translations of Karel Čapek's work finally appear in English;
a British professor's review in *World Literature Today* of a book
that was translated for the second time, comparing translations
(more praising the new than analyzing); and a review of two over-
lapping anthologies in the *San Francisco Bay Guardian*, in which
two translations were compared (using one verb and one adjective)
and one translator was actually referred to as the "leader of what
[the anthology] calls 'the new generation'" of Czech-into-English
translators. So, out of 63 reviews there wasn't a single analysis of
a translation, and the four reviewers who actually took more than
passing notice of translation included a British writer who adores
the author and was every bit as passionate about the new translations as the translators were, a British professor who's writing a
critical work on the author and who is acquainted with the translator, the Canadian Professor Horrendo, and one American whose
analysis was limited to one adjective and one verb. None of these,
by the way, appeared in what are normally considered major book
review publications. And only one review was, to my knowledge,
written by a Czech-into-English translator (it was a short, pre-pub-

lication review, and didn't say anything about the translator), and only two were by translators from other languages (one used one adverb in a medium review, the other—I don't think very experienced—said nothing in a medium review). Which only shows that, under current circumstances, you can't even trust translators to stand up for translators. Or even put them down. Or maybe it's just that editors often cut out what reviewers write about translations; there's only so much space, after all.

The surprising thing is that five of the translations Catbird has published are new translations of classic works, including a novel that is still widely taught and one of the most anthologized European plays of the century (an entire scholarly article was devoted to the horrors of the old translation/adaptation compared to the new). Karel Čapek is not Dostoevsky, at least in terms of American fame, but one still expects more talk about translation when a work is re-translated than when it is translated for the first time.

Eliot Weinberger told me that his *Collected Poems of Octavio Paz*, merely one of the few living Nobel Prize-winning poets and one of the most popular poets in the U.S., received about 100 reviews. "Of those 100 reviews, 90 did not mention me at all. And this is a book of poetry. They quote the poems, but they don't even mention that it was translated, that somebody did it. And then about six more had one word to describe me, like 'in the excellent translation,' 'in the workmanlike translation,' 'in the mediocre translation,' 'in the fluent translation,' 'in the clumsy translation.' And then there were about two or three that actually had a few more things to say about the translation. It doesn't register at all. . . . It's completely invisible."

The fact is that except with respect to new translations of very major works, little or nothing is written for the general reader or even the general scholar about translations or translators. While an author's previous works (or an actor's previous films, for that matter) are often mentioned, it is almost unheard of for a review to mention a translator's previous works. Reviewers never note that a translator might be over the hill or reaching new heights, nor that he has finally found his perfect match or that he is unfit for a particular author. Reviewers aren't asked to read earlier translations by the translator, and a translator is not pictured as an artist with a career or with particular skills and weaknesses. This is simply not part of the similarly underpaid job of reviewing.

To get better reviews, there would have to be a major change in attitude among publishers (presenting their translations as translations and their translators as artists with a history, with special abilities, with an interesting approach, like any artist is presented in the game of publicity), among book review editors (devoting a little more space to translation reviews, possibly paying a little more for them, seeking out translators to review translations, asking reviewers to look at earlier translations and to think about translation issues, even sending out a short list of sample questions and considerations to get the reviewer thinking), and among professors and writers and even translators who are assigned translations to review (recognizing their obligation to treat translation as something that is actually there and even important, and learning how to use the translation as a way to examine the original).

I think this should, in the short run, be considered a subject for affirmative action, making up for centuries of prejudice and neglect, going out of one's way to pay special attention to translations, not in the usual patronizing single-adverb way, but with thought and an attempt to understand and elucidate. Once this became the norm—a dream if I ever heard one—then reviewers could relax and limit their special attention to situations where the translation seems especially important or interesting, which, once it was generally accepted that the art of translation is interesting, may turn out to be a lot more often than people think. In fact, someday there might be biographies of translators, societies of translation critics, televised award ceremonies, a hall of fame in Cleveland or Canton or Kansas City.

Awards are one way translators do receive publicity, although translation awards do not receive anything like the attention given to awards for other literary and performing artists. The most promi-

nent translation awards include those given by PEN American Center: the PEN/Book-of-the-Month Club Translation Prize for a book-
length translation, the PEN Award for Poetry in Translation for a
book of poetry in translation, and the PEN/ Ralph Manheim Medal
for Translation, a lifetime achievement award; one given by PEN
West: the Elinor D. Randall Prize for Literary Translation; one
from the Academy of American Poets: the Harold Morton Landon
Award for poetry translation; two Modern Language Association
translation awards, both called Aldo & Jeanne Scaglione Prizes, one
for literary works, one for scholarly works; the ALTA Outstanding
Translations of the Year awards, which go to between three and
twenty books a year, including fiction, poetry, and nonfiction
(ALTA also gives awards to young translators for works in progress); and the American Translators Association's Lewis Galantière
Prize for translations from any language but German (not prejudice, but there's also an ATA German Literary Translation Prize).
The other major translation prize used to be a National Book
Award for translation, but that no longer exists. The National
Endowment for the Humanities has awarded grants primarily to
professors doing rather obscure, although academically important
translation projects, and it has supported fellowships to the Center
for Research in Translation at SUNY Binghamton. Several of these
translation awards are very new. A list of their winners appears in
an appendix to this book, so that readers can get a feel for who
are the prominent contemporary translators.

Most awards, however, are given for translations from a
particular language, and most of these are given by or associated
with foreign governments that want to spread their culture around
the world. For example, since 1996 the Goethe-Institut, the
German government's cultural presence around the world, has
awarded the Helen and Kurt Wolff Prize for a translation from
German into English. The prize, which is given by the Chicago
branch, is named in honor of the couple who founded Pantheon
Books, which was devoted primarily to publishing translations from
German and other European languages. Other such awards include
the American-Scandinavian Foundation Translation Prize, the

French-American Foundation Translation Prize, the Friendship Commission Prize for the Translation of Japanese Literature, the Korean Literature Translation Prize, the Raiziss/de Palchi Translation Award for translations of Italian poetry, PEN's Gregory Kolovakos Awards for translators and critics whose work brings Hispanic literatures to English-language readers, and PEN's Renato Poggioli Translation Award for a first-book translation-in-progress from Italian. Some foreign governments also award grants to American publishers to cover all or part of their translation costs.

There are also international prizes, including the most recent one, the Karel Čapek Prize, named after my house's leading author, who in his youth was a translator of French poetry into Czech, and there are British prizes dependent on publication in the U.K., not on the nationality of the translator. Most of the British prizes are tied to a specific original language, as well.

You might wonder how anybody could judge translations from all sorts of languages they don't know, especially considering that there aren't any standards for judging translations even from languages one does know. Well, it ain't easy. Krishna Winston, who has judged the MLA literary prize, told me, "I didn't really have time to consciously work out criteria. I trusted my intuition. I would be able to tell whether a book was poorly or well translated, no matter what language it was from." But in talking with her and with other translators, there did turn out to be general agreement as to criteria. Winston told me, "There were only a few translations that really stood out as extraordinary in my mind. . . . [I was interested in] the convincing quality of the prose, and the sense that when there was strangeness it was intentional . . . The significance of the work figured in." Gregory Rabassa, who happens to have served on the same panel with Ms. Winston, told me, "I would tend to look with favor on a hard job done well. Some things translate easily. The other is the book itself. We don't make a silk purse out of a sow's ear." And Rosanna Warren told me, "You're judging people's writing in English. . . . You're also judging, inevitably, the choice of an interesting author, and one's choice can't help but be incredibly, in the worst sense, contaminated. But do I think translation prizes should be abolished. No, I think translation should be encouraged, and one way to encourage it is through prizes and publicity. . . . For all the nonsense in selecting and the inevitable kinds of compromises that go into selection, I still am in favor of it." That's really what it boils down to. Fiction doesn't need a Pulitzer Prize, but translation needs its awards. They may not be well known, they may be hard to judge, but they're all translators have got.

Now that I'm done dumping on the effect reviewers and book review editors have had on the translator's public image, it's time to move on to publishers, and then end up with the worst culprits of all, translators themselves.

With the exception of some small presses and some individuals at big and university presses (most of them translators themselves), the American publishing industry has little knowledge of or interest in translators, or translation. In the scheme of things, translators stand below illustrators, editors of anthologies, even many ghost writers and freelance copy editors. The only people who also are shown little respect are the authors of midlist books (that is, books that are not expected to sell over 10,000 copies), who often have trouble getting calls returned from publicity and marketing people assigned to their books. For publishing people other than interested editors, *translation* translates as "deep in the red."

The status of the translator in the publisher's eye can be seen clearly by how his presence is hidden. The translator's name is rarely put on the front of a jacket or cover, where every author, every editor, and most illustrators' names are placed. Sometimes the translator's name doesn't appear anywhere on the jacket or cover, only on the title page. When you balance the translator's value (almost nobody will be inclined to buy a book because of who the translator is) against the possible harm to sales from advertising that a book is in translation (that something important is lost, that the book is somehow not authentic, that the book is foreign and difficult perhaps) and against the graphic designer's deep hatred for text in a front-cover design, it's no surprise that publishers do what they do. It's simply not good business to care about the translator, and no one wants to piss off graphic designers, whose skills sell a hell of a lot more books than translators' (which is why no jacket or cover omits the graphic designer's name, even though they are generally much younger, less skilled, paid less per book, and spend on each book only a tiny fraction of the time a translator spends—and even though readers couldn't care less who they are either).

The author tour, from city to city, store to store, library to library, with media appearances along the way, is an important part of marketing a literary work. But how many translators are sent on tour? Even when the foreign author is unavailable or unable to speak English, translators are rarely sent on tour. Occasionally, translators might tag along as interpreters, reading their translations aloud while the author stands there playing the role of living authenticity. It's a smart thing to do, because no matter how fluent in English a foreign author is, when he reads aloud, his accent and his inability to get the cadence right make him very hard to understand.

Publishers will insist that translators aren't a draw. Of course not; their publishers haven't tried to make them draws. They hide their names, they're embarrassed they exist. They don't do press releases for them, they don't get them on talk shows or get features written about them, and they do their best to keep their names out of advertisements, even when the translator has obtained a clause in his contract requiring this. How many publishers ever insist that their translators' names are included, not to mention prominently displayed, in their own catalogs, in other companies' book or gift catalogs (even a highly intelligent book catalog such as Daedalus often leaves out the translator's name), in displays, flyers, press releases, and all the rest of the paraphernalia that makes up promotion campaigns? How many publishers try to educate their employees, in marketing, sales, publicity, design, rights and permissions, and, most important, finance, about the value of translators? A well-written internal memo might do wonders to let people know that translators are to be respected rather than despised or ignored. Publishers could bring a couple of translators in to meet their sales representatives, bring them to trade fairs to meet bookstore buyers, have them tag along on calls to book review editors, try to get features written about them in local newspapers, stick a couple of pictures of them in catalogs. If one major publisher did it, it would stand out. It would tell the publishing world it has pride in its translators, that its translators are the best, as is their foreign literature, and that they're putting their time and money where their mouth is. Then other publishers would copy them, and maybe some day translators would be treated as part of the team, rather than as water boys. And *then* people might actually come see translators perform their performances.

But as I warned, the biggest culprits of all in creating the public image of the translator are the victims themselves. Translators bitch about their status, but they don't act as if they feel they deserve any more. Too rarely do American translators write prefaces or afterwords that explain their approach to the work at hand, even when it's poetry or a difficult work of prose. They are more likely to write a short essay about the author and the book, to give the reader background material, a context from which to better appreciate the book. What is rare is giving the reader background material and a context from which to better appreciate the translation, or discussing alternative ways the translation might have been done. It's hard to expect reviewers to understand what the translator is trying to do with his translation, or what problems he overcame, without being told straight out, at least now, when there is so little appreciation of the art of literary translation. A reviewer faced with a good translator's preface cannot so easily ignore the translator's role in the creation of the book he's reviewing.

Probably the best writer of such prefaces is Lawrence Venuti, who feels they are crucial to making the translator a visible artist.

Here's an excerpt from the introduction to his translation of I. U. Tarchetti's *Passion:**

> I culled a lexicon, syntax, punctuation, and orthography from the nineteenth century British novel, drawing up lists of words and phrases from such related works as Bram Stoker's *Dracula* (1897). But I mixed them with more recent usages, both standard and colloquial, some distinctly American. The aim was to immerse the reader in a world that is noticeably distant in time, but nonetheless affecting in contemporary terms—to compel a participation in the emotional extravagance that drives this wildly romantic novel, but without losing the awareness that the prose is over the top. The proof of the pudding should be a vaguely familiar flavor, followed by a slight queasiness.

It's true that many publishers wouldn't approve something like this, except in the case of re-translations of classics, and it is highly unlikely that a publisher would ask for such a thing (I can't say that I've done this myself, although I'm going to start), but most small and university presses, as well as some of the more thoughtful editors at larger houses, would allow it and often even welcome it. But you usually can't force someone to do this sort of thing.

There are other excellent prefaces, some of which I've quoted from in this book, but even these tend more toward the personal than the explanatory or analytical. Venuti's are enlightening both about his translation and about the work, because his approach is a reaction to the author's approach, to what the author was trying to do. Note that I said "reaction," not copying, because Venuti's goals are often different from his authors'. Yet he respects his authors' goals and seeks a sort of integrity between the two sets of goals.

Venuti has written a book entitled *The Translator's Invisibility*, which consists of a scholarly, historical, and theoretical approach to just what I'm talking about here: the translator's public image as someone who is essentially invisible to the reading public. The ultimate translator's attitude toward his invisibility is stated clearly by William Weaver, ironically one of the most visible of all translators due to his essays, translation diaries, appearances, and that most elusive of states for the translator, name recognition. Weaver told Venuti, when "a reviewer neglects to mention the translator at all, the translator should take this omission as a compliment: it means that the reviewer simply wasn't aware that the book had been written originally in another language. For a translator, this kind of anonymity can be a real achievement."* This Romantic concept of the translator's self-effacing role was well stated by the British translator John Hookham Frere in a preface to one of his classical translations in 1840: "The language of translation ought, we think, as far as possible, to be a pure, impalpable and invisible element, the medium of thought and feeling, and nothing more; it ought never to attract attention to itself."*

Venuti considers this attitude "a self-annihilation, ultimately contributing to the cultural marginality and economic exploitation which translators suffer today."* This self-annihilation seems to go hand-in-hand with the translator's role as submissive partner to the author, being the conduit for the author's aesthetic and philosophical ideas. But it's not necessary to play this role both in the actual writing and outside of it. It's not necessary to take pride in being ignored, because being ignored isn't really a compliment, it's simply a reflection of ignorance or laziness on the part of the reviewer. Hell, there's nothing easier than ignoring someone's artistic capabilities when all the people involved in the business and the culture are ignoring them as well, and when translators themselves are hardly standing there waving their hands. It takes courage, not to mention energy and understanding, for a reviewer to take note, to say not just, "Job well done," but in what way the job was well done.

Otherwise you end up with people like the journalist who wrote about a reading of Octavio Paz's poetry by his translator at the Cathedral of St. John the Divine in New York City. According to the translator, Eliot Weinberger, the journalist wrote, "Octavio Paz's metaphors had my mind soaring through the sky, even though his words were being translated by an interpreter." According to this view, the fact of translation makes the author that much greater, because his poetry can survive the shift in languages; it doesn't make the translator great at all.

The fact is that most translators don't want to be thought of as great. They're also part of our culture, they're also Romantics at heart, who believe that it is their responsibility to bring over the author's greatness as competently as they can. They realize how hard it is; most of them are constantly teaching students and seeing how terrible a job even the better students do. They're also asked to vet lesser translators' work. They know how good they are; they don't need anyone to tell them, they don't need the kind of applause a writer needs, because they're not putting themselves on the line in the same way. But neither is a musician, and applause doesn't sound bad to them. Perhaps it is simply the fact that translators don't get any applause, and therefore don't expect it, that they have chosen to see their invisibility as a positive thing, even as a goal. It's consistent with their position, with their work, and it certainly reflects their treatment by the press, by their publishers, often by their authors and their friends. They are doing a job, they are doing their best, and when the result is praised, even if in the name of the author, they know it was their doing. The flip side of everyone's ignorance about translation is that the translator knows he knows better. He is superior. What more can anyone ask?

And then there is the joy I keep talking about. Ellen Watson has done her share of acting, and so for her, acting is the performance metaphor she uses to describe translation: "Getting inside that original author and doing what you do in your body, in your language, that's an exhilarating feeling, even if you're not on stage in front of 500,000 people."

Since theirs is a life of suffering and ecstasy, maybe what translators need is to canonize a few saints. They already have St. Jerome, translator of the Latin Bible. They could add William Tyndale, the first translator of the Bible into English, who before he could finish the Old Testament was tried for heresy and publicly strangled to death in October 1536. His words to an educated acquaintance, spoken even before he began his translation work, could be paraphrased and placed at the top of a flyer to all foreign literature professors: "If God spare my life, ere many years I will cause a boy that driveth the plough to know more of the Scripture than thou doest." And possibly the words of Mervyn Jannetta, head of the English Antiquarian Section at the British Library, might be placed beneath them: "It's puzzled people that [Tyndale] should have got it right and done it single-handedly, and in such a short space of time. And in such adversity. It wasn't as if he was on a government grant."*

Translators could add a more recent saint, Hitoshi Igarashi, a Japanese scholar who in July 1991 was stabbed to death for translating Salman Rushdie's *Satanic Verses*. The book's Italian translator, Ettore Caprioli, could get an honorable mention for having survived a similar attack nine days before.

But what translators really should be doing is getting out there. They could tell their editors they want their name on the front cover, and that they want a little paragraph about their work on the back flap of the jacket, like authors and illustrators get, and that they want a list of books they've translated up front, underneath the list of the author's books. They could write translator's prefaces, explaining their approach to the particular book, even suggesting other ways the book might have, or has been, approached, so that the reader has some context from which to intelligently read what they've done. They could tell their editors that they want to make appearances at bookstores and in the media, if possible. And if their publisher's promotion department isn't willing to do such a thing, they could make arrangements themselves, and send a bill for expenses to their editor. I work with a translator, Norma Comrada, who sets up book signings and talks in her area, and she has been featured, as a translator, in her local daily newspaper as well as in the state's major daily. It can be done, but very few translators try.

When their books receive translation prizes, translators could insist that their publisher add something to the front cover of their book letting people know. This could even be done for other books by that translator. Publishers don't think this sort of award sells books, and they're right, because few readers even know there are such things as translation awards, not to mention which translators have won them.

Translators could also write to local and national book review editors, asking to be considered for reviews of books in translation from their language(s) and also from other languages, if they're interested. In their letter, they could explain the advantages of having a translator review a translation, and they might even consider including a sample to show what they mean. Translators can't expect book review editors to attain enlightenment all on their own.

But first of all, translators could try to figure out what it is they're doing. As Edwin Honig wrote, "It's very hard to get working translators to say what they really think translation is for, or about."* Are they writers or performers? Lawrence Venuti told me that the central question is, "How can the translator be recognized as a writer?" I think trying to be recognized as a writer is part of the problem, not the solution. And beyond this, do translators want to be left alone or do they want to be recognized for their skills and what they produce? Do they want to be professionals churning out translations for a living, or do they want to be able to translate good literature for not so good pay?

The fact is that translators do what they do for a host of reasons, and they think they're doing it for a host of purposes. But they tend to think in terms of individual projects rather than in terms of their art. It's ironic that although translation is an extremely self-conscious artistic act done by exceptionally self-conscious people, these same practitioners do not take the time to figure out what it is they're doing or what they want out of it in terms of recognition. They certainly seem to want more money for what they do, but that is really the last thing they should expect, because what they're doing isn't about money and they're not doing any of the things money-seeking artists do, things like trying to get well-known, networking, selling out.

*   *   *

The best places for translators to start asking these questions and setting some sort of agenda are their organizations: the American Literary Translators Association, the literary section of the American Translators Association, the Translation Committees of PEN American Center and PEN West, and regional translator associations. Other good places include the translation centers at the University of Texas at Dallas, at SUNY Binghamton, at Boston University and other schools. However, because so many of the people who are active in these organizations and centers (other than PEN) are professors, their discussions tend toward the theoretical and they tend to talk amongst themselves rather than reaching out to include authors, editors, agents, marketing people in the publishing industry, foreign publishers, and the like. PEN's Translation Committee includes not only translators, but also editors, literary agents, and even marketing people with an interest in translation. And it's no wonder that many successes, such as the PEN Translators Handbook and getting translators listed on library cards, have come from the tiny PEN Translation Committee rather than the national organizations.

The organization with the most literary translators is the American Literary Translators Association, which was founded only in the late 1970s. ALTA is, however, relatively unprofessional, and it seems to be uninterested in getting many publishers to participate in its conferences or in carrying on an effective dialogue with the publishers who do attend. I have been to a couple of ALTA conferences myself, as one of only a handful of publishers (the others primarily university presses), and I have found little interest in the sort of networking with buyers that goes on in every other industry and, for that matter, art. It's as if hundreds of painters got together for an annual conference and asked only a handful of the lowest-paying gallery owners to attend, and then ignored the gallery owners to talk about art and politics, and how hard it is to get people to buy their work.

The other place where discussions can begin, but where they

should not stay, is in such translation-oriented publications as *Translation Review*, out of the University of Texas at Dallas, edited by Rainer Schulte, *Exchanges* out of the University of Iowa Translation Workshop and Laboratory, and *Modern Poetry in Translation*, both edited by Daniel Weissbort, and the many little journals that come and go, such as Stanford's *Two Lines*. Again, as long as the discussions stay in these rarified places, they will have little effect on the translator's public image. They need to use these fora to work out what they want and to raise translators' consciousnesses before getting their developed ideas out into the more general media, not just in the form of essays, but in the form of action as well.

And they need to start acting more professional. One of the main reasons translators aren't taken seriously is that most of them are amateurs. Translation is not what they do for a living and not what they base their identity on. Few Americans, when asked at a cocktail party, "What do you do?", ever answer, "I'm a literary translator." It's one of the nice things about translation, but also one of the most limiting ones in terms of their public image and their commitment to improving it.

Of course, this is also one of the things that make translators special. Translators are the nicest and most intelligent group of people I've ever had the pleasure to know. Nearly every interview I did with them was a great joy, not just in terms of conversation, but also in terms of hospitality, making arrangements, and the like. Translators have the intelligence of academics without the arrogance and ideologies. The professors among them do not tend to be wielders of power in academe; they tend to be the sort of people who go about their business, teach their classes, work with their grad students, and do their translations. They have the sensibility of artists without the egos and the obsessions. They worship the beautiful, but they see themselves as serving the beautiful rather than being or creating the beautiful. Even though they do impart a great deal of it.

Their being amateurs becomes a problem when they *act* like amateurs, when they feel that doing the work is enough, that they have no responsibilities beyond the keyboard and the classroom, no obligation to promote their books or themselves. Writers can get away with hiding out, but how many performing artists can? Actors and singers tend to go too far in promoting themselves. Translators, and their organizations, need to do more if they want to be considered performing artists. It might seem crude, and at first it will definitely be difficult, but it's the American way, and without at least trying, translators have only themselves to blame for being invisible.

I hope this book will give translators some ammunition with which to argue their case, that is, to show people that matter—publishers, professors, book review editors and others in the media, bookstore personnel, librarians, and readers—why translation matters, why it matters that it's done well, what it takes for it to be done well, what being done well means, and what can be done to better recognize the best artists in the field. Translators can show how difficult it is to be good at what they do (and, while they're at it, explain what they do); they can explain that they are performers rather than creators and should be treated, criticized, and rewarded as such; they can explain that being faithful is not what translation is about, but rather that they have to be polygamists balancing a number of obligations, and how recent and dubious the idea of fidelity to content is; they can explain that translation involves a two-part act: (i) a close reading to deeply understand, to interpret, to become intimate with a work of art, the way an actor becomes intimate with a character; and (ii) the performance of the work of art in a language it was never intended for (whereas a character is intended to be played by an actor); and they can show how valuable the study of translation can be not only for translators, but also for aspiring literary critics and writers.

They can even talk about their work at cocktail parties, rather than assuming people will begin to yawn. It's a lot better than hearing about somebody's latest litigation or operation. Think how much you'd enjoy listening to a musician talk about the way he was planning to play a violin sonata at a concert that weekend. Or an actor's take on a new play he was in. Ellen Watson, a translator who worked in a bookstore, right on the front lines, told me, "I see people who come in, the kind of people that read the book reviews and decide what books to read . . . when I have a conversation with someone like that, they get very interested in the idea of what a translator does. 'My God, I never thought about that; every single word, you have to decide what to do with it!' When you start talking about it, people *are* interested." If you're not a translator and happen to run into one, open him up, make him talk, give him the ol' third degree!

If you are a translator, you could try starting a literary conversation with some form of John Felstiner's words: "At times, it even seems (to the enthusiast, at least) that only those insights feeding into or deriving from the task of translation are exactly legitimate, germane to the poem."* This might seem arrogant, but is it any more arrogant than the literary critic's similar belief?

Like any publicist, or even person, translators can try to focus on the gains rather than the losses of their chosen art. Josef Škvorecký has found that Dickens' magic is lost on his English-speaking literature students in Canada, "yet if a good translation of *Little Dorrit* or *David Copperfield* preserves Dickens' original freshness, its effect on the foreign reader may be comparable to the enthusiasm of the crowds that, a century ago, used to wait at newsstands for a new installment of Boz's latest melodrama."* All around the world people are seeing a Shakespeare who speaks their language, whose jokes they understand, whose words their actors can speak with authority. Translations, even translations of Shakespeare, can be *more* effective, *more* moving, *more* humorous than the original, which is why Shakespeare is the most performed dramatist in France, Germany, and even Japan. Translations aren't something to apologize for, to be depressed about, to attack.

Translators go against economic and social theories in being capable, sometimes even great artists, without much pay, without any fame, and without a hope in the world of winning the pot of gold at the end of every other art's rainbow. Translators can safely say, I'm better than I *should be*. How many other artists can say this? Translators deserve to brag. At first, people might think they're obnoxious braggarts, but eventually they'll assume that they're simply professionals or artists, who are expected to be obnoxious braggarts.

The goal in all of this is what Lawrence Venuti told me: "in order to see the translator in the text, to become aware of a translation as a translation, ultimately it requires a detached critical appreciation of form. You have to realize that there's another text here . . . In order to make the translator visible, the reader needs to be taught a new way of reading."

Venuti doesn't mean that readers need to learn to critique translation. What needs to happen is for readers to learn to *listen* to translations, to appreciate distinctions, to enjoy different approaches, not necessarily be able to articulate the differences. Just as we listen to jazz soloists and appreciate the differences between the way, say, Miles Davis and Dizzy Gillespie approach the same tune, enjoying the differences even though most of us couldn't say exactly what those differences are. It's not so clear with translator's approaches, but if readers—especially close readers such as writers and critics—tried to appreciate such differences and to reward them with increased sales and better reviews, the differences between translators' approaches would grow, and publishers would even start encouraging translators to take chances, to be more individual, while still respecting the original and preserving the work's vision and integrity.

I think that translators are the ones that should lead the way toward this awareness of translation, not because it's their responsibility, but because they're the only ones in a position to do it, the only ones who have the awareness and the ability to articulate it. It seems that this is being done more in Great Britain and in bilingual Canada than in the U.S., or at least it is involving a larger percentage of translators there, but it seems to be more involved with theory than with practicality. It is, as Terry Hale, a British translator, told ALTA members in 1995, a "discourse." But I think that translators who want to be seen need to go beyond discourse among a small, closed circle of specialists. It seems, for instance, that no one but me can write a book about translation without going on about the German theorist Walter Benjamin, but almost everyone can write about translation without mentioning John Felstiner, whose ideas and experiences have far more to do with actual translation and with the visibility of translators. (For those who must know, Benjamin wrote an essay, "The Task of the Translator," about the *Ur*-language that lies behind all languages and which all translations must pass through with absolute fidelity, to form rather than to meaning; this is a highly simplified summary of a complex, highly idealistic essay that deconstructionists and others have passionately embraced and placed at the center of their debates.)

What I think is the most important task for American translators today is to ask themselves a lot of questions. Such as, Why do translators see their work as more of a service than actors and musicians do? Is translation really about self-denial rather than performance? Why can't a great translator be given not only credit, but precedence over a young, unknown author? (And why is it that translators only get top billing when they're translating authors far greater than they can ever hope to be?) Is there something subversive about translation—about what translation brings into our culture, about the fact that its effect on literature is formal rather than philosophical—that might be taken out from under the bed and made to be something closer to a rallying cry? Is translation truly as valuable a way to read and write literature as translators think it is, and if so, how can it become more prevalent in teaching, writing, and publishing? Are there criteria or standards that distinguish good and great translations from mediocre ones, and how can translators start a valuable discussion about them, so that reviewers, not to mention readers, professors, and aspiring translators, will have some guidance? Is it important to take the word "translation" away from the deconstructionists, to goad them into recognizing translation in its own right and not primarily as a metaphor for their cause? Would it be valuable to put forward one translator as the Pavarotti of translation, to market translation by first marketing that translator?

I suppose that's enough questions for one paragraph. Getting people to actually see translation is a tough row to hoe, so tough that all I could do is turn a little earth here and there and hope that earthworms will do the rest. It's hard enough to get writers, not to mention readers, to take notice of translation. Perhaps one famous American writer should come out and say what the French novelist André Gide said back in 1928: that if he were Napoleon, he would require every man of letters in France to translate a foreign work related to his own talents in the hope of raising respect for translation.* But how many famous American writers are in the position this translator of *Hamlet* was in?

Here's what lovers of translation are faced with: an art that has little if any identity (it doesn't even know that it's a performing art!) and that is not the basis for almost anyone's identity (how many people consider themselves connoisseurs of translation?), that is the unconsumable foreground of a palimpsest, that is not supported in the way most arts are supported, by foundations, patrons, or audiences, that isn't written about except for experts, that has no criteria or standards, no rewards or fame. On the other hand, think how much translators can accomplish that no other group of artists can: they can introduce people to their art, give it an identity, create taste in it, seek support, write about it for the public, and work on creating standards. Translators could even expand the audience for their work, and by doing so increase what they're paid. How could a form-oriented art prosper at a time of conceptual art, realism, memoirs, confessionals, and testimonies? It won't come easy; the odds and forces in the publishing industry are all against it. But then, translation itself is impossible, so what are a few more windmills to tilt against?

"Poetry is that which is worth translating," says Eliot Weinberger. "I'd be lost without translation," says Peter Glassgold. Who's afraid of Robert Frost, a guy who couldn't even translate? Maybe the first thing translators need to do is burn him in effigy.

Recommended Reading

I wouldn't have written this book if there had been any good surveys of literary translation for a general audience. There *are*, however, books that will be of interest to people who have made it through this book and, as readers, translators, writers, editors, critics, or literature students, would like to learn and think more about some aspects of translation.

The best books that do exist are anthologies of essays. Unfortunately, most of the translators who write these essays are writing for people like themselves, so that their nitty gritty studies of particular translation problems can be deadly dull, and their theoretical flights can be very demanding or even meaningless to the uninitiated. But some of the anthologies are excellent, particularly the historically oriented ones and a couple on the craft aspects. A star before the title means that the book is in print.

The classic anthology is Reuben A. Brower's classically named *On Translation* (Harvard University Press, 1959), PN241.B7. It's a mishmash of essays by very distinguished translators, including Nida, Fitts, Lattimore, the Muirs, Nabokov, Poggioli, and Hollander (for the more linguistically and philosophically oriented, there are even essays by Quine and Jakobson).

But for the beginner who's simply fascinated with literary translation and the people who do it, the best place to start is my most cited book, Edwin Honig's *The Poet's Other Voice: Conversations on Literary Translation* (University of Massachusetts Press, 1985), PN1059.T7.P6. It consists of eleven interviews with people who have done a lot of thinking about translation, including Hollander, Trask, Belitt, Wilbur, Fitzgerald, Keeley, Paz, Hamburger, and Middleton.

To get an historical overview of translation, you can turn to three excellent anthologies of essays and prefaces by translators from the classical era to today. Two are edited by John Biguenet and Rainer Schulte: *The Craft of Translation* (University of Chicago Press, 1989) P306.C73, and *Theories of Translation* (University of Chicago Press, 1992) P306.T453x. The other is André Lefevere and and Susan Bassnett-McGuire's *Translation/History/Culture: A Sourcebook* (Routledge, 1992) P306.T735x.

And for a close-up look at the decision-making process involved in translating poetry, the best collection is Daniel Weissbort's *Translating

Poetry: The Double Labyrinth (University of Iowa Press, 1989) PN1059. T7I73.

There are several other essay anthologies of value, especially William Frawley's *Translation: Literary, Linguistic, and Philosophical Perspectives* (University of Delaware Press, 1984) P306.T742; another classic collection, William Arrowsmith and Roger Shattuck's *The Craft and Context of Translation* (1961) PN241.A74; Rosanna Warren's **The Art of Translation: Voices from the Field* (Northeastern University Press, 1989) PN241.A76; **The World of Translation* (A PEN Club Symposium, 1970) PN241.C6; *Across the Language Gap: Proceedings of the 28th Annual Conference of the American Translators Association*, ed. Karl Kummer (1987) P306.A65; and Marilyn Gaddis Rose's **Translation Horizons* (Center for Research in Translation, 1996) and *Translation Spectrum* (SUNY Albany Press, 1981) P306.T743. On the more theoretical side, there's Lawrence Venuti's **Rethinking Translation* (Routledge, 1992) P306.R468x; Edwin Gentzler's **Contemporary Translation Theories* (Routledge, 1993) P306.G44X; and Joseph F. Graham's *Difference in Translation* (Cornell University Press, 1985) P306.D45, all of them anthologies as well.

The only general history of translation in English is Louis G. Kelly's *The True Interpreter: A History of Translation Theory and Practice in the West* (St. Martins, 1979) P306.K45. This is still a relatively uncharted area, and one reason why there's less history in my book than I would have liked. There are many other historical studies, but they are more specific, and most of the relatively general ones are rather old. One interesting example is C. H. Conley's *The First English Translators of the Classics* (Yale University Press, 1927).

There are few books by single authors about their experiences as translators. There are none of the usual autobiographies or memoirs that accompany every other performing art (nor are there biographies or critical works focused on a single translator or group of translators). There aren't even essay collections by a single author where the major focus is translation from a doing rather than a critical standpoint, although a collection of Edmund Keeley's essays is scheduled for publication around the same time as this book, by Harwood Academic Press.

There are, however, two fascinating books by John Felstiner, one on translating Pablo Neruda (**Translating Neruda: The Way to Macchu Picchu* (Stanford University Press, 1981) PQ8097.N47.A763), the other on translating Paul Celan (**Paul Celan: Poet, Survivor, Jew* (Yale University Press, 1995) PT2605.E4Z599). Each of the books, and especially the latter, mix writing about translation with biographical and literary criticism; the result is a fresh and enlightening take on literature. And there is also Suzanne Jill Levine's *The Subversive Scribe* (Graywolf, 1991) PQ6044.L48, which is about her experiences translating the works of three Latin American writers, all of whom are very parodic. Her book is marred by the unnecessary use of too much lit. crit. language, but it's still the most fun book on translation I've read.

Another place to turn is the scholarly book about translation or certain aspects of translation. Most of these are collections of essays in book form. One of these is the book that the plurality of translators told me was their favorite or the most important book on translation, George Steiner's *After Babel: Aspects of Language and Translation* (Oxford University Press, 1975). I'm a big fan of Steiner's work and of this book (note how many times I quote from it), but it's not really a book about translation; it's much more a book about language and about literature, and about translation primarily because it is an important place where the two intersect, where literature is viewed through language. But there is a great deal of wisdom about translation in this book, and the book's difficulties are well worth confronting. One final thing that distinguishes this book from the rest is that although Steiner grew up trilingual and knows a host of languages, he is a literary critic rather than a translator.

Lawrence Venuti's *The Translator's Invisibility* (Routledge, 1995) P306.2V46x stands alone as a book that covers a lot of the gamut in its attempt to show why the translator has no public image and why our translation values are the way they are. It's a fascinating book, with lots of history, but it is steeped in contemporary literary theory. Eliot Weinberger's *Nineteen Ways of Looking at Wang Wei: How a Chinese Poem Is Translated*, with comments by Octavio Paz (Moyer Bell, 1987) PL2676.A683.W4X, is a tiny book that does nothing but critique nineteen translations of the same classical Chinese poem. It is devastating and much more valuable than its length suggests.

Some of the best and most recent critical works on translation are Ronnie Apter's *Digging for the Treasure: Translation After Pound* (Lang/Paragon House, 1984/1987) PS3531.O82.Z9.A68; Burton Raffel's three books: *The Art of Translating Poetry* (Pennsylvania State University Press, 1988) PN1059.T7R3; *The Art of Translating Prose* (1994) PN241.R28x; and *The Forked Tongue: A Study of the Translation Process* (The Hague: Mouton, 1971); Willis Barnstone's *The Poetics of Translation* (Yale University Press, 1993) P306.B287; Douglas Robinson's *The Translator's Turn* (Johns Hopkins University Press, 1990) P306.R63 (especially good on practice); Ben Belitt's *Adam's Dream: A Preface to Translation* (Grove, 1978) (which contains essays that amount to another close look at translating Pablo Neruda); Frederic Will's *The Knife in the Stone: Essays in Literary Theory* (The Hague: Mouton, 1973) PN241.W55; and Peter Newmark's *About Translation* (1991) P306.N49 (best on the teaching of translation).

There have been some excellent translation journals, although most of them focus on actual translations rather than writing about translation. Of the ones still being published today, the most valuable are *Translation Review*, published since 1978 by the American Literary Translators Association (PN241.A1 & T7); *Poetry World*, formerly *Modern Poetry in Translation* (PN6101.M63), edited by Daniel Weissbort, who is at the University of Iowa; *Babel*, founded in 1955; and *Meta*, a Montreal journal mostly in French (P306.A1.M47). *Index translationum* is the annual UNESCO guide to trends in translation (Z6514.T7.I4, CD-ROM). Of the defunct journals, my favorite is the shortlived *Delos* (1968-1971). And for actual translations, besides the ones above, *Translation*, a journal out of Columbia University, was very good, but recently went under. Unfortunately, most international writing journals come and go.

And then there's the practical stuff. There's a good deal of writing about practice in the anthologies of essays and interviews, but there are also books that are intended to help translators translate as well as learn the business. I haven't read any of them, so this is a list rather than recommendations. The newest book of this variety is Douglas Robinson's *Becoming a Translator: An Accelerated Course* (Routledge, 1997). Robinson is such a quirky writer, his book is likely to be fun reading. The old standby is Morry's *Guide for Translators* (Schreiber, 1995—the latest of many editions). And then there's Mona Baker's *In Other Words: A Coursebook on Translation* (Routledge, 1992); since she tends to lean toward the political and theoretical aspects of translation (see below), and this is published by Routledge, the leader in translation studies books, this one is likely to go beyond how-to. For the aspiring professional translator, there is no better book to read than PEN American Center's *Handbook for Literary Translators* (1991). Finally, an *Encyclopedia of Literary Translation* is coming out, by Olive Classe (Fitzroy Dearborn, January 1998), but it had not appeared by the time this book went to press

Rather than give you a list of the translation theory books I have been unable to slog through, let me direct your attention to a brand new *Encyclopedia of Translation Studies* by Mona Baker (Routledge, November 1997). I should also add the seminal books on biblical translation as well as contemporary translation theory, Eugene A. Nida's *Bible Translating* (1947) and *Toward a Science of Translating* (1964) P306.N54. That wonderful world "science" says it all.

Standing somewhat alone will be the upcoming *Oxford Companion to Literature in Translation* (no publication date yet).

But probably the most enjoyable things to read about translation are translations themselves, and there are some recent translation collections that are worth looking into. There is a new Norton Anthology, *World Poetry: An Anthology of Verse from Antiquity to Our Time*, edited by Katharine Washburn and John S. Major, with 1,200 pages mostly of translations. Another monstrous volume (but only 750 pages, so far) is Jerome Rothenberg and Pierre Joris's *Poems for the Millennium: The University of California Book of Modern & Postmodern Poetry* (Vol. 1, 1995), which consists primarily of translations by notable translators. Smaller, but together extremely valuable, are the volumes in Penguin's Poets in Translation series under the general editorship of Christopher Ricks, which so far includes D. S. Carne-Ross and Kenneth Haynes' *Horace in English* (1996), George Steiner's *Homer in English* (1996), Donald Davie's *The Psalms in English* (1996), K. W. Gransden's *Virgil in English*, and A. J. Boyle's *Martial in English*. These are collections of English-language translations, adaptations, and works inspired by these classic writers through the ages; the names are the volumes' editors. I hate to tout Penguin paperbacks, because they publish often mediocre translations on cheap paper and in too-small print, but these are fine and readable, although the paper does yellow quickly. Also from Penguin is George Steiner's *Poem into Poem: World Poetry in Modern Verse Translation* (1966), and a similar book from Oxford, Charles Tomlinson's *Oxford Book of Verse in English* (1983).

Two other recent translation collections are worth noting. Both consist of work by poets who are not generally translators and do not on the whole know the language of the original. But it's worth seeing the full range of how they respond to the original, from fidelity to content and/or form to undermining and travesty. They are Michael Hofmann and James Lasdun's *After Ovid: New Metamorphoses* (Farrar, Straus & Giroux, 1994) and Daniel Halpern's *Dante's Inferno: Translations by Twenty Contemporary Poets* (Ecco Press, 1994).

Also of value are collections of poetry in translation from a particular language or counry. The best known of these is a collection of translations from the French by major poet-translators: Paul Auster's *Random House Book of Twentieth-Century French Poetry* (1982), which includes translations by such people as Ashbery, Beckett, Bly, Eliot, Dos Passos, Ferlinghetti, Kinnell, Levertov, Merwin, Wilbur, you name 'em. Some people consider it a sort of Bible of the great years of modernist translation; others consider it a selection of showy and far from the best translations. Since it's bilingual, it's great for the amateur translator; I've spent many late nights with it. There are similar collections of poetry from various languages, although the more unusual the language, the less likely the involvement of multiple and notable translators.

Translation Award Winners

PEN/Book-of-the-Month Club Translation Prize

1997 - Arnold Pomerans: Vincent Van Gogh, *The Letters of Vincent Van Gogh* (Viking)

1996 - Stanislaw Baranczak & Clare Cavanagh: Wislawa Szymborska, *View with a Grain of Sand* (Harcourt Brace)

1995 - Burton Watson: Su Tung-p'o, *Selected Poems* (Copper Canyon)

1994 - Bill Zavatsky & Jack Rogow: André Breton, *Earthlight* (Sun & Moon)

1993 - Thomas Hoisington: Ignacy Krasicki, *The Adventures of Mr. Nicholas Wisdom* (Northwestern Univ. Press)

1992 - David Rosenberg: *The Poet's Bible* (Hyperion)

1991 - Richard Pevear & Larissa Volokhonsky: Fyodor Dostoevsky, *The Brothers Karamazov* (North Point)

1990 - William Weaver: Umberto Eco, *Foucault's Pendulum* (Harcourt Brace)

1989 - Matthew Ward: Albert Camus, *The Stranger* (Random House)

1988 - Madeleine Levine & Francine Prose: Ida Fink, *A Scrap of Time* (Pantheon)

1987 - John E. Woods: Patrick Süskind, *Perfume* (Knopf)

1986 - Barbara Bray: Marguerite Duras, *The Lover* (Pantheon); Dennis Tedlock: *Popol Vuh: The Mayan Book of the Dawn of Life* (Simon & Schuster)

1985 - Helen R. Lane: Mario Vargas Llosa, *The War at the End of the World* (Farrar, Straus & Giroux); Seamus Heaney, *Sweeney Astray* (Farrar, Straus & Giroux)

1984 - William Weaver: Umberto Eco, *The Name of the Rose* (Harcourt Brace)

1983 - Richard Wilbur: Molière, *Four Comedies* (Harcourt Brace)

1982 - Hiroaki Sato & Burton Watson: *From the Country of Eight Islands: An Anthology of Japanese Poetry* (Anchor/Univ. of Washington)

1981 - John E. Woods: Arno Schmidt, *Evening Edged in Gold* (Harcourt Brace)

1980 - Charles Simic: Vasco Popa, *Homage to the Lame Wolf* (Field/Oberlin)

1979 - Charles Wright: Eugenio Montale, *The Storm and Other Poems*
(Field/Oberlin)
1978 - Adrienne Foulke: Leonardo Sciascia, *One Way or Another*
(Harper & Row)
1977 - Gregory Rabassa: Gabriel García Márquez, *Autumn of the
Patriarch* (Harper & Row)
1976 - Richard Howard: E. M. Cioran, *A Short History of Decay*
(Harper & Row)
1975 - Helen R. Lane: Juan Goytisolo, *Count Julian* (Viking)
1974 - Hardie St. Martin & Leonard Mades: José Donoso, *The Obscene
Bird of Night* (Knopf)
1973 - J. P. McCullough: Sextus Propertius, *The Poems of Sextus
Propertius* (Univ. of California)
1972 - Richard & Clara Winston: Thomas Mann, *The Letters of Thomas
Mann* (Knopf)
1971 - Max Hayward: Nadezhda Mandelstam, *Hope Against Hope*
(Atheneum)
1970 - Sidney Alexander: Francesco Guicciardini, *The History of Italy*
(Macmillan)
1969 - W. S. Merwin: *Selected Translations, 1948-1968* (Atheneum)
1968 - Vladimir Markov & Merrill Sparks, editors: *Modern Russian
Poetry* (Bobbs-Merrill)
1967 - Harriet de Onis: J. Guimaraes Rosa, *Sagarana* (Knopf)
1966 - Geoffrey Skelton & Adrian Mitchell: Peter Weiss, *Marat/Sade*
(Atheneum)
1965 - Joseph Barnes: Konstantin Paustovsky, *The Story of a Life*
(Pantheon)
1964 - Ralph Manheim: Günter Grass, *The Tin Drum* (Pantheon)
1963 - Archibald Colquhoun: Federico de Roberto, *The Viceroys*
(Harcourt Brace)

PEN Award for Poetry in Translation

1997 - Edward Snow: Rainer Maria Rilke, *Uncollected Poems* (Farrar,
Straus & Giroux)
1996 - Guy Davenport, *7 Greeks* (New Directions)

The Academy of American Poets Harold Morton Landon Translation Award

1997 - David Hinton: Bei Dao, *Landscape Over Zero* (New Directions); Meng Chiao, *Late Poems* (Princeton Univ. Press); Li Po, *Selected Poems* (New Directions)

1996 - Guy Davenport: *7 Greeks* (New Directions)

1995 - Robert Pinksy: Dante, *The Inferno* (Farrar, Straus & Giroux)

1994 - Rosemarie Waldrop: Edmond Jabès, *The Book of Margins* (Univ. of Chicago Press)

1993 - Charles Simic: *The Horse Has Six Legs: An Anthology of Serbian Poetry* (Graywolf)

1992 - John DuVal: Cesare Pascarella, *The Discovery of America* (Univ. of Arkansas Press); and Andrew Schelling: *Dropping the Bow: Poems of Ancient India* (Broken Moon)

1991 - Robert Fagles: Homer, *The Iliad* (Viking)

1990 - Stephen Mitchell: Dan Pagis, *Variable Directions* (North Point)

1989 - Martin Greenberg: Heinrich von Kleist, *Five Plays* (Yale Univ. Press)

1988 - Peter Hargitai: Attila Jozef, *Perched on Nothing's Branch* (Apalachee)

1987 - Mark Anderson: Ingeborg Bachmann, *In the Storm of Roses* (Princeton Univ. Press)

1986 - William Arrowsmith: Eugenio Montale, *The Storm & Other Things* (Norton)

1985 - Edward Snow: Rainer Maria Rilke, *New Poems (1907)* (North Point)

1984 - Robert Fitzgerald: Homer, *The Odyssey* (Anchor); and Stephen Mitchell: Rainer Maria Rilke, *Selected Poetry* (Random House)

1982 - Rika Lesser: Gunnar Ekelof, *Guide to the Underworld* (Univ. of Massachusetts Press)

1980 - Saralyn R. Daly: Juan Ruis, *The Book of True Love* (Pennsylvania State Univ. Press); and Edmund Keeley: Yannis Ritsos, *Ritsos in Parentheses* (Princeton Univ. Press)

1978 - Galway Kinnell: Francois Villon, *The Poems of Francois Villon* (Houghton Mifflin); and Howard Norman: *The Wishing Bone Cycle: Poems from the Swampy Cree Indians* (Stonehill)

1976 - Robert Fitzgerald: Homer, *The Iliad* (Anchor)

Modern Language Association Aldo and Jeanne Scaglione Prize for a Translation of a Literary Work

1994-1995 - David Ball: Henri Michaux, *Darkness Moves* (Univ. of California Press); Carol Maier: Rosa Chacel, *Memoirs of Leticia Valle* (Univ. of Nebraska Press);

1992-1993 - Estelle Gilson: Umberto Saba, *The Stories and Recollections of Umberto Saba* (Sheep Meadow)

American Translators Association Lewis Galantière Translation Prize

1996 - William Rodarmor: Bernard Moitessier, *Tamata and the Alliance* (Sheridan)

1994 - Tiina Nunnally: Peter Hoeg, *Smilla's Sense of Snow* (Farrar, Straus & Giroux)

1992 - Ruth H. Cline: Chrétien de Troyes, *Lancelot, or The Knight of the Cart* (Univ. of Georgia Press)

1990 - Edward K. Kaplan: Charles Baudelaire, *The Parisian Prowler* (Univ. of Georgia Press)

1988 - Patrick Creagh: Salvatore Satta, *The Day of Judgment* (Farrar, Straus & Giroux)

1986 - Hildegarde and Hunter Hannum: Alice Miller, *For Your Own Good* and *Thou Shalt Not Be Aware* (Farrar, Straus & Giroux)

1984 - William Weaver: Umberto Eco, *The Name of the Rose* (Harcourt, Brace)

American Literary Translators Association Outstanding Translations of the Year

1997 - Stephen Owen: *An Anthology of Chinese Literature* (W. W. Norton); James Magruder: *Three French Comedies* (Yale Univ. Press); Hardie St. Martin, editor (six translators): Roque Dalton, *Small Hours of the Night: Selected Poems* (Curbstone)

1996 - Rosette C. Lamont: Charlotte Delbo, *Auschwitz and After* (Yale Univ. Press); Edith Grossman: Augusto Monterroso, *Complete Works and Other Stories* (Univ. of Texas Press); Joan C. Kessler: *Demons of the Night: Tales of the Fantastic, Madness, and the Supernatural from Nineteenth-Century France* (Univ. of Chicago Press); Victor Perera: Victor Montejo, *Sculpted Stones* (Curbstone).

1995 - Peter Filkins: Ingeborg Bachmann, *Songs in Flight: Collected Poems* (Marsilio); Michael Henry Heim: Milos Tsernianski, *Migrations* (Harcourt Brace); Carol Maier: Octavio Armand, *Refractions* (SITES/Lumen); John E. Woods: Arno Schmidt, *Collected Novellas* (Dalkey Archive); Peter Bush: Luis Sepulveda, *The Old Man Who Read Love Stories* (Harcourt Brace).

1994 - Arthur Goldhammer: Maurice Lever, *Sade* (Farrar, Straus & Giroux); Howard Goldblatt: Liu Heng, *Black Snow* (Atlantic Monthly Press); Giovanni Pontiero: Jose Saramago, *The Gospel According to Jesus Christ* (Harcourt Brace); Carolyne Wright: Jorege Teillier, *In Order to Talk with the Dead: Selected Poems* (Univ. of Texas Press); Lee Fahnestock: *Quiet Moments in a War: Letters of Jean-Paul Sartre to Simone de Beauvoir* (Scribners).

1993 - Norman Shapiro: *The Fabulists French* (Univ. of Illinois Press); Dick Gerdes: Alfredo Bryce Echenique, *A World for Julius* (Univ. of Texas Press); Edith Grossman: Alvaro Mutis, *Maqroll* (HarperCollins); John Barrett: Grete Weil, *The Bride Price* (Godine); Marjolijn de Jager: Assia Djabar, *Women of Algiers in Their Apartments* (Univ. Press of Virginia); Celeste Kostopulos-Cooperman: Marjorie Agosin, *Circles of Madness* (White Pine); Edmund Keeley and Philip Sherrard: C. P. Cavafy, *Collected Poems* (Princeton Univ. Press); Barbara Wright: Jean Hamburger, *The Diary of William Harvey* (Rutgers Univ. Press); Esther Allen with Monique Chefdor: Blaise Cendrars, *Modernities and Other Writings* (Univ. of Nebraska Press); George K. Zucker: Paloma Dias-Mas, *Sephardim: The Jews from Spain* (Univ. of Chicago Press).

1992 - John H. R. Polt: Camilo Jose Cela, *San Camilo, 1936* (Duke Univ. Press); Breon Mitchell: Martin Grzimek, *Shadowlife* (New Directions); Lynne Sharon Schwartz: Liana Millu, *Smoke Over Birkenau* (Jewish Publication Society); Jeremy Legatt: Jean Raspail, *Blue Island* (Mercury House); Twelve Translators: *New Italian Poets* (Story Line); Jack Schmitt: Pablo Neruda, *Canto General* (Univ. of California Press); Sidney Alexander: Michelangelo, *The Complete Poetry* (Ohio Univ. Press); W. S. Kuniczak: Henryk Sienkiewicz, *With Fire and Sword* (Hippocrene); Herbert R. Rowen: Jan Willem Schulte Nordholt, *Woodrow Wilson: A Life for World Peace* (Univ. of California Press).

Endnotes

(Numbers in italics before endnotes represent page numbers where the asterisk appears in the text. If there is no number, the asterisk is on the same page as the last number above.)

Introduction

8 "On Literature," in *Toward the Radical Center: A Karel Čapek Reader* (Catbird, 1990), 317.

9 John Biguenet and Rainer Schulter, eds. *Theories of Translation: An Anthology of Essays* (University of Chicago Press, 1992), 22

Quoted in George Steiner, *After Babel: Aspects of Language and Translation* (Oxford University Press, 1975), 248

Writings on Literature (1824), in André Lefevere, ed. *Translation/History/Culture: A Sourcebook* (Routledge, 1992), 25

Quoted in Suzanne Jill Levine, "From *Little Painted Lips* to *Heartbreak Tango*" in Rosanna Warren, ed. *The Art of Translation: Voices from the Field* (Northeastern University Press, 1989), 30 (my translation).

10 Lefevere, ed., 13

"On the Best Way of Translating" (1683), in Lefevere, ed., 96

William Frawley, ed., *Translation: Literary, Linguistic, and Philosophical Perspectives* (University of Delaware Press, 1984), 42-43

11 Margaret Sayers Peden, "Building a Translation: The Reconstruction Business" in John Biguenet and Rainer Schulte, eds. *The Craft of Translation* (University of Chicago Press, 1989), 13

Preparing for the Best

19 First two and the last sentences and following quotation from Edwin Honig, ed. *The Poet's Other Voice: Conversations on Literary Translation* (University of Massachusetts Press, 1985), 82

20 Suzanne Jill Levine, *The Subversive Scribe* (Graywolf, 1991), 6

21 Ibid., 153

23 Lefevere, ed., 17

28 "On the Best Way of Translating," in Lefevere, ed., 89

30 Eliot Weinberger, *Outside Stories* (New Directions, 1992), 60

The Intimacy of Submission

33 Honig, 72

34 v

Gregory Rabassa, "The Silk Purse Business: A Translator's Conflicting Responsibilities," *American PEN* 4, reprinted in Frawley, ed., 40

36 Hans Erich Nossack, "Translating and Being Translated," trans. by Sharon Sloan, in *Theories of Translation*, 228

The Earl of Roscommon, "An Essay on Translated Verse,' in *English Translation Theory, 1650-1800*, ed. T. R. Steiner (Assen: Van Gorcum, 1975), 75, quoted in Lori Chamberlain, "Gender and the Metaphorics of Translation," in Lawrence Venuti, ed. *Rethinking Translation: Discourse, Subjectivity, Ideology* (Routledge, 1992), 58

37 (Princeton University Press, 1993), xiv

Honig, 194-5

39 Michael Upchurch, "Nazi and Stasi: The Soundtrack," *New York Times Book Review*(December 21, 1997), 12

Quoted in Rosemarie Waldrop, "The Joy of the Demiurge" in Frawley, ed., 41-42

Ibid., 47

Quoted in Haskell M. Block, "The Writer as Translator: Nerval, Baudelaire, Gide" in Marilyn Gaddis Rose, ed., *Translation Spectrum: Essays in Theory and Practice* (Albany: SUNY Press, 1981), 120 (my translation)

40 *After Babel*, 378

45 John Felstiner, *Paul Celan: Poet, Survivor, Jew* (Yale University Press, 1995), 206.

Ibid., 205.

46 John Felstiner, *Translating Neruda: The Way to Macchu Picchu* (Stanford University Press, 1980), 183

Ibid., 198-199

47 W. Packard, ed. *The Poet's Craft: Interviews from New York Quarterly* (Paragon House, 1987), 13; quoted in Lawrence Venuti, *The Translator's Invisibility: A History of Translation* (Routledge, 1995), 246

48 7

49 Honig, 49

The Knife in the Stone: Essays in Literary Theory (The Hague: Mouton, 1973), 76

Honig, 27

David Wevill, "Death's Dream Kingdom," in *Delos 4* (1970), a review of Yves Bonnefoy, *Selected Poems*, tr. Anthony Rudolf, and *On the Motion and Immobility of Douve*, tr. Galway Kinnell.

Lost and Found

52 Quoted in George Steiner, Introduction to *Penguin Book of Modern Verse Translation* (Penguin, 1966), 25

After Babel, 241

"Letter to a Translator, Jenö Tamás Gömöri, Hungarian translator of Mann," translated by Richard and Clara Winston, in *Delos 3* (1969), 210

Dennis Kennedy, ed. *Foreign Shakespeares: Contemporary Performance* (Cambridge University Press, 1993), 22

53 Honig, 85

After Babel, 269

"Preferences in Translating Poetry," in Frawley, ed., 52-3

55 Honig, 14

Ibid., 155

Donald Frame, "Pleasures and Problems of Translation," in *Craft of Translation*, 70

Delos 3, 211

59 Belitt, *Adam's Dream: A Preface to Translation* (Grove, 1978), 33

60 After Babel, 71

Ibid., 34

61 Willis Barnstone, "Preferences in Translating Poetry," in Frawley, ed., 51

Michael Hamburger, *Testimonies: Selected Shorter Prose, 1950-1987* (Carcanet, 1989), 259

In Karl Kummer, ed. *Building Bridges: Proceedings of the 27th Annual Conference of the American Translators Association* (1986), 8

62 Quoted in Burton Raffel, *The Art of Translating Poetry* (Pennsylvania State University Press, 1988), 196

Edmund Keeley, "Collaboration, Revision, and Other Less Forgivable Sins in Translation," in *Craft of Translation*, 54-55

Weinberger, 59

63 *After Babel*, 250

Quoted in Moura Budberg, "On Translating from Russian," *The World of Translation* (PEN American Center, 1970), 151

Richard Sieburth, "The Guest: Second Thoughts on Translating Hölderlin," in Warren, ed., 240

Richard Sieburth, Introduction to Friedrich Hölderlin, *Hymns and Fragments* (Princeton University Press, 1984), 25

The Romance of Infidelity

67 John Dryden, "Dedication" to his translation of Virgil's *Aeneid*, in Lefevere, ed., 24

Friedrich Nietzsche, "On the Problem of Translation" (1882), tr. Peter Mollenhauer, in *Theories of Translation*, 65

68 Zoja Pavlovskis, "Translation from the Classics," in Rose, ed., 100-101

L. G. Kelly, *The True Interpreter: A History of Translation Theory and Practice in the West* (Basil Blackwell, 1979), 71

D. P. Lockwood, *American Philological Association* 49: 125, quoted in C. H. Conley, *The First English Translators of the Classics* (Yale University Press, 1927), 105

Kelly, 59

Antoine Berman, *The Experience of the Foreign: Culture and Translation in Romantic Germany*, tr. S. Heyvaert (SUNY Press, 1992), 4

70 Conley, 50, 56

Alexander Neville, Dedication to Seneca's *Oedipus* (1563; spelling modernized), quoted in *Ibid.*, 69

Sir Thomas Hoby (spelling modernized), quoted in *Ibid.*, 68

Kelly, 218

73 Honig, 91

Ezra Pound, *Letters, 1907-1941*, ed. D. D. Paige (Harcourt Brace, 1950);

quoted in Edwin Gentzler, ed. *Contemporary Translation Theories* (Routledge, 1993), 27
75 Archaïscher Torso Apollos

Wir kannten nicht sein unerhörtes Haupt,
darin die Augenäpfel reiften. Aber
sein Torso glüht noch wie ein Kandelaber,
in dem sein Schauen, nur zurückgeschraubt,

sich hält und glänzt. Sonst könnte nicht der Bug
der Brust dich blenden, und im leisen Drehen
der Lenden könnte nicht ein Lächeln gehen
zu jener Mitte, die die Zeugung trug.

Sonst stünde dieser Stein entstellt und kurz
unter der Schultern durchsichtigem Sturz
und flimmerte nicht so wie Raubtierfelle;

und bräche nicht aus allen seinen Rändern
aus wie ein Stern: denn da ist keine Stelle,
die dich nicht sieht. Du mußt dein Leben ändern.

77 János Csokits, "János Pilinsky's 'Desert of Love': A Note," in Daniel Weissbort, ed. *Translating Poetry: The Double Labyrinth* (University of Iowa Press, 1989), 8
79 John Frederick Nims, "Poetry: Lost in Translation," *Delos* 5 (1970), 109; also the introduction to his *Poems in Translation* (Rutgers University Press, 1971)
Alexandre Chciuk-Celt (Sandra Celt, pseud.), "Poetry Translation Seminar" in *ATA Silver Tongues - American Translators Association Conference 1984* (Learned Information, 1984), 269
81 Everett Fox, "Translator's Preface," *The Five Books of Moses* (Word, 1996)
José Ortega y Gasset, "The Misery and Splendor of Translation" (1937), tr. Elizabeth Gamble Miller, in *Theories of Translation*, 108
85 J. M. Cohen, *English Translators and Translations* (Longmans Green, 1962), 35
86 61; quoted in Berman, 131
Quoted in Ronnie Apter, *Digging for the Treasure: Translation After Pound* (Paragon, 1984), 241
87 Goethe, in Lefevere, ed., 6
Vladimir Nabokov, "Problems of Translation: *Onegin* in English," *Partisan Review* 22, no. 4, reprinted in *Theories of Translation*, 135
88 Ibid., 127
Ted Hughes, "Postscript to János Csokits' Note," in Weissbort, ed., 17
Csokits, 8
(Harcourt Brace & World, 1954-65), 9-10

89 George Steiner, "Introduction," *Poem into Poem: The Penguin Book of Modern Verse Translation* (Penguin, 1966), 34

93 Levine, *The Subversive Scribe*, 34

96 Milan Kundera, *The Art of the Novel*, tr. Linda Asher (Grove, 1986, 1988), 148

99 Milan Kundera, *Testaments Betrayed*, tr. Linda Asher (HarperCollins, 1995), 271, 274

100 Marcel Proust, *Swann's Way*, tr. by C. K. Scott Moncrieff (Modern Library, 1928), 346

101 Honig, 61-2

Alastair Reid, "Neruda and Borges," *The New Yorker*, June 24, 1996, 70

102 Quoted in Felstiner, *Neruda*, 26

Honig, 74

William Weaver, "Pendulum Diary," *Southwest Review* 75:2 (1990), 167

The Obligations of Polygamy

106 In Joseph F. Graham, ed. *Difference in Translation* (Cornell University Press, 1985), 142-143

111 *New York Review of Books* (April 20, 1995), 14

112 Berman, 135

Decisions, Decisions

115 "Observations on the Art of Translation," in Lefevere, ed., 111

116 "Translation As a Species of Mime," in Warren, ed., 27

Belitt, 293

"The Process of Translation," in *Craft of Translation*, 117

117 "The Craft of Translation," in *American Scholar* Vol. 19, No. 2 (Spring 1950), 179

"Pendulum Diary," 154

"Translating Poetry," tr. John Alexander and Clive Wilmer (1985), in *Theories of Translation*, 188

118 *Outside Stories*, 59

Gregory Rabassa, "No Two Snowflakes Are Alike: Translation As Metaphor," in *Craft of Translation*, 6

121 A. Leslie Willson, "Bent: The Role of the Editor in Literary Translation," in *ATA Silver Tongues*, 244

122 Gregory Rabassa, "If This Be Treason: Translation and Its Possibilities," in Frawley, ed., 23

124 "No Two Snowflakes," 3

127 Dinitia Smith, "Competing Versions of Poem by Nobelist," *New York Times* (October 21, 1996), C13-14

Edward Seidensticker, "On Trying to Translate Japanese" in *The Craft of Translation*, 146-148

128 "The Spilling of the Beans" in Josef Škvorecký, *Talkin' Moscow Blues*, ed. Sam Solecki (Ecco, 1990), 204

Ibid.

Raffel, 174

130 Introduction to *Greek Plays in Modern Translation,* quoted in Richard Winston, "The Craft of Translation," *American Scholar* 19: 181

William Weaver, "The Process of Translation," in *Craft of Translation,* 119

132 Felstiner, *Neruda,* 30

133 Reid, 68

Felstiner, *Neruda,* 151

134 Keeley, 143-4

"No Two Snowflakes," 9

138 "Translating from the German," in Reuben Brower, ed. *On Translation* (Harvard University Press, 1959), 94-96

"On Trying to Translate Japanese," *Craft of Translation,* 143

139 Levine, "From *Little Painted Lips,*" in Warren, ed., 37

Raffel, 157

145 Honig, 105

146 Rachel Hadas, *Other Worlds Than This* (Rutgers University Press, 1994), xvii

"No Two Snowflakes," 8

147 Nims, 120

Bettering

149 Honig, 102, 104

152 *Ibid.,* 105

153 *Ibid.,* 187

It's Even Good for You

169 "Slouching Back Toward Babel: Some Views on Translation in the Groves," *Centerpoint* 1 (1975): 57-9, reprinted in Frawley, ed., 34

173 *Critical Poetics* (1743), quoted in Lefevere, ed., 57

W. S. Merwin, Talk to ALTA, October 26, 1995

174 ALTA Speech, November 1994

Honig, 190

Frederic Will, *The Knife in the Stone: Essays in Literary Theory* (The Hague: Mouton, 1973), 112

175 *Ibid.,* 63

After Babel, 359

177 Quoted in Carl Jacob Burckhardt, *Ein Vormittag beim Buchhandler* (Basel, 1944), and then quoted in Alberto Manguel, *A History of Reading* (Viking, 1996), 264

180 Philip Lopate, "Sans Teeth," *New York Times Book Review* (September 8, 1996)

183 Hamburger, 263

184 "'Ziv, That Light': Translation and Tradition in Paul Celan," in *Craft of Translation,* 94

185 ix

"'Ziv'," 94

The Subversive Scribe, xiii
186 Kelly, 53-54
Peden, 27
187 Douglas Hofstadter, "What's Gained in Translation," *New York Times Book Review* (December 8, 1996)
Raffel, viii
188 *Ibid.*
Nims, 109
189 Will, 122
192 André Lefevere, "Beyond the Process: Literary Translation in Literature and Literary Theory," in Rose, ed., 59

No Translator Is an Island

197 Raffel, 130
Ibid., 135
Ibid., 137
198 Arthur Waley, "Notes on Translation" in *Delos 3* (1969), 165-166; orig. appeared in *Atlantic Monthly* (1958)
Quoted in Apter, 155
From Osip Mandelstam, *Selected Poems* (Oxford University Press, 1973), quoted in Raffel, 131-132
199 Honig, 92-93
Octavio Paz, "Translation: Literature and Letters," trans. Irene del Corral, from *Traduccion: Literaturea y Literalidad* (1971), quoted in *Theories of Translation*, 158
200 Kelly, 112
Nims, 124-125
W. S. Merwin, Talk to ALTA
Michael Gormon, "W. S. Merwin Translator Poet," *Translation Review* 9 (1982), quoted in note by Daniel Weissbort, Weissbort, ed., 139
204 Keeley, 58-59
206 Kundera, *The Art of the Novel*, 121-122
208 "Pendulum Diary," 161
209 Levine, "From *Little Painted Lips*," 32
212 Harry Zohn, "Before and After Your Translation Is Printed: Matters Politic, Political, Polemical," in Kummer, ed., 314
214 Honig, 175
215 Hugh Kenner, "Beckett Translating Beckett: *Comment C'est*," *Delos* 5 (1970)
216 *New York Times* (October 8, 1997), E8
218 Willson, 241, 243-245, 248
220 Lawrence Venuti, "The Art of Literary Translation: An Interview with William Weaver," Denver Quarterly 17:2 (Summer 1982), 24
223 "Before and After," 309
232 Venuti, "Art of Literary Translation," 25
Will, 150, 157

Love Is All There Is

238 Hans Erich Nossack, "Translating and Being Translated," trans. by Sharon Sloan, in *Theories of Translation*, 232-3
n.d.
239 Nossack, 228-229
245 Charles Tomlinson, "The Presence of Translation: A View of English Poetry" in Warren, ed., 260
255 Edwin McDowell, "The Media Business; Foreign Writers, Even Nobel Winners, Find Few Outlets," *New York Times* (October 31, 1988)

Performing Without a Stage

259 In *Theories of Translation*, 33
Quoted in Škvorecký, 204
262 D. J. R. Bruckner, review of John E. Woods' translation of Thomas Mann's *The Magic Mountain*, *New York Times Book Review* (October 22, 1995)
John Hollander, "Versions, Interpretations, and Performances," in Brower, ed., 205
Rabassa, "If This Be Treason"
Quoted in Raffel, 166
263 No. 3 (1990), 398-9
266 Honig, 18-19
267 Dolman, "To the Reader" in *Tusculanae*, quoted in Conley, 102 (spelling modernized)
New York Times Book Review (April 29, 1984), 1, 45
269 David Park, *The Fire Within the Eye* (Princeton University Press, 1997)
E. Rodríguez Monegal, *Borges: A Literary Biography*, quoted in *Subversive Scribe*, xii
270 Waley, 163
272 *New York Times Book Review* (December 22, 1996)
New York Times Book Review (August 17, 1997)
273 Wevill, 237
274 Felstiner, *Neruda*, 15-17
284 (Mercury House, 1994)
285 Venuti, "The Art of Literary Translation," 16-26
Preface to translations of Aristophanes, in Lefevere, ed., 41
287 Quoted in Gustav Neibuhr, "Display of Two 1526 Bibles Celebrates Translator," *New York Times* (n.d.)
288 Honig, 59
292 Felstiner, *Neruda*, 32
Škvorecký, 196
295 Block, 24

Index

About the Author

Robert Wechsler has edited numerous book-length translations and is the author of *Columbus à la Mode: Parodies of Contemporary American Writers*. He lives in North Haven, Connecticut.

This book was set in Berling Roman and printed by
Arcata Graphics Co. in Fairfield, Pennsylvania.
The jacket was printed by Phoenix Color Corp.
The jacket and book were designed by the author.

Here's a list of Catbird's books in translation. If you would like to order any of the books, or receive our bi-annual catalogs in the future, please call us at 800-360-2391, e-mail us at catbird@pipeline.com, fax us at 203-230-8029, or send us a letter at 16 Windsor Road, North Haven, CT 06473. Shipping and handling is $3.00 total, no matter how many books you order (at least as of 1998).

Books by Karel Čapek

TOWARD THE RADICAL CENTER: A Karel Čapek Reader. Edited by Peter Kussi, foreword by Arthur Miller, multiple translators. Čapek's best plays, stories, and columns take us from the social contributions of clumsy people to dramatic meditations on mortality and commitment. This volume includes the first complete English translation of *R.U.R. (Rossum's Universal Robots)*, the play that introduced the literary robot. $14.95 paper, $23.95 cloth, 416 pp., illus.

WAR WITH THE NEWTS. Translated by Ewald Osers. This new translation revitalizes one of the great anti-utopian satires of the twentieth century. Čapek satirizes science, runaway capitalism, fascism, journalism, militarism, even Hollywood. "A bracing parody of totalitarianism and technological overkill, one of the most amusing and provocative books in its genre." —*Philadelphia Inquirer*. $11.95 paper, 240 pp.

TALES FROM TWO POCKETS. Translated by Norma Comrada. Čapek's unique approaches to the mysteries of justice and truth are full of twists and turns, the ordinary and the extraordinary, humor and humanism. "Čapek's delightfully inventive tales ... stretch the detective story to its limits and, in the process, tell us much about the mysteries of human existence." —*New York Times Book Review* "One of the Best Books of 1994." —*Publishers Weekly*. $14.95 paper, 365 pp., illus.

APOCRYPHAL TALES. Translated by Norma Comrada. Čapek approaches great events and figures of history, myth, and literature in unexpected ways, making us reconsider not only the familiar tales, but also our own views on such basic concepts as justice, progress, wisdom, belief, and patriotism. "These little nuggets combine broad learning with sharp wit to make powerful statements." —*Publishers Weekly* $13.95 paper, 192 pp.

THREE NOVELS: Hordubal, Meteor, An Ordinary Life. Translated by M. & R. Weatherall. This trilogy of novels approaches the problem of mutual understanding through various kinds of storytelling. "Čapek's masterpiece." —*Chicago Tribune*. $15.95 paper, 480 pp.

TALKS WITH T. G. MASARYK. Translated by Michael Henry Heim.. Never have two such important world figures collaborated in a biography. Tomáš Garrigue Masaryk (1850-1937) was the original Philosopher-President who founded Czechoslovakia in 1918, an important inspiration for Václav Havel. $13.95 paper, 256 pp.

Other Czech Literature in Translation
DAYLIGHT IN NIGHTCLUB INFERNO: Czech Fiction from the Post-Kundera Generation. Selected by Elena Lappin, multiple translators. "[A] new generation of writers is putting pen to paper with not only speed but consequence. This important anthology ... places some marvelous talent on display." —*Booklist.* $15.95 paper, 320 pp.

THE FOUR SONYAS by Vladimír Páral, translated by William Harkins. In Páral's darkly comic world, people will do almost anything to attain their dreams, and freedom is nothing but another fairy tale. $22.95 cloth, 391 pp.

CATAPULT by Vladimír Páral, translated by William Harkins. This twist on the Don Juan story looks at the attractions and difficulties of freedom. "Páral masterfully switches from farce to drama and back again, so that in the end we feel Jost's dilemma even as we're laughing at him." —*New York Times Book Review.* $10.95 paper, 240 pp.

WHAT OWNERSHIP'S ALL ABOUT by Karel Poláček, translated by Peter Kussi. "Poláček studies the effect of power on the values and dreams of ordinary people, revealing their weaknesses and skewering their pomposity with a deftness and dark wit reminiscent of Chekhov." —*Library Journal.* $21.95 cloth, 238 pp.

German Literature in Translation
JEWISH VOICES, GERMAN WORDS: Growing Up Jewish in Postwar Germany and Austria. Edited by Elena Lappin, translated by Krishna Winston. Fiction, memoirs, and essays. "By turns comic and sharp, melodramatic and maudlin, [it] shows the varied range of experience among today's German Jewish writers." —*New York Times Book Review.* $23.95 paper, 304 pp.

DIPLOMATIC PURSUITS by Joseph von Westphalen, translated by Melanie Richter-Bernburg. Harry von Duckwitz pursues ideas and women with the same conflicted, contrary, self-critical volatility he brings to his diplomatic career. $14.95 paper, 300 pp.